The Fire of Freedom

Satsang with Papaji
Volume 1

Edited by David Godman

Avadhuta Foundation
Colorado, USA

© Avadhuta Foundation 2007

All rights reserved
For information on rights contact mail@avadhuta.com

ISBN (10 digit) 0-9638022-6-7
(13 digit) 978-0-9638022-6-2

Published by
Avadhuta Foundation
P.O. Box 296
Boulder, Colorado 80306-0296
USA
mail@avadhuta.com
www.avadhuta.com
(303) 473-9295
toll free: (877) 282-3488

Printed at
All India Press
Kennedy Nagar
Pondicherry 605001
India

Introduction

Hariwansh Lal Poonja was born in 1913 near Lyalpur, a small Punjabi town that was then in India but which later, in 1947, became part of the newly created state of Pakistan. His father, who worked as a stationmaster for the government railway network, was subjected to frequent transfers, and this meant that the family was regularly relocated to different small towns.

In 1919 the British colonial government declared a special holiday to commemorate victory in the First World War. The Poonja family took a trip to Lahore, the biggest city in the region, and it was there that Hariwansh had his first major spiritual awakening. As a mango and yoghurt drink was being distributed to members of the family, Hariwansh ignored his because he had become completely paralysed by a direct experience of the Self. He became unable to drink, speak, or move in any way, and he remained absorbed in this state for three days. In later years he would attempt to describe what happened to him by saying that it was an experience of unalloyed beauty and happiness, but at the time he had no context to evaluate what had happened to him. Once this direct contact with the happiness of the Self had been established, he spent much of the succeeding years trying to regain this experience, or occasionally being spontaneously pulled back into it.

His mother, who was an ardent devotee of Krishna, convinced him that devotion to Krishna would bring him back to this state of happiness. Following her advice, Hariwansh focused his attention on a picture of Krishna with such great intensity, Krishna began to appear before him in a real physical form that was solid enough to be touched. Though no one else in the family could see Krishna, they all saw Hariwansh playing with his 'invisible' new friend. Hariwansh became so addicted to the form of Krishna, for many, many years his principal spiritual desire was to have Krishna appear before him so that he could enjoy the bliss that came from being in his presence.

When he was about thirteen years old, he fell in love with an image of the Buddha that was in one of his school textbooks. It was a picture of a famous statue, now in a Lahore museum, that depicted

Buddha as an emaciated ascetic. Something prompted Hariwansh to imitate the picture in the book, and in the months that followed he deliberately starved himself in order to look like it. He also made himself a Buddhist robe from one of his mother's saris, went out to beg his food, and gave speeches on the Buddha in the town square. His teenage adventures as an imitation-Buddha ended when his mother, who knew nothing about them, found that he had converted one of her saris into a monk's robe.

In the late 1920s part of the house in Lyalpur that Hariwansh's family lived in was rented by Sukdev, a militant freedom fighter who belonged to an organisation that was trying to expel the British from India by force. Sukdev and his friend Bhagat Singh were both eventually hanged by the British for murdering, and attempting to murder, officials of the colonial government. Hariwansh, who had no time for Gandhi's path of non-violence, became a member of their group because he was fully convinced that violence against the British, who were occupying his country, was legitimate self-defence. He had promised his family that he would not take part in part in any violent activities himself, since that would have led to reprisals on other family members, but he was an active public speaker who gave fiery speeches which attempted to persuade people that the British should be thrown out of India by force. After Sukdev and Bhagat Singh were hanged, Hariwansh did take part in what was supposed to be a revenge mission – an attempt to blow up the Viceroy's train – but when this failed, the militant movement in the Punjab fizzled out since almost all its members had by then either been jailed or executed by the British.

Hariwansh was the oldest child in the family. When he was sixteen years old, he went through the traditional arranged marriage and began work as a salesman because his father could not afford to send him to college. His work, which initially involved selling sports goods and surgical implements, took him to Bombay, where he spent most of the 1930s. He earned enough to support both his wife, his young children, and the other members of his family who had stayed in Lyalpur.

In the early 1940s, after the outbreak of the Second World War, Hariwansh applied to be an officer in the British wartime army. He felt that the Punjabi freedom fighters of the 1920s and 30s had been doomed to fail because they had lacked a proper military training and had had insufficient access to arms and ammunition. In applying for a commission, he thought that he would get a good military training which he could later put to good use by fighting the British again. However, soon after he began his training, he realised that this was an unrealistic goal.

During his years as a freedom fighter, and as a married man working in Bombay, Hariwansh had never abandoned his love for Krishna, nor his desire to have regular visions of him. When he eventually attained his commission, he spent his nights dressing up in a sari, jewellery and makeup, and dancing before an image of Krishna in an attempt to persuade him to manifest. He was convinced that Krishna was more likely to appear to a woman.

Eventually, when military service proved uncongenial to him, he resigned his commission in order to search for a Guru who would enable him to see Krishna all the time. His search took him all over India and led him to some of the most famous teachers of the time, but none of them was able to give a positive reply to his standard introductory query: 'Have you seen God, and if so, can you show Him to me?'

Sometime after he returned home, a *sadhu*, a mendicant Hindu monk, appeared at his door in Lyalpur, asking for alms. Hariwansh asked the question again: 'Can you show me God, and if not, do you know anyone who can?'

The *sadhu* replied by saying, 'Yes, I know a person who can show you God. If you go and see that man, everything will be all right for you. His name is Ramana Maharshi.'

Hariwansh found out from the *sadhu* that Ramana Maharshi lived in Tiruvannamalai in southern India. Since he had used up all his money on his earlier fruitless trips to find a Guru, he financed his journey to the south by accepting a job from a company that was based in Madras, a city just a few hours away by train from Tiruvannamalai.

When he arrived at Ramana Maharshi's ashram, in 1944, he discovered, much to his annoyance, that Ramana Maharshi was the same person who had appeared to him as a *sadhu* in Lyalpur. Feeling that he had been cheated, he was about to leave the ashram when he was told by a resident devotee that Sri Ramana had not left

Tiruvannamalai for almost fifty years. Intrigued, he decided to stay.

The first time he spoke to Sri Ramana, he asked him. 'Are you the man who came to my house in the Punjab?' but Sri Ramana remained silent.

Then he asked him his standard question: 'Have you seen God, and if you have, can you enable me to see Him?'

Sri Ramana replied, 'I cannot show you God because God is not an object that can be seen. God is the subject. He is the seer. Don't concern yourself with objects that can be seen. Find out who the seer is.' He also added, 'You alone are God'.

Though Hariwansh, who was still desperate to have visions of Krishna, was not willing to accept this advice, he stayed long enough to have a major experience in Sri Ramana's presence. This is how he described it in *Nothing Ever Happened*:

> His words did not impress me. They seemed to me to be yet one more excuse to add to the long list of those I had heard from swamis all over the country. He had promised to show me God [when he came to my house in the Punjab] yet now he was trying to tell me that not only could he not show me God, no one else could either. I would have dismissed him and his words without a second thought had it not been for an experience I had immediately after he had told me to find out who this 'I' was who wanted to see God. At the conclusion of his words he looked at me, and as he gazed into my eyes, my whole body began to tremble and shake. A thrill of nervous energy shot through my body. My nerve endings felt as if they were dancing, and my hair stood on end. Within me I became aware of the spiritual Heart. This is not the physical heart. It is, rather, the source and support of all that exists. Within the Heart I saw or felt something like a closed bud. It was very shiny and bluish. With the Maharshi looking at me and with myself in a state of inner silence, I felt this bud open and bloom. I use the word 'bud' but this is not an exact description. It would be more correct to say that something that felt bud-like opened and bloomed

within me in the Heart. And when I say 'heart' I don't mean that the flowering was located in a particular place in the body. This Heart, this Heart of my Heart, was neither inside the body nor out of it. I can't give a more exact description of what happened. All I can say is that in the Maharshi's presence, and under his gaze, the Heart opened and bloomed. It was an extraordinary experience, one that I had never had before. I had not come looking for any kind of experience, so it totally surprised me when it happened.

Though he had had a good experience, Hariwansh decided that the teachings of Sri Ramana, which seemed to disparage visions of God, were not for him. He went to the other side of Arunachala, the holy mountain where Sri Ramana had stayed all his adult life, and continued with his Krishna meditations. Krishna appeared to him several times.

Before returning to Madras, he stopped off at Ramanasramam to see Sri Ramana once more. Hariwansh told Sri Ramana that he had been having visions of Krishna, but again Sri Ramana seemed to downplay the importance of them.

After ascertaining that the visions came and left, Sri Ramana commented, 'What is the use of a God who appears and disappears? If He is a real God, He must be with you all the time.'

Hariwansh returned to Madras to start his new job. He intensified his chanting of Krishna's name, coordinating it with his breathing, until he reached a point where he was repeating a Krishna mantra 50,000 times every day. Then, somewhat surprisingly, the gods Ram, Sita and Lakshman appeared before him in his house in Madras and stayed with him for most of the night. After they left, he found himself unable to do any more chanting. His mind simply refused to engage in the repetition of the divine name. Perplexed by this new development in his practice, he decided to return to Ramanasramam and explain his predicament to Sri Ramana.

Once he had outlined the details of what had happened, Sri Ramana responded by telling him that his practice had been like a train that had brought him to his destination. This is how Hariwansh described the meeting in *Nothing Ever Happened*:

'The train [from Madras to Tiruvannamalai,' said Sri Ramana,] 'brought you to your destination. You got off it because you didn't need it any more. It had brought you to the place you wanted to reach...

'This is what has happened with your chanting. Your *japa* [chanting of God's name], your reading, your meditation, have brought you to your spiritual destination. You don't need them any more. You yourself did not give up your practices: they left you of their own accord because they had served their purpose. You have arrived.'

Then he looked at me intently. I could feel that my whole body and mind were being washed with waves of purity. They were being purified by his silent gaze. I could feel him looking intently into my Heart. Under that spellbinding gaze I felt every atom of my body being purified. It was if a new body was being created for me. A process of transformation was going on – the old body was dying, atom by atom, and a new body was being created in its place. Then, suddenly, I understood. I knew that this man who had spoken to me was, in reality, what I already was, what I had always been. There was a sudden impact of recognition as I became aware of the Self. I use the word 'recognition' deliberately because as soon as the experience was revealed to me, I knew, unerringly, that this was the same state of peace and happiness that I had been immersed in as a six-year-old boy in Lahore on the occasion when I had refused to accept the mango drink. The silent gaze of the Maharshi re-established me in that primal state. The desire to search for an external God perished in the direct knowledge and experience of the Self which the Maharshi revealed to me. ... I knew that my spiritual quest had ended....'

Hariwansh went back to Madras where he continued to work as a contractor to the army, but he returned to Ramanasramam whenever he had free time. Within a year or so he completely fell in love with Sri Ramana's form and found it difficult to be away from him for any length of time.

In the middle of 1947, after the border between the new states of Pakistan and India had been demarcated, Hindus and Muslims on either side of the border began a mass migration: Hindus in Pakistan to India, and Muslims in India to Pakistan. Tensions ran high and many people were killed in the ensuing altercations. Hariwansh, who was then staying in Ramanasramam, was oblivious to all of this since he no longer read newspapers or kept up with the news. However, one of Sri Ramana's devotees who knew that Hariwansh's family was living on the Pakistan side of the border, informed Sri Ramana about the situation. Sri Ramana advised Hariwansh to return home to Lyalpur and bring all his family to the safety of India.

Hariwansh was disinclined to go, feeling that he no longer had any connection with his family, or any responsibility for them, but Sri Ramana persuaded him that it was still his duty to take care of them. Reluctantly, Hariwansh left Ramanasramam and brought thirty-five members of his extended family to India on the last train that left Pakistan. Once this train had crossed the border, the railway lines connecting the two countries were pulled up.

The Poonja family, who were little more than penniless refugees, then settled in Lucknow, in what is now Uttar Pradesh. Hariwansh had to remain with them there to work since the family had few resources to support itself. Most of the members of the family who accompanied Hariwansh to India were women who were unable to get jobs. Because of these family obligations Hariwansh never managed to see Sri Ramana again.

In the early 1950s, after Sri Ramana had passed away, Hariwansh returned to Tiruvannamalai with the intention of living there as a *sadhu*, but destiny had other plans for him. After a brief stay in the vicinity of Sri Ramanasramam, he took a trip to Bangalore where he was offered a job as a manager in a mining company. He accepted the appointment, primarily to have an income with which to support his family, and for the next fifteen years, until his retirement in 1966, he worked at a number of mines in Karnataka and Goa.

Once he had given up his job, he began to travel all over India, although his favourite spot seemed to be Hardwar, on the banks of the River Ganga in the foothills of the Himalayas. Although he had never announced himself as a teacher, he had always attracted small numbers of devotees wherever he went. These numbers slowly increased once he began to spend more time among the spiritual seekers who congregated at the various centres that line the banks of the Ganga in Rishikesh and Hardwar.

Between 1970 and 1990 he travelled extensively, both in India and abroad, with most of his trips being at the behest of devotees who wanted to see him. He resisted all attempts to found a centre or an ashram, preferring instead to meet with small groups in their own communities. In the late 1980s, when physical disability prevented him from travelling alone, he settled down in Lucknow, initially at his family's house in the centre of the city, and from 1991 onwards in a house in the Indira Nagar suburbs. It was there that he spent the final years of his life, giving daily satsangs, and occasionally travelling for brief visits to the Ganga. He passed away in September 1997.

In this introduction I have been referring to him as 'Hariwansh' since it is the first of his given names, but throughout his life he has had many different identities. His mother, for example, called him 'Ram' at home, and for a brief period in the 1970s he was known in the foothills of the Himalayas as 'Scorpion Baba' because of his ability to cure scorpion bites. Around 1990 he acquired the title 'Papaji', meaning 'respected father', and this honorific was used by virtually all the people who came to see him in the last few years of his life.

Papaji always denied that he had any 'teachings'. What he did have, though, was an astonishing ability to give people who came to him a direct glimpse of the Self. In the pages of this book one can see him repeatedly cajoling and pressurising his visitors into looking within themselves in order to become aware of the pristine experience of the Self that Papaji said was always there, just waiting to be acknowledged and recognised. His method was not to send people away to meditate and practise, with the long-term goal being some great spiritual experience, it was instead to show people who came to him that Self-awareness was possible here and now if one looked for it in the place where the mind and the sense of individual identity arose.

The dialogues that comprise this book come from conversations that Papaji had with visitors in his Indira Nagar home in 1991. At that time about ten to fifteen people were coming to see him every day. The original audio tapes are not dated, but I have spoken to some of the people who were present and ascertained that the satsangs were in

July and August of that year. Although some of the voices on the tapes were familiar to me, I decided not to identify them in the book. All the input from visitors is simply prefaced by the word 'Question:'.

Since Papaji was mostly talking to westerners, he did not use many of the technical terms of Hindu scriptures and philosophy. However, a few do appear from time to time, and if they are not translated in a bracketed editorial interpolation, their meaning can be found in a glossary at the end of the book.

Papaji always maintained that there was a power in the words of an enlightened being, a power that facilitated a direct experience in the people who listened to them. I believe that this power is still accessible to people who never met Papaji in person, and who have only come across him in videos or through the written word. I once asked Papaji if he accepted that there were 'mature' devotees and 'immature' devotees, meaning people who were ready for an experience of the Self and people who were not. He replied by saying that he only recognised two categories: those who could listen properly to his words, and those who could not. If you listen properly, with an utterly silent and receptive mind, to what he has to say, and look in the direction that his 'teachings' are pointing you towards, the power of the Self that produced those words will reveal itself to you.

David Godman, Tiruvannamalai, 2007

Acknowledgements

I should like to thank Aruna for transcribing all the tapes, for doing the pagemaking, and for supervising the printing work. I should also like to thank the Avadhuta Foundation for providing the funding and the general support that made the transcription work possible, and for waiting patiently while this long-overdue project was finally brought to fruition. Thanks also to the following people who read the manuscripts, pointed out errors and made useful suggestions: Chandra, Dev, Divya, Gita, Leela, Nadhia, Nola, Sarah, Venkatasubramanian, and one or two others who preferred to remain anonymous.

1

Who is thinking?

Question: I'm not clear how to make the best use of you as my teacher. I want to make the best use of my time here, but I'm not clear how I should use my time. What should I be doing that I am not doing at home?

Papaji: Take care of the purpose for which you have come. First, clarify your purpose. A relationship is not really necessary. That we can look after later. Purpose is the foremost, the most important thing.

When you are thirsty, you go to the river. Your purpose is to quench your thirst. It is not to ask the river what kind of relationship you have with it. You don't need a relationship; you only need a purpose.

You came here the day before yesterday and your purpose is to find out who you are. Find this out. Know who you are. If you first know who you are, then you will automatically know who I am. So, your first priority is the question 'Who am I?' Once you have discovered that, you will know the real nature of all the other things and people that you see. First start with this question 'Who am I?' We started on this question the day before yesterday. You need to recognise yourself. Now, what was that question I asked you to ask?

Question: Who?

Papaji: Yes, what was the full question?

Question: Who is thinking?

Papaji: Yes, this was the question I gave you. I told you to find the answer to this question. I asked you to return home to the Self through asking this question, and then to come back and tell me what you saw there.

Question: What do I see there?

Papaji: Yes, what do you see there? *[There was a pause while Papaji wrote 'who' on a piece of paper and showed it to the questioner.]* What do you see here?

Question: I see a word on a piece of paper.

Papaji: This simple word is your question.

Question: What do I see in here?

Papaji: Anywhere. Wherever the 'who' is. Your question is, 'Who is thinking?'

Question: I can see the question.

Papaji: Can you see where the question comes from? Focus on this question and look to see where it arises from. Return back to the 'who'. What do you see there?

Question: I see arising. I see things arising, one from another.

Papaji: Something arose that is the predicate. Now, what is the subject? Who is thinking? Return from this predicate of thinking and focus on the 'who'. This is the finish. Now you are at the root, aren't you? Find out who this 'who' is. What is its shape? What is the shape of this 'who'? What is its form? How is it? What does it look like?

[Long pause]

What is happening?

Question: The question just arises out of nothing, out of emptiness, and disappears back into emptiness.

Papaji: That's right. You say this question disappeared into the emptiness. The question was, 'Who is thinking?' For thinking you need a mind, don't you? Now, the process of thinking has been arrested. It happened when you put the question, 'Who is thinking?' Now the process has been arrested. Then you said, very correctly, that the question disappears. That's what you said. 'There's emptiness.' What else do you say?

Question: It's emptiness; just space.

Papaji: OK, it's emptiness; it's space. Emptiness is there; space is there. This is your inherent nature. You can call it presence or space or anything else. It is obstructed by desire and by thinking. It is always obstructed by desire. Emptiness is just the lack, the absence of thoughts and desires. When you have a burden on your shoulder, you are restless. Let us say that you are holding onto two hundred pounds and that you want to get rid of this trouble, this burden. When you drop it, you have not gained anything. You have not attained some new state that was never there before. You have simply thrown something away that was troubling you and returned to your inherent nature, the inherent state that was there before you loaded yourself up with this weight.

This thinking process, this burden, is a desire that we always carry with us. I am showing you how to drop this unwanted burden. When you ask the question, 'Who is thinking?' you arrest the process of thinking and return back to your true nature, your inherent nature, your spontaneous nature, the pure source that is empty. This is your own nature, and this is what you are always. The mind does not enter there. Time does not enter. Death does not enter. Fear does not enter. This is your inherent, eternal nature. If you stay there, there will be no fear. If you step out of it, you step into *samsara*, manifestation, and there you are in trouble all the time.

Question: I think I have a desire to make a much bigger deal of it.

Papaji: What?

Question: I think I had expectations that it would be some big, great experience, but actually the experience of it is very ordinary. It just feels very clear, very ordinary, and very empty.

Papaji: Yes, from emptiness everything arises. From emptiness all this cosmos has arisen, all this manifestation comprising millions of planets and solar systems. All of these millions of planets hanging in space arose from just one thought that arose from this particle of emptiness. This can happen without affecting the emptiness at all.

Question: Should I try to stay in the emptiness? Thoughts arise in the emptiness. Some of them are attractive; some make me afraid; and some of them are repugnant. I find myself latching onto thoughts and identifying with them. I become those thoughts. I lose sight of the emptiness and the presence until I can remind myself again.

Papaji: If you remind yourself at that time, all is over, all is gone. The best position to take is that of not forgetting. Just play your role, but don't forget that it is all just a drama on the stage.

Imagine a drama company is putting on a play. The person who has to play the servant of the king falls sick at the last moment and cannot come. No other actors are available, so the proprietor of the company steps in to play the role. In the play the king, who is one of the employees of the proprietor, orders the servant around: 'Fetch my shoes. I want to go for a walk.' The proprietor meekly obeys and carries out the orders, but does he ever forget that he is the owner of the company? He is happy to act the role of the servant because all the time that this role is being portrayed he knows that he is really the proprietor.

If you live like this, knowing that you are the Self, you can act anywhere. If you know this, all your activities will be very beautiful, and you will never suffer. Once you have had a glimpse, a knowledge of this emptiness, you will be happy all the time because you will know that all manifestation, all *samsara*, is your own projection.

Where does all this manifestation rise from? When you are asleep, there is nothing there, is there?

Question: There's another kind of dreaming then.

Papaji: I am not speaking of dreaming. We can talk about that state later. For now, I'm talking about slumber, deep sleep.

A few years ago I met a team in Rishikesh. Twenty-five people had come from all over the world: psychologists, physiologists, even parapsychologists. They had a very original proposition that they were trying to test: that there are only two states, waking and dreaming. They said that man is either awake or dreaming and that there was really no such state as sleep.

One of them told me, 'That is what we are discovering in the West. When we put an EEG on a sleeping person's brain we find that dreaming is going on all the time, even during what appears to be deep sleep.'

In India we say that there are five states: waking, dreaming, sleeping, *turiya*, and *turiyatita*.

Question: What is that last one?

Papaji: *Turiyatita*. Waking, dreaming and sleeping are states you understand. After this there is *turiya*, the fourth state. This is the state in which the previous three appear and disappear. Beyond that is *turiyatita*, which means 'beyond the fourth'.

These scientists were going from ashram to ashram, looking for swamis to test with their equipment. Some of the scientists were part of an astronaut-training programme. Apparently, astronauts were not sleeping well in space, so research was going on, looking for ways to improve their sleeping. There was a theory that some kind of meditation or yoga might improve their sleeping patterns.

These scientists were looking for swamis to test. They wanted to put electrodes on their heads while they were meditating to see what happened to the brain waves during meditation. They tried many people and eventually ended up with a man called Swami

Rama. When they arrived he was gardening in his ashram. I was not there at the time, so I got this story second-hand.

They approached him very respectfully and explained their purpose. Then they asked him if he would sit or lie down and meditate while they checked out his brain waves.

He replied, 'You can attach your wires while I am watering my garden. I don't need to sit down to meditate.'

The scientists put wires on his head and discovered that, as the swami had said, his mind was not working while he was engaged in his daily gardening chores. They were so impressed, they took him off for further tests.

If you are knowingly established in the substratum, any amount of activities can go on, and you won't need the mind to do them. The Self will take care of all these things and you will remain in peace at all times.

Let us go back to the three states – waking, dreaming and sleeping – and the underlying fourth state of emptiness. The three states are projected onto that substratum, that background in which sleeping comes and goes, dreaming comes and goes, and waking comes and goes. There is some substratum, some basic foundation on which they all revolve. That foundation, that presence, that space is always there, but while you are preoccupied with outside things, you forget it.

Now, there are three classes of people. In the first category there are those who never ever forget. Under all circumstances they know that everything is taking place in this substratum. These people are the *jivanmuktas*, which means that they are fully liberated while they are still alive in their bodies. The second category get themselves into trouble because sometimes they remember and sometimes they forget. Awareness of emptiness may be there for a while, but then the memory of a friend who has died may rise up and suddenly they are in grief. They have lost the awareness of that emptiness by attaching themselves to a thought. This kind of emptiness is not abiding; it depends on the whims of mental activities. The people in the third category are suffering all the time. They never have even a glimpse of that original space, that emptiness, and so they suffer endlessly. For them, *samsara* never ends or even stops briefly.

If you are a member of the very exclusive number one club, you know that whatever manifests is an appearance in your own Self. When you wake up, manifestation arises, but you know that it is all a projection. When you sleep, no manifestation is present, but you, your Self, will still remain. Something will still be there while you sleep, and that something is your own Self.

Question: I am not aware of that presence while I am asleep.

Papaji: Yes, it is because 'you' are not present. It is the 'you' that you live through that decides these matters. For 'you' presence is only felt when there is some obstruction to the awareness of the presence.

Question: 'When there's obstruction, I can feel presence, but when there isn't, I can't.' This sounds very paradoxical.

Papaji: Your sense of being a person is the obstruction. Everything, all your experiences, or the lack of them, are mediated through this idea of individuality. This obstruction rises from the presence and you either feel the presence through it, or you are aware of its absence. The presence is there all the time, but you don't feel it in your deep-sleep state because this mediator, this 'I', is not there. You don't know how to be aware of anything when this 'I' is absent, so you declare, 'Presence is not there when I sleep'.

You use this obstruction to validate all your experiences but it has no inherent validity of its own. *Shanti*, peace, was there before the obstruction arose, and when the obstruction subsides, *shanti* still prevails. Your inherent nature is this *shanti*. It is there both when the experiencer is there and when the experiencer is absent.

Question: Yes, it's obvious. A fish swims in water all its life, but it doesn't know anything about water. If you want to teach it about water, you take it out of the water, and immediately it understands what water is and how important it is.

What you are saying is that if there is nothing to interfere with the presence, there's nothing to contrast the presence to. And that means there is no means to know the presence.

Papaji: Here we speak of the fish that is still in the river and which cries, 'I am thirsty!' It is ignorance of the underlying substratum that creates the idea of suffering. That space, that emptiness, is your inherent nature. It is always there.

Question: *[begins to laugh uncontrollably]*

Papaji: He's a doctor of... *[Papaji also starts to laugh]*

Question: What a relief! *[Everyone in the room laughs]* I can't believe it's so simple. Hmm. Thank you. Thank you very much. I seem to remember now.

Question: *[new questioner, addressing the laughing man]* Did you forget? I watch myself and I ask myself questions such as 'Who is getting upset?' but I forget all the time.

Papaji: When you say, 'I have forgotten', you are not forgetting, you are suddenly remembering. Every time the thought 'I have forgotten' arises, that is remembrance.

Question: But there is also a point when you are not even aware that you have forgotten. You just get angry, for example, with no thought of forgetfulness or remembrance.

Papaji: You have a relationship with this entity that is forgetting or remembering. There must be a person who is forgetting. There is a person who is the same whether she has forgotten or remembered. So, the person remains the same throughout the process of remembering and forgetting. Find out the 'I' who has the forgetfulness and you will discover the 'I' that never forgets. That real 'I' is consciousness itself. It will not forget anything. It is presence itself. In that presence you don't forget anything. If light is everywhere, nothing can be hidden because there is no area of darkness where things are not clear. When you return to consciousness, everything will be very clear. Nothing will be forgotten or hidden.

There is the sleep state in which you have dreams, and there is the waking state. These are known to you. But there is something beyond them, and that is consciousness. This is your true nature. You don't have to acquire it, gain it, attain it, achieve it, or aspire for it. Since you have never lost it, you don't have to run after it to get it back. It is here now, and it will always be here. It can't be lost. If it is not here now, what is the use of trying to get it? Whatever you newly acquire you will one day lose.

So look for that which is never lost, which is permanent, abiding, natural and always there, here and now. Look into 'now'. Look into presence. Look into space. Look into your own emptiness. Everything is there in this one particle of emptiness. The whole cosmos is there, the whole cosmos. It emerges from there. Return there and see the source of all these phenomena. Then, enjoy life.

2

Throw away the oars

Question: Sometimes the awareness is there, but along with it there is still duality. Sometimes I am so intoxicated by the *shanti* [peace]. I don't care; nothing seems to matter. At other times, though, it makes me sad that there is still duality.

Papaji: For duality to be there, there must be a substratum of non-duality. For duality to be recognised as duality, there must be a non-duality that is aware of the duality.

Question: It perceives the subject.

Papaji: There should be a basis of non-duality to perceive the duality. There is no question of them being different since one is the basis and substratum of the other. What is the difference? When you see duality, what do you see?

Question: Others. Otherness.

Papaji: Yes, but where does this 'otherness' come from? When you sleep, you are alone. When you go to sleep, there are not two people asleep. Only oneness will sleep. When there is something other than you, you can't sleep, you can't be asleep. You have to reject all 'otherness' if you want to go to sleep. You have to reject your body, your mind and your intellect in order to go to sleep. Only oneness is there when you sleep.

Now, you are alone in sleep. In that sleep you create a dreamer and manifestation comes back. You see mountains, rivers and forests. Duality is there again. Then sleep comes back and in that state there are no more manifestations and dualities. Return back to this state. Who has created this duality? Who? From where? From where did this manifestation come? Who created it?

Question: There is only one source for everything.

Papaji: 'One source.' If you know there can only be one source for everything, a place from where so many things come, stay and go, if you really know this secret, how can you be troubled with dualities, manifestations and illusions? How can you be troubled by them? Let manifestation rise, stay or dissolve. This is all your drama, all your cosmic play. If you know this, you will enjoy it all.

[Long pause]

You do not need to meditate; you just need to remove all your doubts. Once the doubts have been cleared, you need not do anything. If a lake is full of weeds, you can't see the water. You can't see your reflection in the water, and you can't see the bottom of the lake. But remove all the weeds, and all will be clear.

First, it's absolutely essential that you understand things properly. Once you do, meditation may or may not follow. Just understand things. Be very, very clear about important things, such as who you are. If you haven't got this understanding, meditation is just going to be another trick of the mind; it will be an act of postponement.

Don't be deceived. Be very clear about things. That's all that is needed. With a truly quiet mind you can do anything.

Question: Is searching for the 'I' compatible with being quiet and thought-free? Or are they two different things?

Papaji: The place of silence is the place where the 'I' rises from. If you want to find out the source of this 'I' and be quiet there, first fix its geographical location. Once you know where something is, you can then decide on the best way of getting there. Before you make a decision about whether you should travel somewhere by air, by sea or by road, you have to have a destination, and you have to know where it is. How far away is the destination? What is the starting point? Once you have satisfactorily answered these two questions, it will be easy to decide the best way of making the journey.

Now, this 'I', where is it? Start with the body itself. Someone inside a body is saying 'I'. All your life you are using this word 'I'. Where is this 'I'? Where is it? First of all take note of the fact that it is there in all the three states – 'I am awake, I dreamed, I slept'. It persists in all these three states, but where does it actually reside? What is its residence? And the person who wants to discover its residence, who is this person? How far away is this person? If the destination, the object of the search, is the 'I', how far away from it is he? These things have to be discovered, clarified.

The seeker, through his search, is seeking what? What is doing the seeking? This too has to be ascertained. There is the seeker, there is the search and there is the sought. First, find out the seeker who wants to do the seeking. This is very important.

Question: *[the man from New Zealand who burst into prolonged laughter in the previous section]* It's as if presence is seeking recognition.

Papaji: *[laughing]* Very good. Yes, you are coming very close. You are coming very close. You are coming close because you understand that it is just a recognition.

Question: It all seems to arise out of vast, empty space, and then disappear back into it.

Papaji: Seeking is there because recognition is not yet established. The seeker is slowly moving through the search for recognition. It is like looking in a mirror to recognise yourself. You find the mirror, see your reflection in it, and recognise yourself. Once you have recognised yourself, you can throw away the mirror, the search, and the idea that there is something to be sought.

In recognition there is no 'who' who recognises, but no one knows this. From time immemorial everyone has been sitting endlessly in meditation. Nobody tells the truth about this process of recognition, about the necessity of it. Prayers are going on in temples and meditations are going on in monasteries, but nobody knows the truth. Nobody dares even to speak it. Everyone is walking on the beaten track, like a flock of sheep. You have to get off the beaten track. You have to take your own track, perhaps no track at all.

Question: It's so vast!

Papaji: In emptiness there are no tracks. There aren't any. Wherever you go, emptiness follows you. And emptiness leads you. Emptiness is on either side of you, above you and below you. Where can you go where you can leave behind the emptiness? Where else can you go? In that emptiness death cannot approach. Gods cannot approach there.

Question: It is. It just is.

Papaji: *[laughing]* It just is. This Kiwi is very strong *[laughter]*. It looks slow, but it is very fast. It has been very nice meeting with you. You originally asked about what relationship you had with me. This is the relationship.

Question: I have got my question answered.

Papaji: The answer! This is the only relationship. There is no other relationship that is permanent, not even with the gods. Your parents cannot provide you with this permanent relationship, nor can your priests. This is the only abiding relationship that you must have. This is the one you cannot shun. This relationship will not abandon you, and you will not be divorced from it at any time. All other relationships revolve around self-interest. Every other relationship is motivated by some interest, some desire. This relationship is sweet, very loving, and of excellent beauty. You will not find anything about this relationship in your dictionary. It is not there. I can tell you this because I am very sure about it. This relationship is not known anywhere. All the others are very ugly relationships, very ugly, very dirty relationships.

Question: I start out wanting to use you and finish up by meeting you.

Papaji: Hereafter, throw away your oars. Throw your oars into the river and you will have a very safe passage. You will sail very safely.

Question: I am very fond of the oars.

Papaji: The breeze is there. The breeze will take care of you. Using the oars is a very tiring job. Let the breeze take care of you.

Question: Fear arises when the thought of throwing away the oars appears.

Papaji: This is the right time. When I say, 'Throw away the oars', this is the right time to do it.

3

It's something that is there all the time

Papaji: *[speaking to a woman who did not seem to be fully aware of what was going on around her because of some internal experience she was immersed in]* We were walking together in the garden. Some music was playing. I looked at you and spoke to you, but you didn't hear what I said. You were the only person there who didn't hear me. You weren't taking part in what was going on because you were attending to something else, something inside you that was far more interesting and attractive. It's true, isn't it? Life could go on like this all the time. You could move through it without leaving any footprints.

Question: Footprints?

Papaji: Your mind was not engaging with anything external. You were not taking any serious part in it because you were absorbed. This is how it should happen. Eventually, you will take part, but at the same tine you will not be taking part. This is the technique to adopt. It will come slowly.

Question: This is how I have been feeling for most of this weekend.

Papaji: You are speaking too softly. Come and sit here. I don't want to ask you to repeat everything you say.

Question: *[after moving closer]* I was going to say that during this weekend I have had the feeling that there is one person who is asking 'Who is Susie?' and another one who is just observing the process. Is this what you are talking about?

Papaji: Yes, this is what I am describing. You are in the transit lounge, watching what is going on. Keep on watching. Everyone is agitated in the transit lounge. You know that. There are announcements that people are trying to catch; much activity is going on; no one is just sitting quietly. See what is going on. Observe it, comment on it if you like, but at the same time get clarity in yourself. Now is the time to do this. You have not read about this anywhere. Why? Because it is not written anywhere. It is not something that you can read in books or pick up from other people.

You are seeking clarity, a clarification of the confusion you have become aware of within yourself. It will come in a few more days, and then you can pack up and go. What you are speaking of is a good thing. Something is happening to you. Some dictation is being given to you, and you are following its commands. You are becoming an instrument, an instrument that is being activated by a power that is not your own ego. It will be a very happy life, a very beautiful life. There will be no responsibilities in it. You will be very happy.

Question: I don't think the ego is absent. Is it? It feels like it is still here.

Papaji: In this state it becomes like a burnt rope. You look at it and its shape appears to be that of a rope, but it cannot be used for anything. If you try to pick it up and tie something with it, it disintegrates in your fingers. It seems to be there, but it can no longer be used.

Question: I see. I'll try to tie something with it and see if it is still working.

Papaji: Don't think at all. Just stay as you are. Meditation is going on. It will do its work. Meditation is going on continuously. Do you see? Are you finding it?

Question: Yes, I find that…

Papaji: This is meditation.

Question: It's interesting. It feels like … some kind of perception … it's interesting … some special kind of perception is happening.

Papaji: Yes, that's what I am saying. It's meditation, but it has become effortless. Some concentration is there, but it is not attaching itself to any object, neither an object on the inside nor anything outside. You are not clinging to any object. Have you noticed?

Question: No. It just feels like meditation. I don't really know what's going on.

Papaji: *[laughing]* Yes, this is what real meditation is like. Usually, there is some attachment to sense objects, a clinging to them, but in this meditation there is nothing to cling to. There is no intention there. That's the important point. When there is no intention, there will be constant meditation. You must be feeling some difference yourself. The mind is quiet. In this state it will be quiet even if you don't meditate. You are somehow different. Haven't you noticed it?

Question: Yes. … I feel … I am knowledge.

Papaji: That's what I am saying. This is something that was known to you. It was a knowledge you had before. How to meditate, how to sit. The knowledge is there. It is coming back to you.

Question: I didn't do anything. I didn't sit and I didn't meditate.

Papaji: This is natural meditation. You don't 'do' it. It's something that is there all the time. It's called '*sahaja*', which means 'natural'. This is *sahaja* meditation.

Question: *Sahaja?*

Papaji: *Sahaja* meditation. This is the natural state. It will become your sister.

Question: This is confusing me, Papaji. You are talking about this, giving a lot of importance to this change. To me it doesn't feel like anything special.

Papaji: This is good. It may not feel special, but it is a special thing to say. *[laughter]* You didn't say this before, before you came here. At the moment, it is not 'special' to you, but if you knew this before, if this 'knowledge', as you call it, was there before, then why did you come here?

Question: I don't know.

Papaji: Now you are saying 'I don't know'. Before you knew all sorts of things. You have nothing to gain any more. Nothing more to get, nothing more to achieve. This is a return to your natural state, a very natural state. Most people can't do this. They don't want to stay as they are. They want to become something else, something they are not, and that makes them disturbed. You are making good statements. 'No change.' This is very good.

[Very long pause]

    I was staying in Rishikesh a few years ago when I was visited by a woman who came from Baroda. Have you heard of Baroda? Her husband was a petrochemical engineer. She came to Rishikesh with about fifty other people to attend a yoga course at Sivananda Ashram. They had a very busy programme. They were living in a house that was called 'Baroda House'. Baroda was once an independent state and this building had been constructed by a member of the royal family so that people who came to Rishikesh from Baroda would have somewhere to stay. It was a very big building.
    They had a very busy programme. At 5 a.m. they all had to get up and attend some yoga class. There were talks, lectures and yoga classes for most of the day, but they had some free time after

1 p.m. I was staying in a cottage that belonged to a temple which was up the hill from Rishikesh. This woman came to visit me there during this short period of free time.

She asked the priest of the temple if there was any swami in residence, and he told her, 'There is no one in orange robes you can speak to, but there is a man who teaches here who wears western clothes. He is a householder. Some foreign people are staying with him in his cottage. You can go and speak to him there.'

She wanted the priest to introduce her, but he said, 'No introduction is necessary. Just go there and join the group. No one will mind.'

There was something about her face that reminds me of you. She would eat and do things, but her attention was withdrawn into herself. She wasn't really noticing much of what was going on around her. Something was pulling her in, and she wasn't absorbing much from the outside world.

There were seven or eight foreigners with me at the time and we were speaking in English. A few Indians were also there. This woman arrived at my *satsang* with several other women who were also on the Sivananda Ashram course. She seemed to me to be the leader of the group.

After some preliminary conversation about yoga, a subject she seemed to be quite knowledgeable on, she asked me, 'Swami, how does one control the mind?'

This is a standard question that disciples have been asking gurus for thousands of years. In all that period it has never been satisfactorily answered.

Arjuna, in the *Gita*, had the same problem. 'It's just like air,' he said. 'How can it be controlled?'

Everyone on the spiritual path is obsessed with this particular question, but on this occasion I didn't give any reply. Instead, I asked a girl from France who was staying with me to make some tea for our new guests. The question was repeated, and again I made no reply. After the tea had been drunk she asked the question for the third time, and for the third time I gave no reply.

Time was running out for them because they had to return to Sivananda Ashram to carry on with their course. They had been there three days, doing this course, and they had still to complete the course before they could return home.

Just before she left she asked the question one more time, and once more I kept quiet.

The following morning, at a very early hour, she came to see me alone, carrying fruit and flowers.

She gave them to me, saying, 'I have found the answer. Even though you never answered my question while I was here, I wanted to come again and repeat it because it was really bothering me. In the middle of the night, at about 1.30 a.m., someone knocked on my door. I assumed it was someone from my group, but when I opened the door it was you.'

I hadn't been anywhere that night. I had been asleep in bed when this story apparently took place.

'You came to my door,' she continued, 'and somehow you gave me the answer. Now I am satisfied. We came here for a month of yoga training as a group. We booked a whole coach on a train and we are all travelling together. I don't want to go back on the coach with everyone else. I want to stay here with you.'

I tried to discourage her: 'You can continue staying where you are. You can finish your course and then go home to Baroda with everyone else.'

'No,' she said, 'I want to stay here with you.'

When I saw that she was determined to stay with me, I asked her to go and see the manager of this ashram I was in since I couldn't let anyone else stay there without getting his permission first. When the manager gave the necessary permission, she moved into a nearby room. Afterwards, she came to my room, sat down and refused to move or even eat. She was absorbed in some inward state and didn't want to bother with the business of ordinary life. She could hear what I was saying, but she didn't feel inclined to stir herself and do anything that I suggested. She did not even speak to me when I asked her to do things.

Her name was Suman. 'Suman,' I would say, 'You are not

eating. You have to eat. I will help you.'

I put food in her hand but she refused to lift the hand up to her mouth. I had to lift her arm as well and place her hand next to her mouth. She never complained about any of this, but she wouldn't do any of the work herself.

I made her open her mouth to put the food in, and then I told her, 'That's all I can do for you. You have to do the munching and swallowing yourself. I can't do that for you.'

She gave me a lot of trouble for two days. She sat there for this whole period, day and night, just staring vacantly and not responding to any of the suggestions that I gave her. I couldn't make her go back to her room. She just sat on my floor and refused to move. There were seven or eight of us staying there at the time. We had four rooms between us. I had a room to myself and the others shared the other three rooms. The manager knew me and usually gave me these rooms every year for three months. It was a good place – up in the mountains, away from the town of Rishikesh.

I wanted to send this woman home to her family, but I knew that in her current state I would have to make all the arrangements myself. I took her in a taxi to Hardwar, purchased a first class ticket to Baroda, bought some sweets to give to her children, and gave her a bottle of Ganga water to take back for anyone who wanted some. I tried to make her eat at the station, but she wasn't interested.

She tried to give me all her money, saying, 'I don't need this any more. I will keep five rupees for the journey. I can get a taxi at the other end and my family can pay for it when I arrive home. Now, everything I have belongs to you. I want you to take it all.'

I refused to take it. Since I could see that she was in no fit condition to look after herself, I spoke to the man who was sharing the first class carriage with her. I had found out her family's phone number, so I gave it to the man in the carriage.

'When the train reaches Baroda,' I said, 'please call this number and make sure that someone comes to collect her. Otherwise she will just wander around and get lost.'

When I explained to the man in the carriage that Suman was having problems looking after herself, he promised to take care of her until her family could take delivery of her in Baroda. Since the train stopped for twenty minutes at Baroda, there would be enough time to make all the arrangements.

'Will she eat?' he asked, and I replied, 'If you put some food in her hand and tell her to put it in her mouth, chew it and swallow, she will probably do it. But don't worry if she doesn't eat. She can easily last until her family comes. There is nothing physically wrong with her. She is just very absent-minded at the moment. Her attention is elsewhere.'

Everything went according to plan and she arrived safely at her house. Her husband sent me a telegram, thanking me for all the trouble I had taken to get her home. He even invited me to come and stay with them. Suman had apparently told him that if I didn't come to them, she would leave and look for me.

This was a very rare case. Someone who got it instantly from the teacher. She came with a burning question – 'How to control the mind?' – and without my saying anything she experienced the state in which mind no longer needs to be controlled. It is the state of no-abiding, the state in which the mind does not abide anywhere. There have been two or three cases like this; they are not common.

I accepted the husband's invitation and went and spent fifteen days with them. Then I took her to Bombay where I visited some other devotees.

These things do sometimes happen very quickly. In some people it doesn't happen at all.

There is a never-ending cycle of birth and death. What is birth and what is death? They are desire. This never-ending cycle is fuelled by desire, the desire to enjoy sense objects in a body. When desire ceases, this cycle also ceases. This apparently endless cycle of birth and death ends with the cessation of desire. It is not only birth and death that end. When desire ceases, the universe itself ceases. It is as if it never existed. That's how it is.

Question: *[new questioner]* I have a question about the mind. It seemed to me this morning that the mind is not just something that one needs to disengage from. It seems that it can take me to wherever I need to go.

Papaji: Mind can be the enemy and mind can also be the friend. It is the mind that binds and it is the mind that liberates. When the mind is attached to objects, which are transitory and impermanent, this is the mind that binds. This is the mind that is an enemy. But a mind that does not abide anywhere, on any object, is a mind that is your friend. This is the mind that liberates. It all depends on you, on what kind of company you keep in your mind. Mind can destroy you, but mind can also be of great help. There is a tremendous power in the mind, a power that you can make use of. When the mind is at rest, it gives us peace. But when it is restless, it creates all this *samsara*, this suffering, this hell. A peaceful mind brings heaven down to earth. It brings peace everywhere. In that state, wherever you walk, that place will be heaven. This is the mind.

Question: It seems to me that there is a choice. The mind can decide whether to create a heaven or a hell. At any given moment that choice is there.

Papaji: Yes, that is your own choice. You have to decide these things for yourself. You can decide, 'I am bound; I have to suffer,' and this creates *samsara*. Alternatively, you can say, 'I want peace. I want freedom. I want happiness. I want love.' When you move in this direction, what a beautiful choice you have made! Make it! 'I want freedom! I want to be free! I want happiness! I want love!' Do it now, today, or at least some time during your span of life. Have a good mind, a friendly mind.

Question: *[new questioner]* When mind is not abiding, does mind still exist?

Papaji: No. When a desire arises in the mind, there arises with it an intention to enjoy sense objects. When this happens you are involved in their enjoyment. The mind works through the senses;

the senses move out to objects that they can enjoy. All these things manifest once desire and intention arise. Your intention makes the mind the agent for the various enjoyments it indulges in. In the middle of all this is the ego, the enjoyer of all the objects that are being pursued and enjoyed. If the ego remains still, mind itself does not arise. It does not cause any trouble. It will not abide anywhere, and with no place to abide, it will return to its source, to the place of no-mind. In that place there will be no mind.

You can function without this mind. You can function very well without it. Earlier today this girl was talking about how this can work. She was talking about the state in which no mind does the work. What did you say? Can you repeat it again?

Question: *[the woman who reminded Papaji of Suman]* I was saying that there is an actor and the observer.

Papaji: Yes, this is how it is. Can you explain it a little more?

Question: It feels as if there is an actor and an observer in the same person. And the body just seems to act by itself.

Papaji: The body is acting and the observer is different from it. The body is receiving direct instructions, but not through the ego. The 'I am the doer' idea is not there. When the doer is not there, one is not responsible for one's actions. No karma is formed in this state. This is no mind. You can work very well without this mind.

Question: *[new questioner]* Why does mind arise again afterwards?

Papaji: If you are careful and vigilant in this state, it is not mind that rises again. Something else is going to rise in its place. What's that 'other'? Now, you only know about the mind. You don't know about what is beyond it. When mind has gone, when mind is finished, you no longer have desires, and when you don't have desires, you return to the source. In that source something else will animate you, something that you have not been aware of before. You can call it *prajna*, wisdom. It will look after you, and it will do a very good job. When *prajna* runs your life, you will just be its instrument. This was explained well in the *Gita*. Arjuna surrendered his mind at the feet of his Master, and then allowed *prajna* to dictate his actions. The command to fight started with the direct command of Krishna. That command worked through Arjuna and carried him through the battle. This word, this state of being dictated to by the divine, can only be known after freedom.

4

Desires will only be a problem when they leave an impression in the mind

Question: It is fairly easy for me to convince myself that I have no desires, but how do I know that it is true? If I need something in the moment, how do I know if it is a need or a desire? I may be eating, for example. I eat a little, and if I still feel a little hungry, I might decide to eat some more. How do I tell if that extra helping of food is a need or a desire? I can convince myself that I need to eat to survive, but when does genuine need cross the boundary into self-indulgent desire?

Papaji: If you feel hungry, you eat. If you feel thirsty, you drink. These are not desires. You eat, you drink, and then you forget about it. Can you remember what you had for lunch two days ago? If you can't, there is no desire involved. It was just something you did, which you needed to do, and then forgot about.

Question: Actually, I don't remember that particular meal, but since I tend to eat the same thing every day, I could make a good guess about what I probably ate at that meal.

Papaji: This amounts to the same thing. If you eat the same thing every day, it's not a desire. You are inhaling air every few seconds. Do you have a problem with this? Do you have a desire to breathe in before you inhale? If you forget to inhale, what will happen to you?

Question: I'll die.

Papaji: So, inhaling is the most important need. Until you have satisfied this one, you can't even begin to satisfy any of the others. But desire is actually something that you keep in the mind, something that troubles you because you are having some problem in fulfilling it. Desire is something that stays in the memory; it's something that you can't get rid of. Breathing is not like this because it goes on automatically. It doesn't nag at you, saying, 'Fulfil my desire to breathe'. Food is somewhat similar. When you feel hungry, you put food in the mouth; you swallow it, and then you forget about it. Once the food has gone into the stomach, you forget about it.

Desires that are not fulfilled are the ones that are going to trouble you. Desires that land in the memory are going to cause problems. They will always be pushing themselves forward, saying, 'I must have this, I must have this'. Pressure to fulfil unfulfilled desires brings about manifestation. It is *samsara*. This is why we are all here again, in yet another birth. If there was no desire, you would not have manifested at all. This desire is bringing you into a body again and again. Desire is attachment, and attachment causes us endless problems. It is better to forget desires completely. Don't let them lodge in the memory.

Fulfilling the necessities of life will not cause you any problems. It is the other ones that will cause you trouble.

Question: Yes, fulfilling desires seems to be an endless thorn. It's jabbing all the time, making me go out to fulfil desires again and again.

Papaji: Desires will only be a problem when they leave an impression in the mind. It is the impressions that are dangerous, not the desires themselves. When a bird flies, it doesn't leave a mark in the air. When a fish swims it doesn't leave any trace on the surface of the water. If we could move through life without leaving any impressions, any footprints, on the mind, we would have no problems at all. These footprints are the problem, not the desires themselves. You store up thoughts in your mind: 'I should have done this; I should not have done that,' and so on. These are the footprints that bring you back again and again to engage with this world process.

There was a teacher who was travelling with his student in the forest. There had been some heavy rain and a small, shallow stream had swollen into a much deeper river. The two of them put their robes on their shoulders and prepared to ford the river. On the bank of the river there was a prostitute who had to reach the other side of the river because she had been booked to dance at a wedding. She was in her full dancing regalia and couldn't cross because it was neck deep. The teacher put her on his shoulders, carried her across the river and put her down on the other side. She went off to her function and the student and the teacher continued their journey.

The student was very concerned about what his teacher had done. He thought to himself, 'My teacher says I must never touch a woman, yet he has lifted a prostitute and carried her across this river'. For quite some time these thoughts were bothering him.

Eventually, ten miles down the road, he turned to his teacher and asked, 'Sir, may I ask a question?' and the teacher said 'Yes'.

'Didn't you tell me never to touch a woman?'

'Yes, I did.'

'Well, what about this woman you helped across the river. She was a prostitute, yet you helped her to cross the river by putting her on your shoulders.'

The teacher replied, 'She wanted and needed help. She needed to cross the river to go to work. She would not have been able to cross the river without our help. I put her on my shoulders and carried her across. I did my job, put her down, and then forgot all about it. Why are you still carrying her? I put her down miles ago.'

The prostitute here denotes desire. The teacher did what was necessary, and then forgot all about it. The student had thoughts about the incident – footprints – in his head, and these caused him to suffer for ten miles of walking. If something needs to be done, do it and forget about it. Don't carry thoughts about it afterwards. These lingering thoughts will bring you back into *samsara*, back into the endless round of birth and death. Whenever there is a desire that leaves footprints, there is *samsara*. Where there is desire of this kind, there is bondage. When there is no desire at all, there is freedom. The desire-free state is nirvana, the pure state of nirvana. Nirvana means 'no desire'.

Question: Does having no desire mean having no thought? When you arrive at the place of no desires, do thoughts arise, or are they absent?

Papaji: Thought itself is a desire. Thought arises because of an earlier desire for something. Desire and thought arise together.

Question: What about abstract thought?

Papaji: What is abstract thought? Abstract thought is 'I am nirvana. I am thoughtless. I am free.' This is abstract thought. Abstract thought is no thought. The state of no thoughts is abstract thought. Why should there be thoughts then?

Question: You say 'Leave no footprints', and I can appreciate the wisdom of what you are saying. It sounds the right and perfect way to live. But what do I do with the footprints that are already there? My memory is full of them.

Papaji: Yes, the memory is still there. And yet, at the same time, you aspire for this nirvana. Let this aspiration be a candle in your hand, a fire in your hand, a torch in your hand. The torch – 'I want to be free' – is in your hand. When you enter the room that contains all these desires, what will happen next?

Question: You see them.

Papaji: This torch you have in your hand is not just for looking; it is also for burning. If you look at a desire, it will burn. Go on. Do it. Pick up any desire that you can find in this room of memories, any thought you like, put it in front of you, and look at it. Hurry up! You have a torch. Shine it on something in your memory.

You have to understand what I need from you. When you have that burning torch in your hand, the thought in front of you gets lit. It catches fire and burns. Look at something in front of you. What do you see?

Question: The desire itself. I see it with the torch.

Papaji: You haven't done it. I will explain again. Take a torch in your hand. Bring out a thought or a desire in front of you and see what it is. May I explain again what I want you to do? Take a torch in your hand and shine it on any object that comes in front of you in your mind. If it is a towel, then you say 'I see a towel'. Just tell me whatever thought is coming up in front of you. I am not asking you to guess or speculate or give some philosophical answer. I am simply asking you to shine a torch into this store of memories that you were just complaining about and tell me what you see.

You are thinking about this as if it is some puzzle that you have to solve. It is not. I am just asking you to tell me what you see. If, as you claim, you have a memory full of old thoughts, it shouldn't be hard to find one. Speak up! There are always twenty thousand thoughts fighting for attention. Pick one up, put it down in front of you, look at it, and then tell me, 'This is the thought that I see'. Come on, tell me. Why is this taking so much time?

Question: Ah … it's only one thought that you want. You want exactly….

Papaji: That's what I am saying. Listen properly. Repeat to yourself what I have just told you, and then reply. Don't waste the time of the others. Take this torch in your hand, shine it, and then tell me what it is illuminating. What is the thought that is at the forefront of your mind?

Question: No thought.

Papaji: Ah, that's it. 'No thought.' You said it was difficult. If you keep this torch in your hand and look for a thought or a desire, everything will disappear. This is the state of nirvana. What else could nirvana be? There, you have no thoughts. If you have no thoughts, there is no time; no time means no mind; no mind means no memory; no memory means no garbage; no garbage means no *samsara*; no *samsara* means no cycle, no cycle of birth and death; no cycle of birth and death means no suffering. This is how to end it all, right now, in this moment. It doesn't take time at all. It can be done right now.

Question: *[new questioner]* When I hold up that torch, I see a desire to be healthy, to have no pain in my body. What should I do with that desire?

Papaji: That's OK. You can keep this desire.

Question: I can keep this one?

Papaji: The body is something on the outside. Maintaining good health and having a desire to stay healthy are not going to create problems for you.

Then, when you have this good health, have a look at what you have. Study it carefully. Ask yourself, 'What is this body? Is the body inside or outside?' Find out what the source of this body is. You say, 'I have a body'. What is the source of this statement? What is this 'I' that claims it has a body? What is your relationship with this body?

Question: I am a body.

Papaji: And then you say, 'I want to have a healthy body'.

Question: Yes, I want a healthy body.

Papaji: OK, so let's go back to my question 'Who is this "I" who owns the body?'

Question: The 'I' who owns the body is healthy at the moment.

Papaji: Go to this 'I' and find out more about it. It will give you very powerful assistance. Return to this 'I' and you will see a very healthy body. Go there and see for yourself. Return to the source of this question, and you will get its answer. Go back to the 'I'. Slowly go back there. You start with 'I want a healthy body'. Go back to the 'I' that wants it and see what is there. What are you getting out of this? Do it slowly, but first understand what I mean, what I am talking about. 'I' is the subject and 'need a healthy body' is the predicate. I am advising you to stay with the subject and ignore the predicate. Begin with this 'I'. Return to its source and finish the enquiry. You don't need to meditate to do this. Just return there following the way that you emerged. As you came out, go back that same way.

Question: OK. The body needs a healthy 'I'.

Papaji: OK. Now find out if this 'I' is healthy or diseased. How about this 'I'? Is it a sick 'I' or a healthy 'I'?

Question: Healthy.

Papaji: If it is healthy, then everything is healthy because I can tell you that this 'I' is everything. Stick to this thing, this 'I' that you are saying is healthy. If you step out of it, there will be suffering, disease, unhappiness and death. Just step out of it and see what happens.

Question: I don't think I want to step out of it.

Papaji: You wrote this letter to me, didn't you? In this letter you said that you could find no words to express your gratitude. You say, 'I have no words to express the gratitude'. So, you don't need words. This is the best kind of expression. Silence is the best expression and the highest state. It is a very rare state to live in. You say, 'I can't find any words of gratitude'. You don't need any words if you are in that silence. There is no word that has so far been found in any dictionary that expresses the gratitude of this silence.

People say, 'In the beginning was the word'. The word goes

right back to the beginning. Then the statement goes on to say 'and the word was God'. So God is also a word. But beyond words, beyond God, who is also just a word, there is something else, something that no one ever speaks about. Everyone can use words; everyone can talk about God or any other word, but that is not the true experience. In the true experience there are no words at all. If you have found this silence, you won't need any words at all. It's a very good place to be. It will be enough for you.

[Long pause]

'I am free' is a healthy thought. If you keep up this thought, everything will instantaneously be healthy. If not, everybody will suffer. The other thoughts that keep you busy all the time are just a disease that stops you from being truly healthy. To ward off this disease, just keep up this thought of freedom: 'I am free; I am in nirvana'. A healthy mind will keep the body healthy as well. And for a healthy mind have the thought 'I am free'. This is the most healthy thought.

When you say, 'I am the body', this is a diseased thought. If you think like this, you are living in the graveyard. All bodies sooner or later have to return to the graveyard, don't they? When you have this 'I am the body' thought, you are living in a graveyard, but the opposite thought, 'I am not the body', is a very healthy thought. Why should you have bad thoughts? If you have a mind that can think, then use it to have good thoughts. There is no better thought than this 'I am free' thought. If you can't stick to this 'I am free' thought, the other thoughts that displace it will put you in suffering. You therefore have this option. The choice is left to you which way you go. You become what you think; you are what you think. If the mind decides, 'I am bound', then 'bound' is what you are. But if the mind decides, 'I am free', then 'free' is what you are. It's entirely your own decision.

It's a very rare choice that is available to very few human beings. There are six billion human beings and countless other species. There are very few of us, but how many mosquitoes are there? How much marine life is there? How many worms? How many germs? How many people or beings are presented with this choice? Out of six billion people and the countless billions of other animals, how many truly aspire for freedom? How many? I would say that twenty would be a liberal estimate. It's a very small number. They are very lucky people. They have a mountain of luck, a mountain of past merits. Only when you have a mountain of merits can you aspire for freedom.

Question: *[new questioner]* Isn't saying 'I want to be free' also some kind of attachment? If you are really free, you don't have to think about it or say it. You are saying that this one thought – 'I want to be free' – can take you to freedom, but isn't clinging to this thought all the time also some sort of attachment?

Papaji: This thought is a symptom, a sign that other attachments have been dropped. When you have detached yourself from everything in the past, present and future, only then will this thought arise. How can you give rise to this? It will only arise after the cremation of all other thoughts. Once it happens, once the other thoughts have been dropped, it has an unstoppable momentum that takes you to your goal.

Look at the case of the Buddha. A prince is asleep in his palace in the middle of the night. The most beautiful woman in the kingdom is lying by his side. He gets out of bed and the thought arises in him, 'I want to be free'. That thought arose because the other thoughts, the other attachments, no longer had any hold on him. He had wealth, youth, health, a comfortable life, a beautiful wife, but nothing mattered to him except this thought 'I want to be free'.

This man had never seen suffering at all because none was allowed inside his palace. Yet, in that moment, 2,600 years ago, an unstoppable thought, 'I want to be free', arose in this prince. All his previous attachments were instantly dropped. There was a horse waiting for him outside the palace gates. The horse made no noise and the palace guards slept through his escape. Some power, freedom itself, helped him to escape because it wanted to claim him.

No ordinary man can have that thought. This thought will rise up, and its rising will end all other desires. In ordinary minds thoughts of enjoyment will come. 'I want to have this. This much I have right now. Tomorrow I will have some more.' This is desire. This is attachment, and this is the state in which virtually everyone lives. Those six billion people I was just speaking of are all planning and scheming: 'Today I have this; tomorrow I will have that.' This is how you are all living, and this is *samsara*. 'I am enjoying so much today, and tomorrow I will enjoy even more.'

You are living in this body like a parrot in a cage. At any moment this parrot can fly away. You are only guaranteed this instant to make this decision. Future instants are not under your control, and they may not even be given to you. Make the best of the present moment because the future is not in your hands.

5

People who want to be busy don't come to *satsangs* such as these

Question: I can see that I still have many doubts. I think I am somehow expecting to have some big experience, but at the same time I look at myself and I see that I haven't changed. I listen to you when you say it is very simple and I think I doubt that too. There is some expectation that it ought to be...

Papaji: ...very hard, very difficult.

Question: Yes, difficult.

Papaji: So you would be more inclined to believe me if I prescribed some hard penance for you. Maybe I should tell you to go to the Himalayas and hang yourself upside down for a long time. I have seen people who do that.

Question: I don't know what to think.

Papaji: This is what people are doing. You can join them and do these idiotic things or you can keep quiet. You can do these yoga exercises if you want to. You can put your head down and your feet up for an hour while you chant your mantras. The mind wants to engage you in activities. It is going to encourage you to do silly things because it likes to be busy. But if I say, 'Don't stir a single thought', you can't do it. And you don't want to do it because you think it is too simple. Just give up all your mental activities for some time and see what happens.

Question: I still have so many concepts, and they are all swirling around inside me. Theories about different states of consciousness, theories about energy and light coming up in certain places, and so on. All these different things.

Papaji: Yes, different books describe these things in different ways. These differing accounts are meant for different kinds of temperaments. What kind of spiritual exercise you pick will depend on your spiritual temperament. Because everyone wants to keep his mind engaged in activities, many different methods are prescribed for all the different types of people. But no one teaches anyone to keep quiet. The teachings that people receive are all about doing things and keeping busy. You can keep the voice busy with chanting or singing, you can keep the body busy with yoga or *pranayama*, or you can keep the mind busy by making it concentrate on an object of meditation. While you are busy in all these different ways, you are never keeping quiet. Religions and teachers can only thrive as long as they have activities to prescribe and enforce. If you keep quiet, the religions will fail, the teachers will fail, and the teachings will fail. Just keep quiet. That is the way to find peace and love among people.

Keep quiet and the whole structure of religion will collapse. Religion teaches you fear: 'If you don't do this or that you will go to hell.' All religions are based on fear, fear of the consequences of not doing what the religious teachers tell you you must do. No religion teaches you to keep quiet, to rest quietly in your own Self.

If you can keep quiet for just a few minutes of your whole span of life, perhaps you will win peace. This is the way to approach reality, liberation, nirvana. Keeping quiet is up to you.

People who want to be busy don't come to *satsangs* such as these. Since they can't sit still even for a few minutes, their temperaments will take them somewhere else. They will go to the hills. They will go to the Himalayas, crying out that they must visit this temple or that one. They will spend weeks walking to

Badrinath or Kedarnath. These places are twelve thousand feet high, and you need to expend a lot of effort to get there. These people who cannot spend five minutes sitting quietly in their houses will happily suffer physically for weeks on their journey to one of these places. If you ask them, they will say that they are going to these places because their religion prescribes such activities. The real reason is that they can't keep quiet for five minutes, so they have to do something else instead.

If a teacher just tells you to stay at home and keep quiet, his business will not flourish. He cannot run his business giving out advice such as this, so he has to tell you something else instead. No religion will survive on advice such as this. No teaching will flourish and no books will be published.

Just keep quiet. This is the way. Without this, you will not find peace anywhere. Doing and thinking will not produce peace.

Question: I have memories of experiences I once had: energy everywhere in the body, intense feelings of bliss, and so on. When I sit here I have an expectation that something like this should happen because of this past memory. My feeling is, 'If it is not like this, then it cannot be real'. This makes it very difficult for me to accept that keeping quiet will be enough. I have expectations of something more, something dramatic and tangible.

Papaji: You should not expect anything at all. An expectation is something that your mind projects. When this happens, your mind just runs after this projection, wanting to fulfil or experience it. While this is going on, the mind is not quiet. So, first of all, you have to keep your mind quiet, and this means that expectations should not arise in the mind.

'Where does this expectation rise from?' Go back to its source and see. Having expectations did not provide you with any satisfaction, any peace. Since you have not fulfilled your expectations and since having them is not making you happy, spend a few minutes of your time on discovering where this expectation comes from. What is its source? If you can't find satisfaction outside by having an expectation, or by trying to fulfil it, look inside and find the place where it arises. Try to locate that place. Instead of running outside, arrest the mind which is running out and bring it back to its source.

You can do whatever you want. You can follow whatever path seems helpful to you. There is no pressure here. Follow whatever path brings good results. The results are more important than the teaching itself. It is better that you work on this problem yourself and come to your own conclusion. You want peace of mind, don't you? Investigate how it can happen. Work on yourself and see. You have been going to see so many gurus and ashrams. Wherever you are benefited, go to that place.

Question: *[new questioner]* Is it all right sometimes to do some sort of exercise? If we feel there is a benefit, should we do them? Sometimes it feels good to do some form of spiritual exercise, and at other times it feels good to keep quiet. Is there some sort of contradiction here?

Papaji: No, no, doing these exercises is not a problem. Since you can't sit quietly all the time, you do some yogic exercises. There is no harm in this. You have to maintain the body. Eating good food and doing some form of yoga can be good for this.

Question: I was thinking more about mental exercises.

Papaji: They can also be helpful.

Question: So, if one feels some benefit, it's better to practise to reach a quiet mind? For example, I have found from experience that if I concentrate on my breath, I feel that after some time it is easier for me to sit down and be quiet.

Papaji: These things can be helpful. Breathing exercises can be helpful because while you are controlling the breath, the thought processes are also being controlled. These exercises are also good for the health. Usually we have sixteen breaths every minute. If you can reduce that to twelve by having longer, deeper breaths, you will improve your health, and if you are watching your breathing at the same time, your thoughts will be less. So *pranayama* [breath control] and yogic exercises are good. They go together. If your body is sick, you can't do anything. You must maintain it properly with good food, sattvic food, and some exercise. There are many exercises that you can do, but a few minutes of yoga every day will always benefit you physically. In America there are programmes on TV every morning that get people to do a few simple exercises before they go off to work.

Question: There are also exercises in which the breath is retained for some time. They also feel good to me. Is it OK to do these practices, or are they dangerous?

Papaji: You can also do this. The ratio should be four-eight-four. Four seconds inhalation, eight seconds retention and four seconds exhalation.

Question: I have heard of exercises where the retention is much longer – a minute or more.

Papaji: Retention of the breath is called *kumbhaka*. While *kumbhaka* is being practised, you cannot think. *Pranayama* also wards off many diseases. Do it in the fresh air, where the air is good. Before you start your meditation, you can do some *pranayama* to calm the mind. Slowing the breath is also good for physical longevity, if that's what you want. Animals that have short lives usually breathe very quickly. Animals that have long slow breaths live much longer. The human life span is calculated to be about eighty years, breathing at the usual rate of sixteen breaths a minute. If you can learn to slow your breath down over a long period of time, you will get healthier and live longer.

[There was a long pause and then Papaji turned to a new person.]

Where are you from?

Question: Arizona.

Papaji: These exercises I have been talking about come from a different method, a different school. The school of *kundalini* yoga. The *kundalini* energy will rise if you do them properly, but to do this properly you need a very special way of life. You have to live in a very clean place where the air is clean and you have to make the body very sattvic. I don't think this is possible nowadays. Very few people can do it. People teach it, but they haven't been able to put the teachings into practice themselves. I have seen one man in Rishikesh who could do this, but he was the only one. The rest just talk about it. There are books about it also. There are Sanskrit texts translated by Woodroffe such as *Yoga Pradipika*. Has anybody read it?

Question: I have seen it. Didn't he call himself 'Avalon' when he wrote it?

Papaji: It's an excellent book, and very well written. It was translated by Woodroffe. I saw it thirty or forty years ago. Good photos and diagrams of all the chakras. It was a very nice book with very good descriptions.

Question: *[new questioner]* What do you mean by a special kind of life?

Papaji: You have to live a secluded life, without contact with many people. You have to have a special diet with very light food, and you have to spend the whole day doing these practices. These exercises will only work if you do them full-time.

Question: What is the difference between the kind of experiences you get from pursuing these exercises and freedom?

Papaji: Through these exercises you can get all kinds of powers: levitation, multi-location, manifesting objects, and so on. You can read minds and you can be clairvoyant – all these things are possible through this power. But all these special powers will function through the ego. 'I am doing this feat', 'I am performing levitation', and so on. The 'I' is still there. Sometimes, some of these powers come to people even if they haven't done any practices to attain them.

I met one man in the Himalayas who could levitate. He could stay suspended in mid-air, but he was restless and without peace.

He told me, 'My guru taught me to do this, but before he died he said, "This is not the ultimate truth. I was not able to find a teacher who could give me this ultimate truth. After I pass away, look for a teacher who can give you true knowledge."'

That man showed me all his powers, and some of them were very impressive. I met another man in Gujarat who was clairvoyant. He could see into your mind and tell you exactly why you had come to see him. These are powers, though. They are not freedom. The powers belong to *samsara*, and the more you indulge in them, the more *samsara* multiplies.

Question: *[new questioner]* Are you saying that these powers take you away from freedom? Or are they a stage that one goes through on the way to freedom?

Papaji: They don't lead you to freedom because they keep you preoccupied with other things, things that have nothing to do with the Self. If you are pure enough and practise long enough, you can learn how to levitate. The instructions are there in Patanjali's *Yoga Sutras*. You can spend years on this, but even if you finally succeed, you are only doing something that every butterfly can do.

Question: The main idea of *kundalini* yoga is not levitation. It is to make the *kundalini* rise to the head. The yogis and the yogic texts say that when it reaches the *sahasrara*, freedom results.

Papaji: Freedom does not rise or fall, nor is it a result of anything rising or falling. People who master *kundalini* yoga can sit in a yogic *samadhi* for months at a time, but this is not freedom.

A few hundred years ago there was one man who could enter *samadhi* for six months at a time. He went to his king and said,

'I can sit in *samadhi* for six months, without eating, and without answering the call of nature'.

The king didn't believe him so he said, 'If you can do this, I will give you anything you want'.

The yogi said, 'I want the horse that you ride. When I come out of meditation after six months, you must reward me by giving me the horse that you ride.' The king agreed to the terms.

Six months passed but the yogi could not come out of his meditation. Years went by and he was still stuck in this state. The king died and his son took over. After twenty years the yogi opened his eyes. Since everyone in the court knew the story of this yogi, he was taken to the king as soon as he had regained full consciousness.

He told the new king, 'I want the horse that was promised to me'.

The king told him, 'I know about this promise that was made by my father but I can't fulfil it because that particular horse died years ago. However, I will happily give you a new one since you have proved your point.'

When the yogi went into this *samadhi*, he had the desire for a particular horse and the expectation that he would be given a horse when he came out of the *samadhi* a few months later. This is not freedom. He suspended his mind and his desire for twenty years, but when they started functioning again, the desire was still there. True freedom is not to have any desire at all.

Does a king ever think, 'I want that building over there', or, 'I want that particular horse'? He doesn't because he knows that everything already belongs to him. Everything in his domain is his already. When, through desirelessness, you reach the Self, you find that everything is your own Self, and in that state the thought 'I want this' or 'I want that' no longer arises because there is nothing separate from you, and no 'I' to want it. When everything is your own Self and nothing is apart from you, how can there be anything separate from you that you desire to own? In that state you will not have to beg for anything.

There was another Indian king who used to give to whomsoever came to him for assistance. After he came out from his prayers, he would give to anyone who had come to see him. A fakir came to see him while he was praying. The king was praying out loud, so the fakir could hear that he was asking for God's assistance on several matters.

When the prayers were over, the king came out and said, 'I've finished praying. Now you can tell me what you want. Whatever it is, I will give it to you.'

The fakir replied, 'I thought I had come to see a king but I have discovered that you too are a beggar. You are begging from God. I came here with a small desire which I thought you might be able to fulfil, but now I see that it is better to beg from the same person that you are begging from. I will take my request directly to God himself.'

Who is not a beggar in this world? Everyone is begging either from other people or from God himself. But there is another way. If you don't ask for anything, and if you desire nothing, then everything will be given to you. People say that God is very happy when you go to him and say, 'I want this', or 'I want that'. When this happens, you get what you want, but then you walk away from God. However, when you want nothing at all, if you ask for nothing and desire nothing, then God himself will be walking behind you, following you wherever you go. Whatever you do and wherever you go, he will always be there. Don't ask and don't desire and everything will be added unto you. Then, you will not need to beg any more.

Question: *[new questioner]* I once had an experience in which I felt that I was dissolving totally. I felt that my body was dissolving, and everything else was dissolving as well. It was the most beautiful and peaceful thing I have ever experienced, but it was so overwhelming I was not able to do anything in the world. All I could do was lie down and do nothing at all. This experience has gone now, but the memory of it is still there. Nowadays, I tend to compare this experience with others. I have this feeling that this state was freedom, or something very close to it, because

I can't think of anything more beautiful than being in that state. My ego, my sense of 'I', had dissolved in that state, rendering me incapable of doing anything. How can it be that people are able to function in the state in which the 'I' has gone? It was my experience that I could do nothing except lie down and enjoy it.

Papaji: You were not near a real teacher at that time. That was your problem, your misfortune. If you had been able to meet with a true teacher at that time he would have shown you another way, a way in which you could have been 200 per cent active, not just normally active.

Question: So it is possible to be in this state and still act normally in the world?

Papaji: Yes, and as I just said, you can be twice as active as everyone else. 200 per cent active.

6

Supreme devotion is not to give rise to a single thought.

Question: Papa, Kavita and I had a debate this morning about *prakriti*. If I understand it correctly, *prakriti* is the five elements plus mind. We were not quite sure whether mind is actually creating the elements. Or alternatively, that the elements are there and that the mind, by perceiving them brings them into existence.

Papaji: They're simultaneous.

Question: If the mind is looking at a fire, it is saying, 'There's a fire'. Are you saying that if the mind is not saying 'There's a fire', then fire is not there?

Papaji: Mind creates everything, simultaneously. First the mind is there, and then, simultaneously, everything else is there. Mind is thought, isn't it? When you wake up, thought arises. The mind rises first, and then everything arises simultaneously.

You are asking about nature, the combination of the five elements. The grossest thing is earth, the first element. Then less gross, more subtle, is water, and so on. The last element, the most subtle one, is ether, space. But where did all these elements spring from? They are all in the mind. Ether, the space element, and the mind are similar in one respect. Everything is in the ether, in space, and all of these elements are in the mind, in thought.

All these things are thought and thought alone. Now, in order to understand *prakriti*, nature, the five elements, you have to find out what the original thought is, the one that contains and brings into being all these things.

These five elements are also in the body. In order to understand the body, you have to understand these elements, and in order to understand the elements you have to understand the mind. Whatever phenomenon you pick, you can get back to its fundamental nature by tracing it back to these elements and the mind that creates it.

Now, just pick out one thought. If you can understand that one thought – what it is and how it comes into existence – you will understand the whole process and nature of the mind.

Question this one thought. Look at this thought and try to see what it is. Find out what the source of this thought is. When you have found that source you will understand the mind, and then you will enter into the source from where everything emerges. There, no one and nothing has ever existed.

This is how the process of nature, *prakriti*, comes into existence. It arises from *purusha*, the first being. All beings are absorbed into this first being and perish there, but that first being never perishes, never vanishes.

Question: When you call *purusha* 'the first being', do you mean a being such as Krishna?

Papaji: Krishna himself once addressed *purusha*, saying, 'I am *purusha*,' but it is not the manifestation of Krishna that is the *purusha*, it is the unmanifest from which it springs. Krishna knew himself to be the unmanifest *purusha*. *Purusha* is beyond all the concepts and perceptions of the mind. A concept can be grasped, but *purusha* cannot be.

Manifestation can be grasped, and so can non-manifestation insofar as it is a concept that is the opposite of manifestation, but what I am talking about is something that is beyond them both. I am speaking of something that is beyond even the non-manifest. That which is beyond it is *purusha*.

Question: Are you saying that it's the equivalent of Brahma, the creator of all this manifestation?

Papaji: No, Brahma is not the equivalent; he is just the creator of manifestation. There is a place where even Brahma perishes, for Brahma is not permanent. Everything, including Brahma and the other gods will perish, but that *purusha* itself will never perish. It is indestructible.

You have been studying the *Gita*. Which translation are you reading? What we are speaking about is in that book.

[Papaji opened her copy of the Gita, *the edition translated by Swami Chinmayananda, and started reading the passage that begins at chapter eight, verse fourteen:]*

14 I am easily attainable by that steadfast yogi who constantly remembers me daily, not thinking of anything else, O Partha.
15 Having attained me, these *mahatma*s do not again take birth, which is the house of pain and is non-eternal, they having reached the highest perfection, *moksha* [liberation].
16 Worlds up to the world of Brahmaji are subject to rebirth, O Arjuna, but he who reaches me, O Kaunteya, has no birth.
17 Those people who know [the length of] the day of Brahma, which ends in a thousand *yugas* [aeons], the night which [also] ends in a thousand *yugas*, they know day and night.

Though the day and night of Brahma, his coming and going in manifestation, take thousands of *yugas* to complete, he is still impermanent. Because he comes and he goes, he is not the imperishable substratum. Brahma's days and Brahma's nights all proceed from the unmanifest and return there.

Question: And that is *purusha*?

Papaji: Yes. The text says that all manifestations proceed from the unmanifest, and at the approach of night they merge into that alone. That place into which all these things merge is the unmanifest *purusha*.

Question: Then the unmanifest is what I am not?

Papaji: *[reading from the book again, starting at 8:18]*

> 18 From the unmanifested all the manifested proceed at the coming of the 'day' [of Brahma]; at the coming of the 'night' [of Brahma] they dissolve verily into that alone which is called the unmanifest.
> 20 But verily there exists, higher than that unmanifest [*avyakrt*] another unmanifested, which is eternal, which is not destroyed when all beings are destroyed.
> 21 That which is called the unmanifest and the imperishable, that, they say, is the highest goal. They who reach it never return.' That is my highest abode [or state].

This is the highest attainment.

Question: This is definitely what I am not!

Papaji: This is the highest attainment. I will read again:

> 21 That which is called the unmanifest and the imperishable, that, they say, is the highest goal. They who reach it never return. That is my highest abode [or state].

And then the next verse says:

> 22 That highest *purusha*, O Partha, is attainable by unswerving devotion to Him alone, within

whom all beings dwell, by whom all this is pervaded.

Are you really reading this?

Question: Yes.

Papaji: Listen again:

> 21 That which is called the unmanifest and the imperishable, that, they say, is the highest goal. They who reach it never return. That is my highest abode [or state].
> 22 That highest *purusha*, O Partha, is attainable by unswerving devotion to Him alone, within whom all beings dwell, by whom all this is pervaded.

Question: *[new questioner]* Do you agree with this, Papaji? That one can only succeed through devotion?

Papaji: Yes.

Question: It is *only* through devotion that one arrives there?

Papaji: By 'devotion' I mean 'supreme devotion'.

Question: What is supreme devotion?

Papaji: Supreme devotion is not to give rise to a single thought. This is supreme devotion. Then you are not carried away. This is the supreme devotion. What else can it be?

'Devotion' really means 'not divided'. The Sanskrit word *bhakti* actually means 'where there is no division'. The opposite word to *bhakti* is *vibhakti*. *Bhakti* means unity, no division. *Vibhakti* means division. In supreme devotion, supreme *bhakti*, there is no division.

Question: No division?

Papaji: No division means not to be divided. Don't divide the mind. How is the mind divided? By giving rise to thought. If you don't give rise to a single thought, then mind itself is not. Thought creates division.

Question: *[new questioner]* But then this supreme devotion and this unmanifested *purusha* are one and the same thing.

Papaji: Yes, that is what is left when division goes. *Vibhakti* means division. Where there is no division, where there is an undivided mind, this is *bhakti*. This is called the supreme devotion. Devotion can be to someone, or to something that is other than oneself, but supreme devotion is only to one's own Self.

There is Self and there is non-Self. There is imperishable and there is perishable. To have devotion to the imperishable and to be one with it is supreme devotion. Without this devotion I don't think anything can happen.

The English word 'devotion' can be very misleading, but I can't think of a good English word that translates this very nice Sanskrit word, '*bhakti*'. Nor can I think of a good word in English that adequately translates '*jnana*'. We usually say 'knowledge' in English when we translate *jnana*. But knowledge is not *jnana*. In English knowledge is of something, some object that you know, whereas *jnana* is merely a subjective knowledge of one's own Self. For knowledge of other things we have other words.

Going back to *bhakti*, you can call it 'love' if you want to. 'Love' is one way of expressing one aspect of *bhakti*, but it doesn't cover all the nuances. There is also a knowledge and an understanding in *bhakti*, a knowledge of what is true and real.

We can say that there are two ways of expressing what the Self is: love (*bhakti*) and knowledge (*jnana*). These are also the ways of discovering it. In *vichara*, in enquiry, you look for the source of thought. You return to the source, merge with the source and abide as the source. This is *vichara*. This investigation is called 'knowledge', *jnana*. Devotion is loving your source. When you love it with extreme, supreme love, you will be taken to that source and you will know it. You must have single-minded love of this source in order to get the true knowledge of it. When you have the supreme love you have the supreme knowledge as well. This is just the same thing expressed in two different ways. One is love and the other is knowledge.

7

Who and where is this 'I' that wants to be free?

Papaji: There are desires for the things of this world, there is a desire for the things of the next world, and then there is the fear of God. These three things are keeping you away from freedom. You say that you have a desire for freedom. If you give up these three, you will find that even the desire for freedom cannot be sustained any more. It will leave you, and freedom itself will remain.

Question: I find it very hard to give up desires.

Papaji: Give up desires for this world and the next, and give up even that being who created you to have these desires. That is the meaning of what I am saying. Then freedom will manifest itself and you will not need to desire it any more.

That freedom is the one thing you can never give up or throw away. It is not like some apple in your hand that can be thrown away. When all desires have gone, including the desire for freedom, freedom remains.

Vyasa begins the *Brahma Sutras* by saying, 'Now let me aspire for freedom...'. This was something new and revolutionary. Before this people would say, 'Let me practise yoga, let me practise tantra, let me read the *sutras*,' and so on. This 'freedom' word, this idea of wanting freedom, was not part of the vocabulary of the people who wanted to do all these things. Vyasa said to himself, 'Now, after many births, I have decided to win freedom'.

This thought doesn't arise in many minds. You can see thousands of people doing all kinds of practices in ashrams all over the world, but I don't think any good is resulting from them. People are busy with their practices, but freedom always remains untouched, unreached. In my lifetime, eighty years of it, I have seen many big ashrams all over the world. The world is full of swamis, ashrams, spiritual books, teachings and devotees, but where are the results? Who is attaining freedom as a result of all this?

It is a very rare mind in which the candle of enlightenment will ignite. This candle will burn very rarely. Many people go to ashrams and gurus saying that they want freedom, but they are not really serious. People come here with the same claim, but I don't believe most of them.

Several centuries ago there was one swami in an ashram in Maharashtra. Hundreds of people used to come to see him every day. One of his students, an illiterate, asked, 'Six hundred people are coming to see you every day. Will all of them attain *moksha*, liberation?'

The illiterate was Kalyan and he looked after the ashram cowshed. Many of the other devotees were educated people who were helping the swami to compile a book.

'No,' said the swami. 'They will not all attain it.'

Kalyan then asked, 'Well, how many will? Five hundred?'

'No.'

'Two hundred?'

'No.'

'Twenty?' asked Kalyan.

'I will tell you tomorrow,' said the swami.

During the night the swami wrapped a stained bandage around his leg, and when the devotees came in the early morning, he claimed that he could not stand up. They had all come to help him with his literary work before they went off to their own jobs.

The swami said, 'I have a very poisonous carbuncle on my leg. I will probably die because of this poison. That is what the doctors are saying. But the doctors also said, "If you can find someone who is willing to suck out the poison for you, that person will die and you will probably get better."'

One by one all the early morning visitors made some excuse and hurriedly left.

'I have to go to court today,' said one. 'I just came for your blessings.'

'We are just about to start a pilgrimage,' said others. 'We just came for *darshan* before we left.'

Everyone made some sort of excuse and left. Eventually, Kalyan came in and said, 'Swami, there are no people here today. What happened?'

The swami said, 'Kalyan, the whole night I was suffering with this painful carbuncle. The doctor says I will die unless someone sucks out this poison. The problem is, whoever sucks out this poison will die instead of me.'

Kalyan said, 'Swami, why didn't you wake me up as soon as you felt the pain? You cannot be allowed to die. What is the use of my own life? You are taking care of so many lives. What is the use of my life? You must take it.'

He jumped forward and started to suck at the stained bandage. Much to his surprise, he found a very sweet taste in his mouth. The swami had just put a bandage on his leg and stained it with honey.

'This is the answer to the question you asked me yesterday,' said the swami. 'No one is coming here for freedom. They are coming here for blessings for their marriages, their court cases, and so on. Nobody wanted to look after me. No one was willing to sacrifice his life for his teacher except you. You will get this freedom, and not them, because they are not serious enough. You will get my robe and you will get my ashram when I die. I will write to the king, who is also my devotee, and tell him of my decision.'

If you are serious about freedom, about liberation, you must want it to the exclusion of all else. Let this desire burn unquenched night and day. If you are seriously interested in freedom, this desire must be there all the time. It will take you to freedom, at which point all desires will go, including the desire for freedom.

If a fruit is hanging on a tree, it means that it is not fully ripe. When it drops off of its own accord, the ripeness is complete. When your spiritual ripening has been completed by this constant desire for freedom, you will naturally drop into freedom itself and desires will no longer trouble you.

You have already wandered through the world of desires for many lives. Millions of people suffer endlessly because they keep on chasing their desires. If you want freedom with all your heart, you will give up all these desires and want freedom alone because you will know that any other kind of desire just brings you trouble. There are very, very few people who come to that decision and stick to it. These are the ones who make it.

Question: Papaji, can there be any desire without thought? Is there ever a desire but no thought?

Papaji: Thought will take you to some outside object. All thoughts are of objects. The subject 'I' thinks a thought, which is an object. When you think, a subject-object relationship is immediately established. Every object in this process is something that belongs to the past. It is not the reality of who you are here and now. Desire freedom and it will take you to the place of no thought.

Question: What I am trying to say is that if I have a seed of a desire hidden inside me, and I then see the object of my desire, a thought immediately arises, 'I want it'. It's an unconscious and involuntary coming together of thought and desire. Do you understand what I am trying to say?

Papaji: That's what I am saying. All thoughts and desires bring into being a relationship with the past. Thinking is clinging to objects that you take from your memory, your record of the past. You have a subject-object relationship with the past because you, the subject, are always grabbing at objects of desire, which are memories you have of your past. Have instead the thought, 'I want to be free'. Want it intensely enough and there will be no subject, no object, no past and no future.

Question: This thought, 'I want to be free', is it like a seed that can germinate inside me and grow?

Papaji: Who and where is this 'I' that wants to be free? There is no 'I' either inside the body or outside it. When a doctor does a postmortem, he doesn't find an 'I' inside the body. If you x-ray a body, you don't find an 'I' anywhere inside. You are using the word 'inside' because you are presupposing that you are the body. And following on from that supposition, you are also assuming that there must be an 'I' inside it.

If you question these suppositions by asking, 'Whose body is it?' you will say to yourself, 'It is mine'. Does not the 'I' who owns things exist prior to the ownership of his possessions? Think about this and you must come to the conclusion that the 'I' must have existed before the body came into existence. If the 'I' existed before the body, then it did not simply come into existence when the body was born. The 'I' does not have a birthday that corresponds to the first appearance of the body. Question this 'I' that thinks that it was born on a particular date.

If the 'I' exists on the outside, it would have been discovered by now. Explorers have been everywhere, even to the moon, but they have not found an 'I' anywhere. People have searched in themselves for the 'I', but no one has found it there either. Why not? Because it doesn't exist either inside or outside.

8

Grace is always encouraging you to seek it

Question: Is enlightenment an act of grace?

Papaji: Grace? Yes. Only grace. It is not won by any gymnastic feat, any physical effort. If it were so, anyone could get it by effort. Anyone can make an effort, but it is not enough. Grace alone is enough.

There are two types of grace: *Atma kripa*, the grace of the Self, and Guru *kripa*, the grace of the Guru. *Atma kripa* rises from within, from within the Self itself. The thought 'I want to be free' is a manifestation of the grace of the Self. Having a determination to be free is a gift of grace from the Self. The scriptures say that you need a mountain of merits to win the grace of the Self. Not just a rock or a small hill but a mountain of merits that is higher than Mount Meru, supposedly the highest mountain in the world. So, when your accumulation of merits is higher even than the Himalayas, then this desire will arise. This is the working of the grace of the Self. This grace can arise within you and show you who you are, but most people don't understand this power, don't understand the language in which it is trying to speak to you.

When this happens, the Self arranges for you to meet someone who will speak to you in your own language, someone who will appraise you of the fact that the Self is within you, and that you have to seek it there. This is the grace of the Guru. Even when the grace comes from what is apparently an 'outside' source, the form of the Guru, it is still only pointing to the Self within, the power that will take you into the Self.

Grace is always encouraging you to seek it. Through grace a desire for freedom has arisen in you; through grace you have been enabled to travel here; grace is making you ask this question; even the question itself is grace. There is nothing beyond or outside it. That means that your effort is also grace. The fact that you can make the effort, the fact that you want to make the effort – these are all manifestations of grace.

You can choose to make an effort by being determined to find out who you are. That is the effort of self-enquiry. This arises from the determination, 'I will find out who I am'. The other way is the path of grace, of surrender: 'This is all Your grace. I am in Your hands.' This path, this attitude, will invoke the power that will look after you and take you to the Self.

Different temperaments take different paths. Here in India we call them the monkey way and the cat way. The baby monkey holds onto its mother by effort, by a strong grip. The mother cat picks up her kitten and takes it wherever it needs to go. Whichever path you choose, it is all grace because the decision 'I will win freedom for myself' is just as much a manifestation of grace as the decision to leave everything to the divine, the power of the Self.

Question: Do we have a choice between *Atma kripa* and *Guru kripa*? Is it something we can decide for ourselves?

Papaji: Your temperament will choose for you. If you try to make a choice that is opposed to your temperament, it will not work. It's in your bones. The path you choose and follow will be a consequence of your temperament. There are three *gunas* – call them qualities of mind – that govern character and personality: *sattva*, [purity, harmony], *rajas* [activity] and *tamas* [dullness, sloth]. These *gunas* will drive your behaviour; they will direct you along the path that is most suited to your temperament. If you are dominated by *rajas*, you will be attracted by activity. You will be drawn to activities such as yoga or tantra, things that will keep you busy. Such people are always thinking, 'I can do it. I have to do it.' People with this *guna* end up doing therapy and yoga, things that will keep them busy and occupied. This is not so bad because 95 per cent of the people in the world are in *tamas*. They don't do anything at all. They live and die without coming to this spiritual line at all.

If you are in *sattva*, you are a very focused person. You will have a sharp discrimination and you will be able to find the Self by being still, without thought, rather than by rushing around, looking for it.

You cannot choose your *guna* any more than you can choose your genes. Your genes are the result of thousands of generations of physical reproduction. Your *guna* is likewise the result of thousands of lifetimes of experiences. Your genes decide the way you look; you don't have any choice in the matter. Your *guna* determines the quality of your mind, and this is just as determined as your genes.

Arjuna, the warrior, tried to deny his nature on the battlefield when he said that he was not going to fight, but Krishna told him that he had no choice in the matter. This is how it is.

9

In true love everything that is not yourself drops off

Papaji: In English we say 'falling in love'. When you fall, you start in one place and then end up somewhere lower down. But in the kind of love that I am speaking of, there is no fall, no descent to a lower level. It is in the other kinds of love that there is a fall.

Question: Do you mean there is a fall into desire?

Papaji: Desire is always a fall, but in the love I am talking about, there is never a fall. You remain as you are. This is true love. To express the other kind of love everyone says, 'I fell in love'. In this physical kind of love it is you who fall. In true love it is everything else, except for you, that falls away. In true love everything that is not yourself drops off. When everything has fallen away, this is real love. When you walk away from all other kinds of love, you find true love.

Look at what happened to the Buddha. He was lying next to the most beautiful woman in the kingdom. Physical love was there. Affection was there, but it wasn't enough for him. There was another kind of love that was missing in his life. Though he had everything he could possibly want in the world, he got up and walked out. When this call comes from true love, it cannot be resisted. Kings have left their kingdoms and their queens in search of this love. This is the supreme love that I am talking about.

Question: *[new questioner]* Sometimes I find it difficult to read holy books because they are full of descriptions of these wonderful states. I read them and I think, 'Well, I haven't experienced that state, that experience'. This leads to thoughts and desires, judgements about where I am on the path. Since they give rise to feelings of inadequacy, I prefer not to read such books.

Papaji: This is a good judgement, one that you have made after reading many books.

Question: Well, I haven't read that many.

Papaji: Then you are lucky. *Maya* has a big net that can catch fish for her in many different ways. When a man turns his back on the world, on *samsara*, there are many traps waiting for him. He can get caught in many different ways. He may leave his friends, his relatives and his community, but he may end up in the trap of a new community, an ashram. Or he may end up in the trap of reading spiritual books. Getting lost in these books is a big trap. Wherever you go, *maya* has a trap that is waiting for you. If you worship, you can get trapped in the rituals of worship. If you follow the path of yoga, then yogic *samadhi* will be a trap for you.

Do you understand? You can go into *samadhi* and feel very pleased with yourself. You think afterwards, 'I am having long *samadhi*s. I can stay in these states for six hours at a time.'

You can be a *bhakta* who does *japa* all day, but your rosary will end up becoming your trap. You will think, 'I am counting beads all day. I am doing very well.'

Not even the gods are free from these traps of *maya*. For Vishnu, the preserver of the universe, *maya* appeared as Kamala. Siva left his *tapas* for Uma. Brahma got caught up in his creation. Who is free of these traps? No one. Because whatever you do, whatever you think of, whatever you imagine is a trap of *maya*.

However, let me tell you that all these traps are imaginary. Once you truly know that they are all traps, you know that they are all in your imagination. There is no door that is locking you in. You are free to walk away from whatever trap you find yourself in.

Buddha walked out of his trap and found freedom. He lived in an isolated pleasure garden and was kept apart from the normal world. An astrologer had told his parents, 'This man cannot stay in this world'. His mother had also had a dream about this. After his birth his parents, the king and queen, tried to keep him completely apart from the normal world. He had a beautiful garden full of dancing girls, and for a wife he was given the most beautiful woman in the kingdom. In his private little world there was no suffering, no old age, no seeking except the seeking of physical pleasures.

One day he wanted to see what was outside his wall. He just took the decision, 'I want to see what is on the other side of this wall'. He made a secret trip outside and for the first time in his life he saw suffering, old age and death. He went back to his palace and decided that he had to renounce his world – his kingdom, his family, his beautiful wife – in order to find the secret of suffering and how to transcend it. He renounced everything and walked out, secretly, in the middle of the night. It is said that the locks of the palace unlocked themselves when he wanted to leave. It is said that the earth itself became soft like butter so that the guards would not hear the noise from the escaping horse's hooves. Why and how? Because freedom loved this man. Freedom fell in love with this prince who had exhibited such tremendous renunciation. Freedom itself arranged his escape.

He must have been chosen by the supreme power for this escape, this destiny of ultimately escaping his traps and finding freedom. Who, in a similar situation has ever got up and walked out? Even the gods stayed sleeping with their goddesses. This man woke up, was chosen to wake up, because he had the courage to walk away from everything.

10

I am the unique principle which makes the rose grow

Papaji: The *Vedas* are thousands of years old. It is said that they are the oldest books in the world. The word '*Veda*' means 'knowledge', so these are the books of knowledge. But even these *Vedas* say that knowledge cannot be spoken about. They say, '*neti-neti*,' 'not this, not this'. Whatever you want to say knowledge is, the *Vedas* reply with '*neti-neti*'. Though the *Vedas* claim to be the books of knowledge, they concede that truth is something that cannot be spoken about.

Question: At the beginning of the *Tao Te Ching* the same statement is made: 'The Tao which can be spoken of is not the real Tao.'

Papaji: Truth is always unsaid. We can aspire for it, but we can never say what it is. But remember, we should not aspire to attain, gain or achieve anything. Why not? Because these things we attain are perishable. They become our possessions, and possessions are things that you will one day lose. If you attain something, that means there was a time prior to the attainment in which the attainment was not there. If that attainment was absent at some point in the past, it is something perishable; it is something that will one day leave you and go away. The emptiness that is there in the beginning, the emptiness that is there in the middle, and the emptiness that is there at the end – this is the enduring truth. This is knowledge; this is the true knowledge. The other kinds of knowledge can be read about, spoken about, understood and practised, but they are not the true knowledge. So, all these things that can be understood, known and attained, leave them alone because they are not the truth. The truth is something else.

Question: *[new questioner]* Is it possible to achieve supreme devotion through effort or only through non-effort?

Papaji: Give up all kinds of effort – mental and physical. When all these types of effort have left you, there will be no attainment, no achievement left.

Question: You are saying that it can only happen through non-effort?

Papaji: If you don't try to make any effort – physical, mental, intellectual – what will happen? Just try to imagine what would happen. I received a letter about this from a French girl recently. She didn't speak any English. Her husband translated our conversation for her. I will read you some portions from her letter.

> *I spent a wonderful day with Maya three days ago. What a joy to be near her and share the same understanding, the same aliveness...*

I do not know what she means by 'aliveness'.

> *...knowing oneself to be. I have the feeling that I have known Maya forever, and it is very true. She is really my own heart and my own light and my sister. I love her and the aliveness takes billions of forms, but what happiness when it recognises itself as being the one in the appearance of whom I still name 'the other'. Maya will translate this letter...*

> *...This morning, very early, tranquilly lying in my bed, I thought of my children far away. Then there*

> *was a burning and devouring question, 'What am I really, now, at this precise instant? What really are my children in this precise second?' No image, no concept sprang from this question, but suddenly I knew the answer, behind words, images and concepts. I saw very, very clearly the no-movement, the no-time, the no-distance, the no-possibility of separation. Just the same everywhere, the same in everything, the same in all things, the same being-principle, now, just now without beginning, without end, without form, with no colour, but alone, real, the substratum of everything that is conceivable. This vision was the cry of being, knowing itself to be and knowing itself to be only being.*

In a fraction of a second, out of time. How can she find out this thing? When you put yourself in the experience and do it, then you can see in the fraction of a second. And then she says, 'no time'. If you do it, then you will know this is out of time. If not, you will call it within time.

> *I returned to my point of origin, the original place-without-place that I have never left as this place is me, is 'I' itself. Caught by this shining truth, a very deep joy flooded me.*

I was speaking earlier of true love. True love doesn't go up or down; it is transcendent.

> *Caught by this shining truth, a very deep joy flooded me. It was as if the room had been bathed by the sweet, unsoundable peace of 'I', unique. I clearly saw that I am only the being-principle, moving everything, just now. Being, now itself. I am that 'now'. I am that same being. I am that being-principle without any name, without any form, without any colour, without*

any shape, without movement, but giving the name, the form, the colour, the shape, the movement to everything that appears in the consciousness 'I'.

I suddenly felt without the slightest doubt that I am the unique principle which makes the rose grow, the birds sing, the water flow in the forest, which paints the thousand colours in nature. At the same time I am all, and yet I am nothing in particular. Without the 'me', being, nothing is. Knowledge of that-which-is cannot rise up except through me.

It's a bit crazy, Master, what I write to you. It's very difficult to transmit, but nevertheless, I am trying to do it because with your love, with your grace, which is also light and wisdom, there is the conviction that the writing is also yours, which is why I am able to do it. 'I am only that.'

The conviction 'I am only that' becomes more and more steady. I am the being-principle, the original principle from the beginning, the principle 'I' and nothing else. I occupy all and am everywhere. I am everything. I am in everything. I am all. There is no place for two, no possibility of any distance, of being far away.

In a fraction of a second my children far away have rebecome myself, nothing, but appearing in myself, the living principle. So, no name, no more children far away, separated or living anywhere else. I am the unique being-principle, now living and manifesting itself through what I name 'my children', living and manifesting also through the billions of forms, creating billions of universes in order to recognise myself as unique.

If it is this way, I am as I have always been forever, and if there is then evolution it can only be the evolution of the understanding knowing itself more and more deeply, being only that. I am only the being-principle, alone and unique without a second.

Knowing myself to be the unique being-principle, fear has gone away. Where could it take root? Who can make who afraid, as I am alone? I am alone, and at the same time I live through the form of my daughter, my son, my friends and the marvellous Master Poonjaji. I am also the being-principle in the forms of animals, vegetables, minerals and rocks. Master, my own Self, I feel very deeply that at present for Nicole there is only one thing to do in order to accomplish whatever arises in a day. Not to forget to see myself as the one and only being-principle in all that I touch, I see, I feel, and especially to live life myself as the unique principle itself, seeing itself in what I still call others; and if forgetfulness arises, not to forget that forgetfulness is also the being-principle because other than that nothing exists. The being-principle, emptiness, silence, now are the same. There is no difference between them.

With my profound respect and my sincere love, Nicole.

[Very long pause]

You asked a question. You asked the question, 'Is effort needed for freedom?' I gave you a reply and then I read out this letter to you. It shows that if you want freedom, you don't have to make any effort. If you want to run a 100-yards race and win, you have to make a big effort. If you want to win a gold medal like Ben Johnson, you will have to make a big effort, but this is different

Question: Sometimes, though, I feel that I should make an effort: reading, doing something, breathing exercises – anything.

Papaji: If breathing can produce this result, the asthmatics are ahead of you. They breathe much harder than you.

Question: I've been involved in a lot of therapy groups. Lots of 'doing' went on there. I did groups in which we looked inside. That required effort. I did groups such as primal therapy, in which you are going back to find your source.

Papaji: Looking at yourself doesn't need any effort. First of all, who is looking at the Self? And what is this Self that you are looking at?

Question: That's the question. What is the Self?

Papaji: You say that you need effort while you are looking at the Self. Who is looking at the Self? Find out who is looking. Find out who is looking at the Self.

Question: My consciousness, my awareness.

Papaji: Yes, but what is this awareness, and how does it differ from that which it wants to see? How does this awareness differ from what you are going to look at? There are not two awarenesses.

Question: The awareness doesn't differ, but it wants to be free. The awareness wants to be free or enlightened.

Papaji: The complaint is not coming from awareness. Awareness is not saying, 'I want to be aware'. Awareness...

Question: ...wants to be more aware. *[Laughter]*

Papaji: That's her problem, not yours. Leave it to her. Leave her alone and watch what happens. Just watch what awareness is doing. Just watch.

Question: Sometimes it takes an effort not to make an effort.

Papaji: What do you mean?

Question: Something always wants to do something.

Papaji: Imagine you have a load of 200 pounds on your head. You are suffering and toiling with this extremely heavy load. Is this enough weight, or should you add some more? You want to get rid of all this weight, so you go to a teacher and ask him what you should do.

'This is a serious problem,' he says. 'Here are another twenty pounds of apples to put on your head. This will relieve you of your problem.'

Now you have 220 pounds on your head and you are suffering even more.

You go to another teacher and tell him your problem. His solution is to add twenty pounds of bananas to your head load. Now you are up to 240 pounds.

The next man says 'Raisins. And maybe almonds. Put twenty pounds of raisins and almonds on top of your head and your problems will be over.'

The different items you are being persuaded to load on your head are all the different techniques, all the different practices you are being told to carry out. Weight is being added on weight, but none of it is doing you any good.

But what if you decide one day to just shake your head, to tilt it a little so that everything on top of it just falls off? Once you have decided that you no longer want all this weight on your head, all you have to do is let it drop to the floor. This doesn't require any effort or years of practice, and it doesn't require that you join some ashram or commune. If you go to an ashram or a commune, the first thing that will happen is that somebody will tell you that you have to do some practice, that you have to add some more weight to the top of your head. Nobody is going to tell you to let all the weights fall off by themselves, because if they did that, they would all be out of business. They would lose all their money.

I was in Washington a few years ago. I went to a pastry shop late in the evening and picked out lots of different pastries. I thought I would take them back to my hotel room and eat them there. When I went to the cash counter to pay for them, I told the girl who worked there that I was planning to snack on them in my room.

She was shocked. 'What a pile of junk food you have collected here! You are not supposed to eat this much junk all by yourself. You are too old to live on a diet like this. Look at all this stuff: ice cream, pastries, jellies. Throw it all away. It's better to sleep on an empty stomach and have a good breakfast tomorrow.'

I was surprised at her strong opinions. If I had told her boss that she was telling his customers not to buy his products, she would have got herself into trouble.

However, I took her advice and left everything in the shop. I just put it down and left. You can accumulate things endlessly, things that will do you no good, things that are just burdens on your head. To get rid of them, you don't take on new burdens, you just let go of the ones you already have.

Making an effort is easier for you because this is what you are accustomed to. I tell you to not make an effort but you can't accept this advice because for millions of years you have been making efforts. You have been trained in effort, and you want to continue in that effort because this is all you know how to do. You come to the spiritual path and you think you can succeed here by effort.

I am telling you not to make an effort. For freedom you don't need to make an effort, you just need to keep quiet. Forget everything you have learned so far. I will tell you the way. Forget everything that you have heard or read; forget any advice that people or prophets have been giving you. Forget everything and look at your own Self. Forget everything that has happened up to the present moment, and then tell me, 'What do you lack?' If you forget everything, everything you have read, heard and done up till this present moment, what's left? May I wait for your answer?

Question: I don't know what's left.

Papaji: No! No! You must try to know. This is the time to know. It's very easy to know this.

Question: I would be in my being.

Papaji: All right. You say, 'I would be in my being'. What effort did you make to be in your being?

Question: It's the biggest puzzle because I know I am in my being...

Papaji: Stop here! Stop here! 'I know I am in my being.' Stop at this point. Stop here! This is the full stop. What else is there? That is the end. That is the goal. That is the destination you have been looking for for thirty-five million years.

My dear young boy, since you are obsessed with making efforts, I will suggest some effort to you.

Question: Yeah, OK.

Papaji: We have arrived here without effort, forgetting everything that you have heard, read or done. Then you said, 'I am in my being'. Now come here and I will give you some effort. From here, from this place of being, I want you to try to make the effort to step out of this being. I want you to try by your efforts to get to that place where you can say, 'I am not in my being any more'. Go on. Start from this being, this place you have arrived at. This is a zone, a zone of being, that you have arrived at without making any effort. You arrived here by forgetting everything. Now you are in this centre which is called 'being'. Everything is being there. You wanted to make some effort, so I am asking you to make a tremendous effort to step out of this place and say, 'I am not being any more'. Do it step by step. Say, 'I am now stepping out of it'. Step out of it and look behind you. Is anything following you? Don't close your eyes. It's effort time. Make this effort! Make this one step. What's a step? Lift up a foot, move it forward, and then plant it on the ground again. Then you shout out, 'I have planted my foot in non-being! Here is the non-being! I am not being any more!' Shout out to me when you plant that foot in the place of non-being.

Question: Here is the non-being.

Papaji: Now lift the other foot. One foot is in non-being, and the other foot is where? You are in being, so I told you to make an effort to run away from this being. OK?

Question: It feels impossible.

Papaji: Impossible? For impossible works effort is needed. To be was possible, and you have done it. Now, return to your natural state. Lift up a foot and say 'Yes'.

Question: I don't know if I am getting this. I feel a bit stupid.

Papaji: Just do it and see. Decide for yourself, 'I'm not being. I'm not being.' Decide for yourself to leave this being and look behind you. Who is following you? Look behind you. Who is following you? Who is all around you? What is behind you?

Question: Many things are behind me.

Papaji: No. Just as your body is a form, this is a form. Just outside of this body, what do you see? – behind, in front, on all sides, above – what do you see?

Question: Nothing.

Papaji: Nothing. This is called 'being'. This is called 'being'. Now, try to avoid it. Avoid it now. Wherever you go, step out of this being. Step out of it so that it doesn't follow you. Make this effort. Look behind you and don't allow it to follow you. Push back the emptiness that is following you. Push it back. You can't.

Wherever you try to run, you are in being. Whenever you try to step out of it, you are in being. When you try to escape from being, wherever you put your foot down, you are still in being. You come from being and you are always in that being. When you make the effort to pretend that you are not being, you will suffer and you will be rewarded by death. Death is waiting for all the beings who, through effort, think that they are not being.

11

What comes and goes is a trap

Papaji: I was in Sant Sarovar many years ago with my sister. She was on her way to Badrinath. When she found out I was staying in that ashram, she came to see me and stayed for some time. Some swami was staying in the cottage next door. He was conducting *satsangs* and many people were attending. I hadn't been to see him because in the morning, when people came to his *satsangs*, I was usually walking by the Ganga, or having a bath there. My sister went to this swami's *satsang* and she told me that many other women were going. He was, by the way, quite a well-known swami in Vrindavan. He was young and he could sing very well, and this attracted many people, particularly women. My sister went to see him every day for about a week. On one of her visits the swami asked her why she had come to the ashram.

'My brother is staying here,' she said. 'I have come to visit him and spend some time with him.'

'Why don't you bring your brother to *satsang*?' he asked.

'I will tell him you are here and I will bring him tomorrow,' she said.

My sister came home and said, 'I promised the swami that I would bring you to *satsang* tomorrow. You must come.'

How could I say 'no'? I went with her and found myself in a room with about sixty other people.

When the *satsang* was over, the swami asked, 'Have you all experienced bliss? Has everyone experienced bliss?'

Many people were calling out 'Yes! Yes!'

He asked everyone one by one, and everyone said 'Yes', but when it came to my turn I said 'No'. He looked surprised.

'Everyone here has said that they experienced bliss. We experienced so much bliss in today's *satsang*. You are the only one who is saying he did not experience it. People experience bliss here every day. What is the problem?'

I told him what the problem was. 'Yesterday these people came here and probably they all said that they experienced bliss, *ananda*. Today they came here and again they said they experienced bliss. Where did the *ananda* go in between? Where did it run away to? And what about today's *ananda*? They will walk out of this door and in a few minutes or a few hours they will say, "The *ananda* has gone. It is not there any more." That which goes away when you walk out of the door is not here even while we are inside the room. *Ananda* has not really come to any of these people. If it had been the true *ananda*, it would have been there all the time. *Ananda* is not something that comes and goes.'

He was quiet for a while and looked very thoughtful. Then he went inside another room and came back with a small book. I saw him holding it, but I didn't bother to look at what it was.

The swami said, 'I don't know if this *mahatma* is alive or dead but he is saying the same thing that you are saying. I read this book recently, and he said exactly the same thing.'

Then he told me the name of the book and the name of the *mahatma* whose teachings it contained.

I smiled. 'He is my Guru. I am his disciple.' That's all I said.

This swami was a good man. He came down from his platform and invited me to take his place. 'Sit there and please tell us something about your Guru and his teachings. This is the first time I have heard this teaching. You are saying, "Experiences that come and go are not an experience of the permanent state. The permanent state never comes or goes, and it is not experienced at one time but not at another." Please talk to us about this.'

I went to the front of the room and addressed everyone there.

'What comes and goes is a trap. It is a trap of the mind. Mind has created many traps for you, and these temporary bliss states are one of them. These experiences come from your own inner desires, your own ideas of what a spiritual experience should be. You want bliss because you think this is what ought to happen on the spiritual path. Your mind obliges you and produces some bliss for you to enjoy. It's all a trap, and no one ever got enlightened by falling for these traps. If you know that they are traps, you will not walk into them. It is enough for you to know that anything that is temporary, anything that comes and goes, is a trap. With this knowledge you can acquire the discrimination that keeps you away from the transient. This rejection of what is impermanent, irrespective of how pleasant it might be, will work against the mind's habits of looking for pleasure and bliss, and it will take you back to your natural state.'

The mind likes to keep busy, you see. It will set up some goal for you, and then it will try to accomplish it. It will make these brief bliss states your goal, and then it will make you work hard to attain them. And then you will think that you have accomplished something good, something spiritual. This is just postponement. You are postponing enlightenment until next year, or your next life.

Question: *[new questioner]* What's the difference between this kind of trap, this type of *samadhi*, and the bliss that you sometimes talk about, the bliss that is natural and automatic? When I am drawn inside, there is an automatic inwardness that pulls me in, and there the mind gets very peaceful. It feels very single-pointed and very calm. I know that everyone here experiences something like this in your presence, though not necessarily all the time. So my question is, 'What is the difference between the *samadhi*s of bliss that one strives for and the bliss and peace that we seem to feel quite naturally in your presence?'

Papaji: The peace that you feel is the result of not doing anything. That is the difference.

Question: That's true. That's right.

Papaji: By not doing anything, by not striving to attain anything. It's the result of an instant, a moment, in which you decide to relieve yourself of all your activity. At that time, in that moment, you have peace and happiness. This is the moment that gives you happiness.

How does the feeling of happiness normally come to you? It comes in the moment that some particular desire has been fulfilled.

You say, 'I want the latest model Mercedes because my neighbour has just booked one. I also want a new apartment facing the beach. These are the things that will make me happy. I want them.'

You set to work to fulfil your desires. You get a loan from the bank and some help from your friends. Everyone joins in with your new enthusiasm. Your wife wants a new car; your children want a new car; everyone wants the new model car. By now you are convinced that you will never be happy with your old Ford. The new car eventually appears and you park it on the street where everyone can admire it. Everyone is happy when they see the new car in front of your house.

This process is the same one that yogis go through to attain bliss, except that the desires and the goals are different. There is a desire to experience a blissful state; they work hard to attain it through their various yogic practices; a blissful experience results, and when they come out of it, they feel very pleased with themselves because they have attained the object of their desire.

Now, where did this happiness come from? The experiencer remained the same before, during and after the experience. Nothing has changed there. The car is made of steel, rubber, and so on. There is no happiness that is built into the machine, a happiness that becomes yours when you buy all this metal and rubber. What has really happened? How did the acquisition of this new car produce a feeling of happiness within you?

In the beginning you were troubled by a desire to have a new car. This desire nagged at you and troubled you all the time you were working to collect the money to buy one. But when you took possession of the car, you suddenly felt happy. Why? It was because the desire to obtain a new car was no longer there. It was the sudden absence of desire that made you happy, not the acquisition of a new possession.

When desire is no longer there, you are happy. When desire has ceased to exist completely, you are happy all the time, and this is liberation. Liberation is not the result of your meditations, of your visits to pilgrimage places. It doesn't come from going into caves in the mountains, from giving to charities, or from reading the *sutras*. So long as desire is there, *samsara* is there. So long as desire is there, suffering is there. Everyone can see this in his daily life.

Who is happy in the waking state? I believe the answer to that question is 'no one'. The kings and the millionaires have everything but they are not happy. From the richest man down to the poorest no one is happy because there is not a single man whom this serpent desire has not bitten. This desire is a serpent, and there is no one who has escaped her bite.

Consider your waking state. If it is such a good, restful and peaceful state, why do you reject it so readily to go to sleep? Why reject it if it is such a good state? Everyone needs to sleep because the desires of the day have tired us out. The mind needs a rest at the end of every period of waking because its busyness has worn you out. Everyone feels happy and peaceful during that state of sleep. There is happiness and peace there because the mind is no longer bothering you. There are no mental transactions there, just the contentment that comes from not having any nagging desires. Because there are no transactions there between subject and object, mind and phenomena, you feel rest. When there is no subject-object division, there is peace and rest.

Even in the state of *samadhi* there is a subtle transaction going on between a subject and an object: the subject who is meditating and the object that is being meditated on. This relationship must be there. I, the meditator, am one entity, the subject, and the object of meditation is something else.

To get rid of this subject-object relationship, why not begin to question who the meditator is? Find out who the meditator is, and find out why it needs to meditate. This is moving in the opposite direction. Instead of moving downstream with the mind by connecting to an object that you experience, move upstream to find the source. Don't go with the flow. Go in the opposite direction, upstream, and find out who the meditator is. Perhaps you will find the answer that will settle your accounts here and now. But this decision, the decision to go upstream to the source, doesn't come to most people. Whatever you do, you never question who is the doer of your actions, the one who performs meditation. When you enjoy, you get lost in the enjoyment, but you never question who is experiencing the enjoyment in that moment. Everyone attributes the enjoyment to the object that is being enjoyed – such as the new car – which is transient, not permanent. This is how *samsara* comes into being. We never attribute the happiness or the bliss to the person who is experiencing it. We only attribute it to the object he is enjoying.

You only experience enjoyment of objects in the waking state. But it doesn't matter how much enjoyment you are getting from these waking-state objects, you always reject them when you go to sleep. The most beautiful experience may be there in the waking state; the most beautiful person, the one who is most dear to you may be there in the waking state, but you will reject them all when you go to sleep. You go to sleep alone, without experiences, without the people who are most dear to you, and in that state you have peace, having forgotten everything that came before. To have true peace, you have to be alone, separated from everything you love and enjoy as separate objects. The happiness and the peace you experience in this state cannot be attributed to anything perishable. This bliss, the bliss that does not depend on enjoying an object or an experience, is imperishable, permanent. No matter what else is destroyed, this will remain. Nobody knows where this happiness is because everyone is looking for it in the wrong place.

All beings need to be happy. All beings are looking for happiness, but no one knows where it is. Men, birds, animals, and even plants are looking for this elusive happiness because it is their fundamental nature to be happy. No one wants to be in suffering. Even the land itself, the earth we walk on, wants happiness and doesn't want to suffer. The bird doesn't like to be injured, and nor does the animal. All are seeking this elusive happiness, but where is it to be found?

I was speaking earlier of traps, of traps of the mind. Happiness is not to be found in any of these traps of the mind. It is to be found when the mind is absent, and one day you will all know it. Everyone gets a taste of this, an experience of it, when he goes to sleep. When sleep comes everything vanishes, but you remain, alone and at peace. When you wake up you say, 'Oh, I had a very good sleep. I was very happy and content. I didn't even dream.'

This sleep state is just one of the three dull alternating states. It is not the final state of freedom or liberation, but it is a state in which the mind activity and objects have vanished. The sleep experience should teach you that when the mind stops transacting its business, peace prevails. When the mind stops jumping outwards to objects and desires in the waking state, you have peace and freedom with full awareness. This is the highest, transcendent state.

How can it be attained? Some people have done it. Many people have tried to attain it through yoga, *samadhi*, meditation and so on, but who gets permanent results?

It can be done, though. The means is not important, what is important is the result. It can be done.

Question: You have said that *samadhi* is the trap for the yogi, and that the rosary is the trap for the *bhakta*. What other traps are there for the devotee? I have heard you talk about devotees not being 'unsmelled flowers', and that this prevents them from reaching the goal. Is this another trap?

Papaji: The 'unsmelled flower' is not a trap. It is a different analogy. The unsmelled flower means a mind that doesn't have a single thought. That state will work for you. It is complete in itself. It is enlightenment, and you don't need anything else.

'How to tackle the mind?' This has been the topic of this morning. Mind in its thought-free purity is the unsmelled flower. Only the unsmelled flower can be offered to God and be accepted by him. When you bring in thoughts and concepts, your mind is no longer 'unsmelled'. It is no longer a pure offering for God.

A devotee who wants to see God starts counting the beads on his rosary. The hands are moving the beads while the mind is moving around through all the sense-objects that it is encountering. The mind is somewhere else while this is going on. It is not quiet and it is not controlled. The problem of the mind has not been tackled and solved.

The thought comes, 'I have to meditate'. When this thought, this intention, comes, the flower of the mind gets smelled. When you think 'I have to meditate', you enter a routine, something that you may continue with for your whole life, and while you are following this routine you forget the original purpose of finding freedom. You forget it altogether. I have seen many people who are like this. They engage in meditation, prayer and various rituals, but they forget the ultimate purpose of these rituals.

I say, 'If there is no thought in the mind, who are you in that moment?' If you don't give rise to a thought, if you don't stir a single thought from the ground itself, from the source itself, who are you in that instant? Don't let a single thought stir and see who you are. Don't think, 'I have to meditate', or 'I have to perform this ritual'. If a thought does arise, investigate it. Find out where it has come from. If you do this intently, this thought will vanish. If you do this properly, when this thought vanishes, all will be over. When this thought vanishes, all ideas such as 'I have to meditate' and 'I have to perform this ritual' will vanish along with it. You are in the source. You are the source. This investigation will take you to the source where the thought will disappear. Any other thought, any other practice, will take you away from the source, to somewhere else. You will hold it, and continue to hold it forever. You will get attached to this thought, this method, and you will hold onto it forever. This is what is happening in all the monasteries. It is what is happening every day with all the people who are attached to practices. These attachments don't produce results. There is just an attachment to the method while the purpose – freedom – is lost sight of.

Our true purpose is realisation of the Self, enlightenment, the freedom of being the Self. If you start off by thinking 'I must attain Self-realisation because I am not realised right now, and I want to be', then you are immediately imposing on yourself the thought of bondage. Your quest for freedom has already been caught up in this idea that it is something you don't already have. You accept this thought, 'I am in bondage', and then you go looking for a method or a book or a teacher who can help you to remove this idea of bondage that you have just imposed on yourself.

No book will get rid of this idea for you. First of all, ask yourself, 'Who told me that I am in bondage?' Where is the bondage? Question the bondage itself. Question the bondage by investigating who it is who appears to be in bondage. 'Who is bound?' Ask this question of yourself and it will take you to the place where the concept of bondage came into existence. It will take you to a place that no book and no teacher can tell you about.

All you have to do is remove this impediment, this idea that there is someone who is bound and who needs to work hard to transcend this bondage. Instead of working hard to find light or wisdom, find out what this impediment is, this idea 'I am bound' that puts you on the spiritual path in the first place.

'I am bound' is the mental substratum on which are built all your ideas about enlightenment and spiritual practice. You take your stand on this substratum and from there you develop and follow all your methods and practices. If you don't remove this initial impediment, the idea 'I am bound,' your practices will continue forever.

Spend some time on investigating this idea 'I am bound'. Work on this.

Question: It doesn't seem to me that this initial idea of being in bondage is something I impose on myself. As a person lives his life, he starts looking at what he is doing, and he eventually gets dissatisfied with it. The sense of limitation is already there, and from this there arises the thought, 'Is it possible to not be limited?'

Papaji: You borrow this limitation from someone else. It is a borrowed thought, one that other people keep giving you and imposing on you. Right from the beginning of your life you are indirectly told about your limitations. When you are very young your mother tells you, 'I am your mother, and this is your father'. Later your parents will say, 'These are your relations, and this is the religion you have to believe in'. All these ideas are given to you, and you accept them all unthinkingly.

Question: Yes, people say, 'You are like this' and 'You are like that'.

Papaji: Limitations start and the innocent child quietly accepts them. First your parents indoctrinate you, then your priests and then society in general. These limitations that you accept for yourself come to you from different sources. You have not learned the truth for yourself, so you have been accepting the opinions of other people.

Some people, the truly sane ones, will find the time to question all these ideas, all these limitations that other people are trying to impose.

Such a person will say, 'I want to be free. From whom did I get these limitations, these ideas?' He will push away these superimposed limitations, and he will see his true nature. This is the process.

12

The knowledge 'I am free' is a fire that burns up any thoughts that approach

Question: Sometimes I know I am free, and I live that way, but at other times I just feel worried and tired. I am afraid of being hurt or sick. I feel I am lacking something, and I forget who I really am. Is there going to be a time when I live permanently in a state of real knowing?

Papaji: You said 'sometimes'. Sometimes you feel free and sometimes you don't. That's what you said. So what happens? Who steals away this freedom? Who takes it away from you? It must be some thought that enters into this freedom. That thought trespasses on your freedom, catches you, and takes you away into your past. If you are careful, if you are vigilant, you can prevent these trespassers from distracting you.

Everyone has moments of uncaused happiness and peace during their lives. They may only last for a few seconds or a few minutes, but everyone knows what I am talking about. One feels free; one is content; there is no suffering; thought is absent. At that time one must be very alert, very awake; one must be aware that thought will try to make an encroachment on your peace. Most people do not maintain this alert awareness and they are robbed of their peace. If a thought comes and manages to rob you, it shows that you were asleep when the robber came. If you always keep aware and alert, nothing can disturb you or rob you of your peace.

When you are truly aware, no thought can even enter and trespass on your freedom because that ultimate state of awareness is a fire, a fire of knowledge. Anything that tries to enter that fire is consumed and burnt to ashes. The knowledge 'I am free' is a fire that burns up any thoughts that approach.

'I am free' means 'I am free of the thought process that jumps around and connects to objects'. In this state nothing can impinge on your freedom or trespass on your peace.

This is a habit that no one has told you about. No one has tried to impose this one on you. It is something that you have to acquire for yourself. For the first time in your life, for the first time in thirty-five million years of repeated incarnations, you have the chance to acquire this habit. Everybody is asleep. Everybody is being robbed of their peace millions of times, but no one wakes up and apprehends the thief.

These robbers give you the endless trouble of birth, suffering and death, but if you are vigilant and keep them out, even Yama, the Lord of Death, will have to give up and leave you alone. If you are simply aware, watchful and alert, nothing can disturb you. Did you listen to the letter from that French girl Nicole that I read out? She spoke of a trick that I like very much. Listen to this:

> *Master, my own Self, I feel very deeply that at present for Nicole there is only one thing to do in order to accomplish whatever arises in a day. Not to forget to see myself as the one and only being-principle in all that I touch, I see, I feel, and especially to live life myself as the unique principle itself, seeing itself in what I still call others; and if forgetfulness arises, not to forget that forgetfulness is also the being-principle because other than that nothing exists.*

Do you get it? This is the result. This is exceptional.

Question: I understand it, but sometimes it's so hard to live it.

Papaji: It looks hard because the people around you are all behaving differently. You have also behaved like them for all of your life. To live a life that is simple, natural and spontaneous, how can it be hard? It only looks hard because everyone is trying to live life differently. It is, in fact, the easiest way to live because it's your own nature. It may be hard in the beginning because no one in your community lives like this. They are all sailing in the same boat together, going in another direction. You have to stop following what other people are doing and walk your own path. Your path will be the solitary way of the razor's edge, not the path of the crowd. Take up this path if you want to. If you don't like it, go with the crowd in their boat. There is no pressure from me on this. You can do as you like. No pressure, no compulsion, no requirements. Whatever you feel is beneficial, whatever you think is wise, do it and see what happens. If you then discover that you like this alternative way of living, then follow it. This way, it will be your decision. If you do follow this path, you will stand alone and you may end up fighting the world, but sooner or later the world will follow you. But in the beginning nobody will like what you are doing. Many people have faced this dilemma, and many of them have got into trouble by choosing a different way, a different path. They have been put on the cross for telling the truth. They have been stoned to death for telling the truth. What was their crime? Only telling people what is the correct way to live. They spoke in the market place about truth and were given poison to drink. Or they were executed on a cross or stoned to death. They just spoke the truth, but telling this truth in public is a very rare event. Most people will not listen to what they have to say, and for these people, *samsara* will continue.

The thought 'I have to liberate myself' never comes to most people. This thought never even enters the mind. If such a thought does arise in the mind of one person, a hundred thousand people will come along and try to discourage him from doing anything about it. This man will probably end up listening to them because he doesn't dare to go it alone.

13

Whatever you experience, reject it

Question: We were talking yesterday about being trapped. You mentioned the yogi getting trapped in *samadhi*, the *bhakta* in his rosary, and so on. You also said that community was a trap.

Papaji: Yes, all those traps we mentioned yesterday were external.

Question: Right.

Papaji: I remember what we discussed. The rosary, reading books, following different methods, and so on. Today, let us deal with internal traps. These things we talked about yesterday are all external traps. Let us talk about the internal ones.

What are they? There are five internal traps. Number one is the body; identification with the body made out of food [*annamayakosa*]. Then the vital body [*pranamayakosa*], the body made up of the vital breath, the *prana*. This one is inside, isn't it? Then there is the mental body, the mind [*manomayakosa*]. Next there is the sheath of the intellect, the intellectual body [*vijnanamayakosa*]. Finally, there is the bliss body [*anandamayakosa*]. In this body there is an attachment to bliss. All of these so-called bodies, these sheaths that the 'I' functions through, are traps. Freedom is beyond external traps. These are internal traps. People say 'I am the body', or 'I am the vital breath', or 'I am the mind', or 'I am the intellect', or 'I am bliss'. We have

87

to cross beyond all these internal identifications before we can face freedom. External and internal traps both have to go.

Question: You are describing how we end up identifying with one of these bodies. I feel there is a self-consciousness inside me. Is this identification with a 'self' one of these internal traps? You have been telling me lately to understand the 'I'-thought. I have been looking and getting very quiet with it. Yesterday, though, you told me to ask 'Who is in bondage?'

Papaji: Yes, this 'I'-thought is the primal thought. It is from this that everything starts. From here bondage starts; from here ignorance starts; from here *samsara* starts. When you come to this 'I'-thought and concentrate on it, you return to the source of thought, and there thought itself vanishes.

Question: Is it useful to isolate the 'I'-thought by rejecting, one by one, all the things that it associates and identifies with?

Papaji: Whatever you experience, reject it. Wherever you find yourself, reject that place. Whatever you perceive, conceive or see, reject them all as 'not this, not this'. Separate yourself from all these things. In the end you will arrive somewhere, at some knowledge, at a knowledge that cannot be rejected. You will be very stupid if you try to reject this knowledge because it is truth itself. Through ordinary discriminative knowledge you can reject all the things that you are not, but then you will end up with a knowledge that cannot be rejected. You have to face that knowledge which can never be left or discarded. That is your reality.

Reject all the things that you identify with one by one. 'I am not the physical body. I am not the mental body. I am not the intellectual body. I am not the blissful body.' When all these identifications are no longer there, the 'I' itself will vanish because it only remains as an entity that is relative to another entity. Finally, the individual 'I' will remain unassociated with anything else, and then it will vanish. And duality will go with it. Where this 'I' vanishes, in that place true knowledge arises.

Question: *[new questioner]* That 'I' can't exist by itself, can it? That 'I' can't exist alone.

Papaji: No. It can't exist except in association with other things.

Question: I've been waking up in the morning, some mornings anyway, and watching the 'I'. I watch myself grab an object. I watch the mind latch onto an object. It seems to need to do this to stay alive. Some mornings, though, there's a sense of space all around me, a quiet space, but then the mind just grabs at that space, that quietness and makes an object out of it. It wants to objectify the quiet space and the silence.

Papaji: Yes, that's how it manifests everything. This is how manifestation takes place every day. When you question this 'I', manifestation will end, along with 'I' itself. Then something else will remain, something that was a witness not only to all the manifestation but also to the dissolution of the 'I'.

Question: Sometimes there is a phase in which there has been an awareness of the individual self-consciousness rising and falling. There's just the awareness of it. At other times it seems that the sense of self-consciousness is the perceiver itself, rather than that which is perceived by self-consciousness. Do you follow what I am trying to say? There have been times when I have actually just been watching self-consciousness.

Papaji: Watching?

Question: Murray's consciousness.

Papaji: How can consciousness watch consciousness? How can it?

Question: By consciousness I mean Murray, the mind of Murray, grasping.

Papaji: This is the individual ego then.

Question: Sometimes there is just an awareness of ego, but at other times there is the feeling of being the ego, of being the perceiver.

Papaji: When you are seeing everything – 'I am conscious of this' – this is the ego consciousness, not consciousness itself. When you are aware that this is the ego, then this ego will vanish. This is the nature of the ego. Then you will be something else; you will be the witness of the ego. It is there that I am taking you. Beyond the five *kosas*, which are the five inner traps. That is the place you need to find. Even when you just begin to look, you will start to experience enjoyment. That place is in everything.

Question: *[new questioner]* Is it that the ego vanishes, or does it just lose its importance?

Papaji: It has no importance if it is there or not there.

Question: But it's still there?

Papaji: If you are aware, if you are aware that it is there and that it will not harm you, then let it be there also. When you can use the word 'I' – 'I will do this', 'I love that' – knowing what this 'I' truly is, you can use it and it can be allowed to stay. A tiger is dangerous in the forest, isn't it? But the same tiger in a circus obeys its master. The master points his finger: 'Stand up!' 'Sit down!' 'Sit on the chair!' and the tiger meekly obeys. It is the same with the ego, if it is a tamed ego. The tiger in the wilderness can be a dangerous man-eater, but the tiger in the circus is just there for fun, for amusement.

Question: *[new questioner]* Sometimes when awareness is there I get the feeling that the ego is resisting it. That the ego likes to see what it can do to test awareness. There can be quietness for a while, but then the ego will come along and say, 'Come on, give me some entertainment, some stimulation'.

Papaji: That is how you have trained yourself. That is how you have trained your ego. You have trained it to do things and want things.

I had the opposite problem when I was young. I wanted to go inwards and enjoy the peace and happiness that was always there, but the people around me didn't like me doing this, so I had to teach myself to go outwards and become interested in the things of the world. I had to expend a lot of effort to make the mind go outwards and get attached to things. Even then, I was not able to do it very well. If I had any practice at all when I was young, it was the practice of trying to be attached to the world. I forced my mind to develop an interest in these things because it only had an interest in going within. I don't know what happens with other people, but I do know that the mind automatically follows its own interests. My interest was to fall into this inner happiness and stay there.

Don't find fault with your mind or your senses. They are just moving towards whatever interests them the most. The senses and the ego will flow towards your attachments. To make them move in a different direction, you have to give up these attachments.

I was attached to going within, to falling into states of bliss all the time. The people around me didn't like this so I started to practise not being in peace, not being in happiness. It was very hard work.

When I was in the army, I was so happy and blissful, my superior officer thought I was drunk all the time. He told my servant not to give me more than two drinks a day, but my servant replied, 'He doesn't drink at all'. I wanted to behave well, but my mind never listened to me. It was too attached to these bliss states. How could I do what people wanted me to do? My mind was never out of this happiness that was always pulling me inside.

I never meditated, and I never did any spiritual practice. When you people meditate, you sit and close your eyes because you think that this will help your meditation. I close my eyes and sit as well, since that is what everyone else here is doing, but I am not really meditating.

To know yourself you don't actually need to control the mind, and you don't need to sit in meditation. Nor do you need any books. To return to the Self, why should you need a map? No map is needed, no book is needed, no track needs to be followed. If you want to go somewhere else other than the Self, you will need a map. To be as you are, to stay as you are, why should you need a map or a guide? You are already there. What exercise is going to bring you any nearer? What *sadhana*? What bodhi tree do you need to sit under?

14

Nobody is a seeker after liberation because nobody exists

Question: Last night I was sitting outside a temple, the Hanuman Temple in Aminabad. I was just sitting quietly. It was night time, and I was just looking at the market. I find these Indian scenes are very intense for me. Suddenly I felt my mind, my American mind, breaking. I suddenly saw that you cannot use the mind to understand the mind. Up till now I have always been using the mind to understand the mind, but I suddenly saw that it can't. I saw that this couldn't be done. I felt that the mind was just a little cloud on top of me. I was separate from it, and it somehow felt very clean. But the whole process was also a little strange.

Papaji: Yes, it's a monkey temple. Mind is a monkey, so this is a temple of the mind *[laughter]*. Hanuman is the symbol of the mind. The monkey has the same habits as the mind, but at least it has a tail to balance with. If you have a tail, it's all right. You can control your movements. You can jump from branch to branch without falling off. A mind that is balanced is a trained mind. It knows that its true nature is consciousness, and that gives it the balance to move well. If the monkey mind knows that its true nature is consciousness, that the mind is consciousness itself, there will be no problem. The balance will be there.

Hanuman, the mind, knows that he is one with Ram, consciousness, the reality. That is his secret. When mind knows that, all will be well. The ten-headed Ravana signifies multiple and uncontrolled desires. The power of consciousness, the power of a mind that is united with consciousness, can destroy the kingdom of desires and its ruler. This is the meaning of the story of the *Ramayana*.

There is another Hanuman temple down by the River Gomti. It's nice there as well. There is a statue of Neem Karoli Baba in that one. He used to visit the old temple that was there before. During a flood that old temple was submerged and destroyed, so the government has made this new one.

Question: *[new questioner]* Why am I so affected when I visit these Hanuman temples? I went with Andy to the one in Aminabad last night. Every time I go there I feel a strong devotional bliss. I don't know why because I don't feel that I have much of a connection with Hanuman. I'm not like Bihari [Ram Charan] or Ram Dass in that I don't feel devoted to Hanuman, but I still experience this *ananda* when I go there. Why do some places affect me like this, apparently for no reason?

Papaji: There are some places that the mind is attuned to.

Question: You say sometimes that bliss is a trap. How does one go beyond bliss? How does one escape the trap? How does one go beyond bliss so that it doesn't become a trap?

Papaji: Unless you have enjoyed bliss, how can you reject it? There must be bliss all around you; you must be drowning in bliss so that you become allergic to it. *[laughter]* Only then can you decide 'I want something better than this'. Unless you have had money, how can the idea come to you that it is better not to have money? It is only when you have a surplus and when you see that the surplus is not doing you any good that you feel you want to give it up. If you have a lot of money, you can see how you get attached to it, and how much trouble it can cause you in the long run. It is the same with bliss.

Question: When the bliss is there, it seems that there is also equanimity of mind. The mind seems to be quiet and balanced. That's a hard thing to want to give up.

Papaji: Mind is, no doubt, very happy when it is in bliss. It is very difficult to cross this barrier. Very difficult. Even some saints don't get past this point. It is said by some that *Brahmananda* [the bliss of *Brahman*] is the highest state, but there are others who feel that there is something beyond even this. This *ananda* can be a very nice experience, and many people settle for it, but when you know there is an ultimate truth beyond it, you should not stay in it.

Question: *[new questioner]* Is there still an experiencer who is in bliss? Do you have to move on because there is still an experiencer?

Papaji: An experiencer must be there. That relationship will be there: the experiencer and the object experienced. To transcend that duality, the prescription is to go beyond it.

Question: But for this to happen, the 'I' itself has to go. One has to reach the state where the 'I' is not there.

Papaji: Nobody can stay in bliss, but it is a rare one who can reject this bliss. The aim of man, of all beings, is happiness, so it is hard to give up states like these.

Question: *[new questioner]* Papaji, you say that we have to reject these states. For me this is difficult to grasp. If I reject something, I reject it with my mind. I can reject one of these five traps of the mind that you were talking about, but the mind that is doing the rejecting, the 'I', must still be there for this rejection to take place.

Papaji: This is from the perspective of the mind. There is another perspective. Do you know the story of the tenth man? Ten men crossed a fast-flowing river. When they reached the other side, one of them counted all the others to make sure that everyone had survived the crossing. He counted them all but omitted to count himself.

'One of us has drowned!' he cried out. 'One of us has drowned!'

The other nine went through the same exercise, and all of them made the same mistake of failing to count themselves, so all of them became convinced that one of their party had drowned. They started crying and weeping because they were all convinced that one of their friends had died.

Some passerby came up to them and said, 'Why are you crying? What is the problem?'

He was told that they were all grieving because they had lost a member of their party. When it was explained to him how they had reached this conclusion, the new man lined up all the ten travellers and counted them, and as he did so he made them all call out the numbers one by one. As the tenth man called out 'ten', they all realised that no one had drowned, that they had all been there all the time, and that their suffering and weeping had been based on an ignorant assumption. Usually, this story is told to drive home the point that when one discovers the Self, one is not attaining something new. One is merely giving up the suffering that was based on the wrong idea that something was missing.

Your ideas of spiritual practice – the idea that I must reject this or that – are also based on an ignorant assumption, the assumption that there is a doer, a meditator, who must do something in order to find something and experience it. You suffer and you meditate endlessly because you never address this erroneous assumption. The ten men in the story ran around weeping, saying, 'One of us is missing! One of us is missing!' You run around thinking, 'I must do something! I must do something!'

Who has to do something? Who is meditating? Instead of looking for results by meditating or rejecting attachments, just look towards the one who is meditating. Find out who he really is and then everything will stop.

Question: In pure awareness is there just the knowledge that one is not the surface wave but the underlying ocean?

Papaji: One knows that one is also the waves.

Question: Also the waves?

Papaji: Yes, everything. The wave thinks that it is different from all the other waves. It says, 'I have a name, a shape, I have movement in a particular direction'. The ocean, knowing that all the water is itself, just enjoys the dance.

The waves can think, 'I am independent; I have many friends in front of me and behind me; we are all moving along together'.

The waves might even decide to have a *satsang*. They may get together and say, 'Let us go off together to find the ocean. Let us meditate together and try to find out where the ocean is. I have heard it is very wonderful there.'

So, they travel along, looking for the ocean, and hoping that they will one day find it.

The ocean doesn't know anything about this. It just knows that the still, silent depths and the froth on the surface are all itself.

Question: I used to get afraid. I thought that the unhappiness I felt was due to the wrong identification with the waves. Now I am beginning to understand that bliss arises when the wave identifies itself with the ocean.

Papaji: Yes.

Question: I am beginning to understand that bliss is there when the individual, the wave, identifies with the larger entity, the ocean. That means that when ocean just knows itself as ocean there is no longer the bliss that comes from 'I am experiencing myself to be the great ocean'. Is this correct?

Papaji: Yes.

Question: I find this hard to grasp. In fact I cannot grasp it at all. This state in which there is neither experiencer nor experience. If I am just ocean, is there no experience, no happiness at all?

Papaji: The truth is, there is neither ocean nor wave. No name, no form: that is where you find the truth. You are not the ocean because the ocean is just a name. No name and no form is the ultimate truth. Where there is a name and a form there is falsehood.

Question: So name and form arise from awareness? And without awareness there can be no name and no form?

Papaji: Name and form are false. Where there is a name and a form there is falsehood. There is no truth in them because they are both perishable. Wherever there is a form, there is something that is going to perish. All forms have to perish, but if I talk like this too much, you will all run away. You will all run away because you want something to hold onto. You will run away into meditation. That's a good trap for you, because there you can have your association, your identification, and still think that you are doing something spiritual.

I tell you, 'No one is bound. There is no bondage. Nobody is a seeker after liberation because nobody exists. Even liberation does not exist. Who are you? Who is the one who is going to meditate?'

Now what are you going to do with this information? What can you do?

Meditation, levitation – these things you can do and know, but how can you do and know what I am talking about because there is no one there either to do or know?

Last year a Zen teacher came from Tokyo to Hardwar to see me. He didn't even go to his room to unpack. He brought his bag with him and sat down in front of me. This was last year, in June. Somebody had given him my name. He made a very elaborate Japanese bow and sat down.

He addressed me and said, 'You are Rama and I am the demon. Kill this demon.'

I looked at him and said, 'I have killed both of them'.

That was enough for him. He understood.

He prostrated again and said, 'I can leave now. I am going

back to Japan.'

I said, 'No, no, you have only just arrived. You must stay a bit longer.'

'Oh no,' he said, 'you are a very dangerous man. If I stay, I will fall in love with you. That's why I have to leave.'

And he left.

15

You have forgotten the purpose for which you incarnated

Papaji: All the prophets have said, 'You are a sinner. When you are happy, you are actually sinning.'

They address you like this and you accept it. You have accepted it completely. But if someone says to you, 'You are free', you don't believe it because you have been conditioned for so long into believing that you are a sinner. This idea of sin is now in your genes, in every drop of blood in your body. It pervades you completely. Generation after generation you have been listening to various people say that you are a sinner. You have believed all these people, and for generation after generation you have been working to free yourself of these sins.

If somebody now says, 'You are free. You have always been free and you have never been bound,' you are not going to listen to him.

So, the teachers start by saying, 'Yes, you are bound. You have karma and you have to meditate. Join some ashram and meditate so that you can get rid of these defects.'

It's only foolish people, though, who talk like this. It is not wisdom to be told that you are a sinner and that you are bound. Who is bound? Where is this bondage? No one ever sees it, but everyone believes in it. This idea puts you in the traps, which are all the methods that are given to you to escape from this bondage.

I am not going to tell you that you are bound. Instead, I am going to take you to the place where you will know there is no bondage. There you will scratch your head in a puzzled way because there is nothing for you to do there. There you have no relationships and no identifications.

There are clothes on your body. You are wearing them, but they are not you. They are your belongings, but they are not you. When you say 'My clothes', you know that the clothes belong to you, but are not you. When you say, 'My body, my mind, my intellect', and so on, have the same understanding. Know that they are your belongings, not who you are. You, the owner of them, are different from them. When you say, 'My mind is happy', or 'My mind is not happy', you are implying an owner of the mind. Who is this owner? To whom does this mind belong? This is what you have to find out. It's not hard. It's very easy to work out.

Question: *[new questioner]* Is the awareness you talk about the same as innocence? This child-like quality of innocence that we value so much?

Papaji: Yes, I believe so. You have to be innocent. A free man is always innocent. He is childlike. Like Socrates. All these people who were free, they were, first of all, very innocent. They speak the truth from that place of innocence.

Question: *[new questioner]* I think it is hard for me to say 'I am free, and I have been free all along' because I am too proud to admit that I have been stupid for so long. That seems to indicate a lack of innocence. How can I be more innocent?

Papaji: Innocence is your inherent nature. Cleverness is something you have acquired. You have acquired your cleverness from your parents, from your society and from your religion. They all make you so clever, you end up forgetting your innocence. You were born innocent. You never noticed any differences between your own people and the neighbours. You were loving everyone, and everyone loved you. People loved you so much, they came up to you and kissed you and gave you chocolate.

As you slowly grew up, all this changed. You learned to be clever; you lost your innocent nature; you even lost God. And that's when your suffering started. Now, you have acquired all this cleverness. You have discovered cheating and deception. You see differences between one man and the next and make negative judgements.

Who told you about all these things? When you were a young child, you didn't see any differences between your family and the neighbours, between one country and another, between one religion and another. You didn't see differences in those days. Look at the children who come here and play. They still have it. You can see it in them. But you have lost your innocence because of the society you live in, the parents and the priests who told you things that are not true. Now you want to return to your original innocence. You are not going to gain anything new, are you? You are just going to return back to your original innocence. When you give up all the things that have made you clever, you will go back to your own nature, your own state. That's what we call freedom. This freedom is 'freedom from'. You are free of everything you have acquired, everything that you have learned, everything that you have known, everything that you have read, everything that you have heard.

Innocence will come back to you if you don't impose any of these things on yourself. Just keep quiet. Don't have any expectation whatsoever. Don't even have the expectation of freedom, or realisation. Don't expect anything and innocence will show up by itself. Your nature will reveal itself once all this camouflage has been dropped. All you have to do is remove the impediments.

Just sit down. Allow your true nature to show up and reveal itself. You don't do this by making any effort, because when you are making an effort you are holding onto something. Clinging to it. Effort means clinging. Just stay very quiet and very still. All things will leave you and innocence will reveal itself. It's a revelation that will reveal itself to itself by itself. It will reveal itself when you are prepared for it.

What is this revelation? Leave it alone. Don't think about it. Just keep quiet and don't do anything. This is the requirement that has to be fulfilled. The circumstances under which this will happen will present themselves to you if you have the merit and the good luck. If the previous merits, the *punyas*, are right, this will happen. If the *punyas* are there, the *jiva* will come to good parents, to a good family. It will grow up and at some point it will be prompted by these old *punyas* to ask, 'I want freedom'. When all these things come together, you will be helpless to resist. You will move from place to place, seeking this elusive freedom. This desire for freedom will trouble you, and you will not be allowed to rest without attempting to fulfil it. You will not be distracted by any attachments, by any kind of luxury. Kingdoms may be offered to you, but you will reject them. Buddha was given all these things and he rejected them all because he had the *punyas* and circumstances to attain freedom. And what circumstances! Good mother, good parentage, good circumstances, and an unquenchable desire to find the truth. Having these things in this life depends on the merits you have earned in previous lives. But all are moving in that direction. Everybody, all *jivas*, are returning home. There's no doubt about that. On the way, though, many of them get distracted by other things.

Question: *Jiva*. What exactly do you mean by *jiva*?

Papaji: The *jiva* is the soul, the transmigrating soul that travels from one incarnation to another before it returns home.

Question: *[new questioner]* Isn't this also an illusion?

Papaji: You will know this afterwards, but not in the beginning. In the snake and the rope analogy, you see a rope and imagine that it is a snake. But you don't discover that you have been imagining this until you get closer and realise that the snake is non-existent, that you just imagined it by superimposing an untrue idea on a piece of rope. While you think it is real, it will give you fear and suffering.

All *jivas* are going home to the Self, but because they imagine themselves to be real, separate entities, they forget about going home and get distracted by other things.

There was once a king who had no children. Since he was getting old and had no heir to succeed him, he decided to adopt one who would be the ruler of the kingdom when he died.

He thought to himself, 'If I don't have an established heir in place when I die, there will be a lot of trouble in the kingdom after I die'.

He called one of his guards and asked him to make an announcement that he would open the gates of his palace the following day from 6 a.m. to 6 p.m., and that all the people of the kingdom could come in and be interviewed for the job of being the next ruler. No one would be prohibited from coming in.

The next morning crowds of people assembled at the gate, each of them hoping that he or she would be the next ruler. They were greeted by the guards and the courtiers.

One of the courtiers announced, 'You are about to meet the king and be received by him. You must look good when this happens. Look at you all! Some of you are just dressed in rags. We will clean you all up, give you a nice bath, feed you and give you some nice new clothes, and then you will be presentable to the king. Come with us.'

Everyone was taken into the palace and offered all the facilities that the king enjoyed. For this one day all the visitors had the run of the palace, which meant that they could take and consume whatever they wanted. Those who were interested in perfumes collected bottles of perfume; those who were interested in clothes collected many items of clothing. Other people luxuriated in the king's baths, ate his food, and watched his dancers and singers perform. This went on all day and everyone forgot what he or she had come to the palace for. The king waited in his throne room, but no one went there to see him because all the candidates were too preoccupied with enjoying themselves with the king's luxuries. At the end of the day, at 6 p.m., when no one had shown up to claim the throne and the kingdom, the king withdrew his offer and asked everyone to return home.

If anyone had gone to the king immediately, without getting sidetracked, all these treasures would have been his or hers permanently, not just for a few hours. But everyone forgot the purpose for which he or she had come to the palace.

This is what happens to *jivas*. The throne of the kingdom of liberation is waiting for anyone who wants to walk in and claim it, but these *jivas* all get sidetracked into enjoying pleasures and accumulating possessions. At the end of their lives they die and get reborn again and continue with their pleasures and sufferings.

You are all so busily engaged with your attachments and desires, you have forgotten the purpose for which you incarnated. You have forgotten that you came here for liberation. What good will these desires, attachments and possessions ultimately do you? What will you leave this world with? Nothing.

Alexander the Great conquered all the known world of his day. All the riches and territories of the world were his while he was alive, but when he died he had nothing. And he knew this. Before he died he gave an order: 'When you put me in my coffin, leave my hands on the outside. That way everyone will know that I am leaving here with nothing.'

Make the best use of this moment in time, this moment that you have in which you can look at your own Self and not at the objects of your desires. This moment may never come back. If you postpone because you want just a little more enjoyment before you go to the throne room of your own Self, you will be lost, you will be washed away. Your chance will not come again. You can see your own true face only in this moment, not in the next or the last. You have to do it now, not later. In this instant of time you have to devote yourself to your own Self.

To accomplish this you don't have to study, you don't have to practise and you don't have to go to the Himalayas. Just this moment, here and now, is quite enough. Put your face inside and you will see it. Don't waste this moment. It is a very precious one. I am not going to discourage you. In fact, I congratulate you for being here. There are six billion people in the world, but there are only twenty people here today saying, 'I want freedom. I want to sit on the throne of freedom.' Well done! All I ask is that you don't postpone. You have been postponing all your life – 'I will do it later today, tomorrow, next week, next year', and so on.

Postponement is the mind. Mind is the past. Mind is manifestation. Manifestation is *samsara*. And *samsara* is suffering. You have to choose and decide what you want, and you have to choose in this instant of time, not later on. In this instant look at your own Self. If you allow this moment to slip, it will become the past. Don't allow it to slip.

16

Don't load yourself up with the *Ramayana* of everyone else's lives

Papaji: The knower in you is aware not only of the knowledge that it knows but also of what it has forgotten. You say, 'I forgot such and such thing', don't you? So, when a knowledge of forgetfulness is there, the knower must still remain. That knower doesn't go anywhere. The knower is imperishable.

Question: What about consciousness of the knower and the knower itself? Are they the same or different?

Papaji: They are the same thing. Knower and the consciousness of the knower are the same thing. How do you establish a difference between them? Consciousness and knowing are the same thing.

Question: I find this knower rather boring. It interferes with the innocence of perception.

Papaji: That is because, for a long time, you have been using this knower for the wrong purpose. In fact, you are attributing the knower to something else. The true knower is the same always. It does not change. When you know the knower, you will know that nothing changes except your concepts. Whatever change you see and experience is all a construction of your mind. You become what you think about. Nothing happens unless you have first thought about it. Instantly it happens. All manifestation is just one part of you. All this creation, billions of years of past and future, is just one thought. When this one thought comes into existence, past, present and future are instantly created. Thought creates it all.

Question: What thought is this? Is it the thought 'I am'?

Papaji: Yes, this thought has to venture out. And when you question it, it vanishes. The questioning will take you back to where there is no thought, where nothing has ever happened. It will take you to the root where there is no tree. The tree is on the outside. What I am talking about is on the inside. There is a question that will take you down to the very root. What is this thought? It is the question 'What is this "I"?' You must return back to the root of 'I'. This is the one thought I was talking about. Everything depends on this 'I'-thought. The past, the present and the future – billions of years – are all within this 'I'-thought. When we investigate, all these aeons of time are over. Investigate and everything will be over.

Question: *[new questioner]* How to investigate without effort?

Papaji: Effort is manifestation. Effort is towards something outside. When the thought 'I' arises, manifestation happens. This is effort. When you say 'I', and look to see what it really is, this is investigation. When you utter the word 'I', instantly everything is there: past, present and future. Just look at this 'I'. This is what I call investigation. Just look at it. Face in the reverse direction. The 'I' created manifestation. Now, look at it and reverse the order. From manifestation go back to 'I'. Put yourself into reverse gear. Don't engage the forward gear. When the forward gear is engaged, you are caught in the cleverness of the mind. All questions such as these, all arguments come in this category of cleverness. Reason and reasoning are also part of this cleverness.

First do what I am saying and then see the result for yourself. Then you will know for yourself and you will be able to talk about it from direct experience. How can you talk about sleep unless you have experienced it for yourself?

If you have never been to sleep, you can question endlessly, 'What will happen when I go to sleep? What goes on there? What is this happiness that people say is experienced in sleep?'

No one can really tell you about this. It is something you have to experience for yourself. We could spend all morning defining sleep and talking about it, but how will this help you to understand this state? Just go to sleep and see for yourself.

It is the same thing with freedom. Thousands of books have been written about freedom, about enlightenment. But is there any man alive who has attained freedom just by reading a book? Enlightenment will not come by reading a book. It may come by throwing away the book, but not by reading it.

Everyone is seeking instant enlightenment. A desire for freedom arises and you go to a bookstore or to an ashram to find an answer. If you go to an ashram you will be given a change of clothes and a change of diet, but I don't believe that this has got anything to do with freedom. Food, clothes, communes, ashrams, caves in the Himalayas: none of these has any connection with freedom. It's not in these things, these places. It's something else completely.

People think, 'If I go to the Himalayas and find a solitary place, I can sit down and get enlightenment'. You will not find solitude by a change of geographical conditions. The friend who troubles you here will go along with you in your head wherever you go.

I saw a *baba* once in the Himalayas. He looked to be about eighty years old, and he belonged to some place in the Punjab.

I said, '*Baba*, what have you been doing?'

He replied, 'I came here a long time ago. I ran away from my home. When I was sixteen years old, I went away with some *sadhus* who came to my village. I wandered around for a long time, but now I can't walk well, so I settled down here. I sat down here when I discovered I couldn't travel any more. Some people from my village found me here and told me the news of my family. Brothers have married and have children. Land has been bought and sold, and so on.'

Then he said to me, 'If I return now, who will give me his daughter to marry? I am too old. I don't want to go back home. If I go back to my village, people will say, "He's coming back after sixty years. Why did he go away in the first place?" So, I don't want to go back. I will just sit here and live the rest of my days on this spot.'

Many people are like this. They run away, thinking that some good will come of a new way of life, but it doesn't turn out that way. I have met *sadhus* who were working on getting *siddhis*, and I have even met *sadhus* who have attained some of these powers, but I have not come across a *sadhu* in the Himalayas who has attained freedom. I have wandered extensively in the Himalayas, but I have never seen or encountered a liberated *sadhu*. I have seen much better people as householders, both in India and in the West. They are doing much better than the people who live in communes and ashrams. Householders live a regular life in the world. I have seen a few who have been successful. They are much better than these *sadhus*. This is how I feel, and this has been my experience.

I therefore don't suggest that anyone run away from his work or his family. Do your work. Neither working nor not working has anything to do with freedom. Just spend a few minutes on yourself, wherever you are. Running away is time-consuming. The time you spend on running and on finding a new place can be better spent on yourself, here and now.

I knew a man who used to go to the Ganga to sit for one hour of meditation there. His village was ten miles away, which meant a lot of travel to and from his house to the river. He thought to himself, 'Why don't I build a hut here? If I have a place here, I won't have to waste all this time coming and going. I can then spend more time here and meditate more.'

This man decided to shift his house to the banks of the Ganga. He ordered some bricks for the wall, some wood for the doors, and some cement to hold it all together. In those days there was no road and no trucks. If you wanted materials such as these, you had to get them carried in on the backs of donkeys. All these things had to be carried in on the backs of these animals. Materials arrived, masons came and went, and he had to keep track of all these deliveries and workers by writing accounts. He was so busy, he didn't even have enough time for his one hour of daily meditation.

He thought to himself, 'I used to come here every day and have a very peaceful hour of meditation. Now, when I get a chance to close my eyes, my head is full of bricks, donkeys and workers. What have I started?'

The next day, when his workers came, he asked them all to demolish his little house and throw all the pieces into the Ganga. He decided to go back to his village and live the way he lived before. He came to the conclusion, 'It's better to walk here, sit here for an hour in peace, and then go home again'.

There are many people like him all over the Himalayas – people who spend lots of time and money trying to get their physical circumstances right so they can meditate properly. The result is lots of ashram buildings and not much meditation. Even when these people do finally get their nice building constructed, they end up spending a lot of their time gossiping. I have encountered people like this all over Rishikesh and in the surrounding areas.

People in the ashrams there catch hold of you and ask you the same questions again and again: 'Where are you working?' 'How many children do you have?' 'Are you married or not?' If you are not married, not working and have no children, you will be asked, 'Why are you not married, why are you not working, why don't you have any children?' It goes on endlessly. All the people in these ashrams know all the personal details about everyone else who is there, but none of them knows anything about freedom. They are too busy gossiping to discover what it is.

'Look at that woman over there! She has already left four husbands and now she is on her fifth!' A good story like this will interest them far more than meditation. The people who sit in these ashrams end up with not only the burden of their own memories and experiences, but the extra weight of everyone else's stories as well.

Live in your own house and be quiet. That is my advice. Don't load yourself up with the *Ramayana* of everyone else's lives. Stick to your own little story. It is quite enough. Why load yourself up with other people's worries and histories? Every time I go to an ashram in Rishikesh I am told stories of renegade swamis and scandalous incidents about the people who are going to listen to them.

Instead of getting involved in all these dramas, stay where you are. Live comfortably, have a good life, eat well and maintain your health. Then, in whatever free time you have – it might be just half an hour or an hour – devote it to looking at your own Self. Don't waste your time going to ashrams or communes. Wherever you are, just devote some honest time to yourself. All you have to do is go home, back to your own Self. Say to yourself, 'I have to return', and just devote time to this project whenever you can. This will be enough. It will drag you home. Just don't forget the real reason why you are here. That's all.

Do you remember the story I told you about the people who went to the palace because the king wanted to appoint one of them as his successor? They forgot the reason for going to the palace and instead spent their time there bundling up things to take home and enjoying the various pleasures that were on offer. They all forgot why they were in the palace, and in the end they were all asked to leave.

Don't spend all your time eating, drinking, wearing fancy clothes, listening to music and so on. You can waste your whole life on things such as these. And most people do. Keep a balanced life and remember why you are here. You can have a shower; you can have a good bath; you can dress well; you can eat well – but don't forget to meet the king. He is waiting for you. He has allowed you to enter his palace. The gate to freedom is open. He wants you to walk through it, and he is waiting for you on the inside. Unfortunately, no one goes in because everyone is distracted and seduced by something outside that gate. This is not good, but this is what is really happening. Two thousand six hundred years have passed since the Buddha ignored all the attractions of his own palace and walked through that door to freedom. Who is following him? No one.

All are enjoying, eating and dancing. Whose fault is this? Freedom is waiting for you with extended arms, but you are not responding to the loving embrace that it wants to give you. You are otherwise engaged. What you don't understand is that when you try to get happiness from all these objects of pleasure, you are really searching for the happiness of your own Self. Your search is simply misdirected. You are all looking for happiness, but you never find it because you are all looking in the wrong place. If you find the correct place to look, instantly you will get it. That instant is the moment you drop all the pleasures of the king's courtyard and walk directly into the throne room to meet the king. How much time do you need to do this? How much time does it take to turn your back on all these enjoyments in order to accept the invitation of the king? In this story, the gate was open for twelve hours, from six in the morning until six in the evening. In your lifespan you have eighty years. You can enjoy that life, but remember that the most important thing you have to do in this incarnation is to run into the king's throne room and claim that prize. Don't postpone. Don't think that you have time to do it later. Make it your first priority. Reject transient pleasures and run inside to meet your inner king. Once you have done that, the whole kingdom will be yours.

While you are waiting in the courtyard, you have a special dispensation to use the king's property for one day. If you become the king by accepting his invitation, it will all belong to you for the rest of your life. You won't have to ask if you can use the baths because they will all be yours. When you become one with the Self by claiming your freedom, you will have no more desires because everything will be your own Self. There will be nothing apart from you that you can desire or want. Take this one instant to accept the invitation of the king and receive his love, and from then on you will be happy all the time. The whole world will be your own Self and you will revel in the enjoyment of it.

If you just spend your life enjoying yourself, thinking, 'This is mine', at the end of your life you will be sent away because you will have failed to take advantage of the offer and the invitation of the king who is within you. And when you go, you will not be allowed to take any of the things you were guarding as 'mine' with you. All these things, your enjoyments and your possessions, are deceiving you. Everything you touch is biting you, but you don't notice and you keep coming back for more. Touch anything in this world and you will find that it has a sting in it. The rose may look beautiful, but when you try to grab it, you get impaled on the hidden thorns. You have to be very careful with what you do, what you smell, what you use.

[Long pause]

You are going to meet your own Self, your own very close relative. No one is closer to you than your own Self. This Self is your eternal friend, your deathless, permanent and most beautiful companion, but you don't know and appreciate this because you don't look at it properly. You don't have the correct eyesight for this. Go near to it, have a glimpse of it, test it, and if it doesn't pass this test of permanence, reject it. Make your own choice, but at least go and see it for yourself. Don't merely rely on hearing about it from others. Advance towards it, get face to face with it, and if you don't like it, reject it.

Question: *[new questioner]* How can one not like one's own Self?

Papaji: All people, by their speech and behaviour, are saying that they don't like it. People like nonsense; people like things that are not permanent. No one likes his or her own Self because all are liking what is not the Self, those things that are impermanent. When you think and behave like this, you are divorcing yourself from your own Self. Are any of these things that you value so much going to stay with you? Sooner or later they will divorce you and you will be alone again. Everyone goes through these divorces again and again, but nobody learns from them. Still you go sniffing after all these things that are impermanent. Life after life you carry on doing this because you are addicted to behaving like this.

What to do about it? I have just told you what to do. Approach it and go face to face with it. Give it one instant of your life. Steal one second out of the eighty years of your life and use it to face your own Self. You can keep the other seventy-nine years, eleven months, twenty-nine days, and all the minutes and seconds except this one. This one second will be enough to glimpse your own Self. And if you don't like it, reject it.

Question: *[new questioner]* How do I see it? How?

Papaji: I have to be very clear about this. First I said that you are seeing your own Self, which is not one centimetre or even one millimetre away from you. You asked me this question from that place. It is that place from where this question arises. The place from where this question comes is so near and so dear. That place is so close to you, even the idea that there is a place separate from you is not there. Go back to where this question arises. Not the place where the question is seen and recognised, but the place where it originally arose. This is prior even to the arising of the breath. To ask a question you need breath, don't you? So prior to the breath, prior to the appearance of the question, what is that place where it all comes from?

That place is within you; it is your own Self. But when you ask 'How?', automatically you move away from it. These three letters H-O-W take you away from that place, so it's better that you don't use them. Why waste your time on them? They are just distracting you, taking your attention away from this place. Don't choose this word at all. Don't use the breath and don't use the word. Find this place that is prior to both. If you get it, you have got it. If you lose it, you have lost it.

17

This question 'Who am I?' will give you an answer that you have never heard before

Question: So what is the use of all these questions? Can you say something about the usefulness of questioning?

Papaji: Questions are useful. You have to ask them to remove doubts and to get useful information. If you are in a forest and you don't know how to get out, you have to ask people there. There are two kinds of people who do not need to ask questions. One is a foolish man. He need not ask. In fact, he doesn't know what to ask about. The other is a wise man. He has solved his problems, so he doesn't need to ask any more. In between there is this community of seekers. People in this group have to ask. They are searching for something, and they need help.

Question: But you are making it so clear that no searching can get you to where you are already. All the searching is so useless. I see now that all the searching is not leading me anywhere. However, I am still in the jungle, and I still want to know the way out. Or I want at least to find the way to someone who can help me to get out.

Papaji: Yes, you need to ask because you are not the foolish man, nor are you yet the wise man. You are in the middle. You are in the forest; you don't know the way out; you are not comfortable in the forest; and you need a guide to help you find out how to leave. You know that nightfall is coming and you are aware that you are in a dangerous place where you might become prey to wild animals. You know that you are in danger and you want to get out before it is too late. So, why not seek help and ask for directions if you know that you want to leave?

He who knows not and knows not that he knows not is a foolish man. Leave him alone. Shun him. Don't stay in his house or have anything to do with him. The second category is he who knows not and knows that he knows not. The third category, the wise man, is someone who knows and who knows that he knows.

These are the three categories. It depends on you which one you end up in. Make a choice. The people who are in groups one and three are happy, but for different reasons. It is only the number two people who worry because they know that they are in trouble. They sense the danger they are in and they decide that they have to do something to avoid it.

The people who are happy in their current circumstances are the foolish ones. The ones who know that the forest of enjoyments and pleasures is a dangerous place are the seekers.

Questions need to be asked. Questions reveal your own state. Questions will reveal what you want and what you need to do and know. However, to be useful, questions have to be on the right topic. If you ask about other people, things external to yourself, your questions will be endless and ultimately pointless.

There is only one wise question, one sensible question, and this is the question that you will ultimately have to ask yourself. This question 'Who am I?' will give you an answer that you have never heard before. This question is one you can put to yourself; you don't need any outside authority to give you a reply. But no one asks this question. Everyone asks about other things, other people. These inessential questions are all about the past. All questions that go to the mind for an answer are about the past. If you can ask the question 'Who am I?' and find the answer, you will be taken out of the past. The solution to this question cannot be found in the past, in your memories or experiences or knowledge.

No one asks this prime question. Instead people occupy themselves with asking, 'What is this?' and 'What is that?' People sometimes ask 'Who is God?' but even this does not address the fundamental question that needs to be answered. No one has faced this one true question properly.

'Who am I?' 'Where am I?' 'Who is this I?' These are all the same fundamental question. If you find the correct answer, all other enquiries will end. It is not only enquiries that will end. All phenomena will end, all suffering will end, all manifestation will end. This question doesn't take time to ask, and finding the answer doesn't happen in time. The answer is found in an instant that is beyond time. The answer is not miles and miles away. Asking the question will not just quieten the mind, it will take you to the source of all questions. This question does not lead to a quiet mind; it makes the mind vanish completely. Mind will disappear, leaving you free. This is called freedom: freedom from all questions, freedom from all sufferings, freedom from the repeated cycles of birth and death. This is the one question that needs to be asked.

Question: *[new questioner]* You say that in the moment one identifies with the 'I', all things arise. There have been occasions when I have felt totally in the 'now', totally free of all thoughts, but in that moment there is no awareness that manifestation is no longer there. I occasionally feel the 'I' rising and attaching itself to ideas and concepts, but when I feel the mind subside, when 'I' is no longer connecting to thoughts, I don't feel that nothing is there.

Papaji: The rising of phenomena and the non-arising of phenomena are both concepts. Rising and non-arising will also disappear. Presence and absence will disappear.

Question: So how do you know that they arise with the 'I' when there's no rising or non-arising?

Papaji: I say that presence and absence are relative and that in the final experience, the final knowledge, they both disappear. Some schools of thought say that the ultimate reality is a void, an emptiness. They put stress on this void. They cling to emptiness, to the idea of the void, but this is just another idea. Let emptiness arise; let forms arise; it is all mind.

It is the mind that has created emptiness. Emptiness is just a projection of the mind. Where has this projection of emptiness come from? One must discover this to avoid getting attached to the concept of emptiness. The mind clings to whatever it has projected. If you have the idea that emptiness is the ultimate state, mind will create this state for you and let you enjoy it. It will let you taste this emptiness and feel satisfied with it. This is a project with a predetermined end. You project the goal with your mind, and then that same mind enters that state and tastes it.

Let forms rise or let them not rise. Let emptiness arise or not arise. You are not concerned with either manifestation or non-manifestation. Where will these mental states come to rest? Where will they subside to? That is somewhere else, something else; it is undescribed, indescribable, untouched. It is an untouched zone, an untouched region. *[Laughs quietly to himself]*

Question: But will it not also tap me on the shoulder and say, 'Here I am'? Will this untouched region not one day announce itself to me? At the right time will it not come?

Papaji: You will never get a message from there. It will not clap or tap to announce itself. It is a place of no return, a place from where no messages emanate. But everything dances on it. Manifestation and emptiness are both dancing on it. Manifestation and emptiness are both dancing on it, not knowing what lies underneath.

Question: *[new questioner]* When I am sitting and looking at the way my mind works, I see my ego getting carried off in all directions. I sit and I see, 'I am angry about this', or 'I like this', or, 'I remember that'. Or I see myself doing something that I know I shouldn't do and I feel hurt or embarrassed. What is the consciousness that is seeing all these things?

Papaji: Discrimination.

Question: Discrimination?

Papaji: Don't discriminate. Let these things come and let them pass away.

Imagine you are standing by the side of a busy road. Cars are passing you in both directions, but you are not interested in them because you have no connection with them. Suddenly a car that has the number of a friend of yours passes you, and that grabs your attention. You look at the car to see if your friend is in it. Many cars passed without attracting your interest, but this one grabs your attention. Your attention gets dragged along with the car, doesn't it? This is how discrimination works. Many cars passed and were ignored, but when one that interested you went by, you used your discrimination and let your attention catch the car and be taken down the road with it.

Who is discriminating in this way? Who is choosing to follow one thought and not another? Ask this question. This question will stop the moving mind. It will stop the process of choosing one thought to follow and not another.

Question: I see that there are some deep patterns in my mind. I feel I am programmed and that I have no real choice on how I think or behave.

You told me once, 'You are a sinner because you have been trained to be a sinner. You believe it and live that way. So, all your life you are going to sin.'

So I decided to try a little experiment on myself. I decided to sit quietly and see what this 'me' was when it didn't have any ideas about itself. I found it very hard. There's no sense or feeling of 'me' without something else being added onto it.

Papaji: You must get rid of this idea that you are a sinner because it is just an idea that gives you trouble. 'Sin does not reach me. Sin has never lived in me. I am free of all sins.' This is who you really are. That is the real you. That is your place and that is your nature. That is your being. All the rest doesn't belong to you. It is just a bunch of ideas that you have collected from outside agencies which you have subsequently accepted as your own. I don't say that you are a sinner. I know who you really are. You are me, and you are free. That's what I say, and that's what I say to you. You have just been told that you are a sinner, and you have believed it.

Question: That's what I am trying to say. Yesterday you told me that I had been trained as a sinner, that I had been trained like a seal. When people say this to me, I believe it, and I start to behave as if it is true. It affected me very deeply when you said this because I know it is true.

Papaji: It is not just you. The whole world is affected like this. It is in the blood of each generation, and it goes on indefinitely. But it is all imagination. It is a pile of straw that you can destroy with a single match. But you have been so trained to think about sin and good and evil, you even think that setting fire to this pile of straw might also be a sin. It is all these ideas about good and bad, right and wrong, that stop you from striking the match. Your impediments can all go in a bonfire that is lit by a single match. That fire is freedom. Burn everything with this fire of freedom.

Very few people come to this path, and very few people are able to strike that match that will burn everything.

18

Self is closer to you than your own breath

Question: I still feel I need to make some effort, and the effort I feel I need to make is to let go. I am also thinking about self-enquiry. When one asks the question, 'Who is it that thinks this thought?' or, 'Who is feeling this feeling?' is this not effort? Can you call this effort?

Papaji: Freedom is eternal. Liberation, enlightenment, is eternal, natural, and here and now. This is freedom. Your own real nature is eternal, ever attained, and the only effort you need to make to discover this is to remain without a thought. Whatever thought arises, that thought will take you somewhere else. You cannot win freedom through thought. Thought will take you somewhere else, to some object which is not the Self. You can call this 'effort' if you want to. You just need to check the tendency of the mind to run to objects and cling to them. Just imagine what will happen if this doesn't occur. What will happen then? Give me an answer.

Question: Nothing will happen. There will just be a silence.

Papaji: Yes, there will be silence. Nothing more. If nothing is happening, what is it called? Is it not freedom? If nothing is happening, is this not called freedom? Is this not your nature? Is this not the light you are looking for? Is this not wisdom? Thought is troubling you because it is running towards objects, towards the enjoyment of sense objects. If you can check and halt this tendency, this is called freedom. If you cannot check it, there will be manifestation and suffering. If you cannot check this cycle of thought, you will be caught in the never-ending cycle of births and deaths. You can choose whichever way you want to go. Don't be afraid of it because this is your nature. Sooner or later you have to return to it.

What did you ever get from clinging to objects? From the beginning of creation until today, what did any person ever get from it? What did any person born on this planet or any other planet get from running away from Self-nature? Has anything worthwhile been accomplished by this? If you want happiness, if you want peace, if you want to abide in the eternal nature of your own Self, in freedom, in wisdom, there is only one way: you have to check the thought process.

Once you have known this trick, you can allow thought to wander wherever it wants to go. Establish yourself in the Self, and then it won't matter where your thoughts go. When you have that wisdom, that knowledge, you and your thoughts can wander freely wherever they want to go. But there will be a great difference from before: there will be no fear. When you take the coiled rope to be a serpent, there is fear, but when that superimposition is absent, fear is also absent. Differences will go in that state. Fear will go.

What kind of effort is needed to return to your own nature? If you want to go somewhere else, obtain something else, achieve something else, meet someone else, then you have to make some effort, but to remain as you are, what effort is required? You only have to make an effort if you are setting out to acquire something that you don't already have. If there is some object that you don't possess, and you want to own it, then you have to make some effort. If you don't own a car and you want to own a car, then you have to make some effort to possess one. You have to go to work to earn money, or you have to arrange a loan. When you have the money in your pocket, you have to go to the showroom to collect the vehicle. All this is effort, and effort like this is necessary whenever you want to obtain an object, something that is separate from you. But what effort is necessary when the thing you want to know is what you are already? To be as you already are, what effort is required?

No time is needed. No effort is needed. This is a problem for most people, though. Instant availability, without any effort, presents a problem for many people because everyone is accustomed to making efforts to attain or acquire the things that they want or need. There are things that are so near to you, so natural to you, you never think that you need to make an effort to acquire them. Take breathing, for example. No one thinks or makes plans to breathe. No one works hard and saves up to acquire a breath at some later date. Breathing is there all the time, naturally and effortlessly. You don't have to make any effort to breathe in and out; it just happens naturally. When you were young, no one had to teach you how to do it. Every child knows how to inhale air and exhale it again afterwards. No lessons were required. But then the child grows up and someone says, 'I will teach you *pranayama*. Come and join our ashram and we will teach you how to breathe properly.' Suddenly, breathing, something you have done effortlessly all your life, becomes a complex subject, something you have to train yourself to do.

Making effort to reach the Self is just like this. Self has been there all your life, naturally and effortlessly, but you were too busy looking at other things to notice it. So, when someone comes along with a method and a plan to reach it and attain it, you think that this is the way to proceed.

Self is closer to you than your own breath. It is that through which the breath moves. It is inside the breath. Breathing may require a little effort to execute. Muscles in the chest have to expand and contract, even if you are not aware of them for most of the time. But even this minimal effort is not required to be aware of the Self. It is there all the time, effortlessly. You miss it only because your mind is always pointing in a different direction. You are looking outwards instead of inwards.

The face of the mind is always looking outwards, going

towards so-called enjoyments. But are they really enjoyments? Wherever the mind goes, it will just get a painful kick. All the things that you call enjoyments just result in your mind getting a kick. So, what do you do? You drop that thing and pick up something else, which also gives you a kick. This goes on until the end of your life. No one has ever got any real and permanent satisfaction from enjoyment of these external objects.

You pick up some object that doesn't give you this satisfaction. You drop it, thinking, 'Not this one. I will pick up another.' This process goes on indefinitely – picking up and dropping, picking up and dropping. This is what constitutes life here on earth.

This goes on because no one knows the source of happiness; no one tries to find it; no one even speaks about it. Instead, everyone runs after external enjoyments and just ends up with endless suffering.

From where does this concept of happiness arise? Nobody directs his mind back to that place in his search for happiness. Direct the mind towards that place from where the happiness arises. If you do this, you will be very happy. The mind will be free. Instead of chasing after ephemeral things, it will be glued to it, clinging to that happiness. It will never return from there, and it will never want to. But no one tries to do this.

Talks like this have been going on for thousands of years; talks about the fountainhead of happiness and how one can discover it. It's in all the ancient scriptures, and it has been continuing ever since. Here and there some results have been achieved, but not many because most people simply don't believe it when they are told the truth about happiness. They disbelieve because they are convinced that they have to make a big effort to attain happiness, and when they make that big effort it always takes them to something outside themselves, to something which is not the happiness of their own Self.

They don't stay as they are. They disturb the stillness with an idea and then use effort to chase it all over the place. It all starts with a disturbance in the mind. Something disturbs the stillness at the base of the mind and trouble follows.

Very few people have known the secret of happiness by finding its source and origin and abiding there. And when they speak about it, no one believes them. *Samsara* continues because no one believes the simple truth of happiness, the beauty of being without thought. It is an absolutely effortless process, and it happens instantaneously. This place is available to everyone, here and now, in this present instant. 'Now' really does mean 'now'. Not before and not later. Anyone can dive into this lake and find it.

Question: Papaji, you say that it is freedom to have no thoughts arising. When thoughts or desires arise and one just sees them as movements of the mind, is that also freedom?

Papaji: These are contradictory statements. When the thought of freedom is there, this is also a thought. Mind is fully engaged with this thought. How can another thought be there at the same time? Two people cannot occupy a chair at the same time. They have to take it in turns. When one person is sitting in a chair, where is the other person going to sit? Thought and freedom from thought cannot be there at the same time.

It is enough for the mind to be fully engaged with the thought 'I want freedom'. If this is so, there will be no room for any other thought. Two thoughts cannot stay together at the same time. You cannot think of Boston and Lucknow at the same time. Try it for yourself and see. You can switch your attention very rapidly from the thought of Boston to the thought of Lucknow, but you cannot think of them both at the same time. When you think of Boston, your attention is in Boston, even though you might be physically present in Lucknow. It is the same in meditation. Your mind is wherever your thought is. If your mind is preoccupied with something, you are in that place. If you can be in no-thought, instantly you are in the place of freedom, but if you are in a train of thought, you are somewhere else, preoccupied with something else.

Mind and thought are quicker than the speed of light. It takes several minutes for the light from the sun to reach the earth, but when you think about the sun, you are there, instantly. A few years ago you might have spent some time with someone you loved. A thought about it comes into your mind and instantly you are back there with that person. You race into the past, going from the present to ten years ago in a single moment. You can make use of this property of the mind to find freedom. It does not take years of travelling and searching to find the source of the mind. Have a very strong determination to be there, look for that place where thought arises, and instantly you are there.

You can make use of this very strong determination to win freedom. With this you can reach the source. This strong determination may only come to you once, but once can be enough. If it can come once in a good human birth, it will be enough. After millions of births you get a good human birth, and in that life you get this rare determination to find freedom. It is a very rare conjunction of events.

For thirty-five million years you have moved from life to life, from species to species, until you finally arrived at a human birth. For freedom you need a rare conjunction of events: a good birth in a good family in a good country, and a desire for freedom. This desire for freedom will take you to *satsang*, either with your own Self or with someone who has known the Self and who can show it to you. *Satsang* is the place where freedom is transacted. It is not just a place where people chatter about the truth. It is the place where the business of freedom is transacted between the Master and the student.

This is a rare conjunction of events that needs a lot of merit and a lot of luck. So many things have to happen for this to take place. All those lifetimes bring you to this point. Then, when freedom is attained, you may see all these lives, all these births that have brought you to this moment. I saw this happen to me. When I sat on the banks of the Ganga, I saw all the species I had taken birth in.

Question: What animals were you?

Papaji: All of them: worms, germs, everything. As they passed before me one by one I recognised, 'First I was this thing, then I was that thing'. I was sitting on the banks of the Ganga while all this was going on. It was not a dream because I was in the waking state. All my past lives passed before me. I saw all my lives, and at the end of the sequence I saw the picture of my own Master, and then the sequence of lives ended.

There were lives on other planets as well. I saw what kind of people lived there. People wonder if there is life out there on other planets, but I don't. I know because I have seen it and experienced it first-hand.

Question: Are there any planets where everybody is free, and know they are free?

Papaji: No. Freedom is only available in this land, on this planet. Everyone has to come here if he wants freedom, including the gods. Even the gods have to come here. This land is the one where freedom happens. All the other places are for enjoyment or suffering. Everyone ultimately has to come here.

The mystery of all these lives takes place in a fraction of a second. It's like a dream in which a long complicated story can happen in a fraction of a second.

There is an old story that illustrates this. A king had just returned victorious from a major battle. A neighbouring country had attacked his territory and he, along with his generals and his army, had repulsed the attack. The king was sitting in his court, chatting with his generals. He was very exhausted and tired. When his Master came in, the king immediately offered him his seat. He dismissed all the members of his court, saying, 'My Guru has come. I want to speak to him. Please go.'

As the members of the court were leaving, the king fell asleep for a few seconds because he was so tired. By the time they had all left he was fully awake again. Sometimes a short nap, even of a few seconds, can have a very refreshing effect.

He addressed his Guru, saying, 'I have a question. We have just returned from a military expedition. As you walked into the room, we were talking about what had happened. There was a big battle and I felt completely exhausted from it. As everyone was leaving I had a brief nap. Just a few seconds. But in that dream I was a beggar. I lived the life of a beggar for many years, begging for my food on the outskirts of a village and living in a nearby forest.

'One day I walked into the village and out the other side. One of the other beggars asked, "Where are you going?" and I replied, "Today the king has had a son. He has promised that he will feed everyone who comes to his palace. We don't have to beg today. We can go and feast at the palace. I even hear that he is going to give away free clothes to everyone."

'I went to the king's palace and everyone received gold coins, sweets and silk clothes. Everyone was very happy because the king had been so generous.

'I thought to myself, "I am very dirty right now. I will go to the well and have a bath before I put on these new clothes and eat the king's food." I went to the well and started drawing a bucket of water. As I was pulling a dog came by and took away the packet of food that I had left on the ground. I chased it, and as I was running, I tripped over a rock and fell. When I hit the ground I woke up, and here I am sitting with you in this palace.

'I suffered so much as that beggar. I was so hungry, I was willing to chase a dog and fight him over a packet of food. I spent many years in that village. It seems to me that I was seventy years old when I tried to chase that dog and finally woke up. My question is: "Which is real?" While I was a beggar, it was all very real. My suffering was real and my begging was real. Chasing a dog was my reality. Begging food from the king was my reality. I had a community of beggars and that was my reality as well. Now I am the king and it is my turn to feed the beggars. Sitting on this same seat, which is where I had my dream, I had seventy years as a beggar. Now I sit here as a king. Which is a dream and which is real?'

His Guru told him, 'Both are real. While you were a beggar, you were a beggar. You were no longer a king. You had no kingdom. Then you came to this state and rejected that state.

Now you think, "I have returned to reality by leaving that dream". But this state that you are in now, which also looks very real, is also a dream. While it persists it will be real for you, but one day you will wake up from this dream as well.'

The king had had a brief nap, suffered for seventy years as a beggar, and then woken up. That life all took place in an instant of time. When you wake up to the Self, you will know that all your lives, all the thirty-five million years that you spent passing from birth to birth and suffering endlessly in each incarnation, were just a dream that took place in an instant of time. You will wake up and know, 'That was all a dream. All those lives were just a dream.'

The wise man knows this, but the ignorant mind does not. But if ignorance is removed, wisdom will be there. Wisdom removes all this ignorance. The state of begging will go and it will be as if it had never existed. This is the ultimate destiny of everyone. Everyone is going to wake up sooner or later. This is your birthright as a human being. You have been given this body so that you can make the decision to wake up and be free. However, you are not making up your mind. You are not making this choice. You are still chasing the dog in your dream, thinking you are a hungry beggar. You are not seeing your own kingdom and you are not seated on the throne.

This body is a temple, and God is seated inside you. But you are not going to see him because you are always going outside. Because you are not aware of God inside, you run after other, outside things. This human body, this temple that has been given to you, is a very rare birth. If you reject it and the opportunities it gives you, it will be a tremendous loss. You don't know when these circumstances will come to you again. Nobody knows. You don't know if this desire for liberation will ever come to you again.

Don't prolong your journey, thinking that it will all culminate in some future life. You have no guarantee that you will ever get these favourable circumstances again. Here you are, in a human body, in *satsang*, with a desire for freedom. Make the best use of this desire for freedom. Cut short your journey. It doesn't take time. I'm not prolonging it, you are. I am not telling you that you have to go on a long journey, that you have to do long meditations. I don't say that you have to join ashrams in the Himalayas. I am not sending you anywhere, and I am not asking you to change your routine of life. I am not telling you to change into robes and cut your hair. Live well and continue to do your work. Show to the world that it is not necessary to run away in order to find freedom.

I don't encourage people to run away from home, to abandon their situations, whatever they may be. A businessman can be a better businessman; a soldier can be a better soldier. I don't believe in escapism. When people leave their life situation, usually no good results. They get spoiled. People who run away because they don't enjoy their old life will not enjoy their new life either. Stay with what you are doing because what I am talking about doesn't take much time, and it doesn't need a change of location. Monasteries are not needed for freedom. Freedom doesn't demand anything. There are no physical preconditions that you have to meet in order to be ready for it. It is available anytime, anywhere. You just have to pine for it.

Make a decision: 'I want this'. That's all. If you really do want this, and if your desire for it is not contaminated or diluted by any other desire, you will succeed. Whoever makes this strong decision and sticks to it will get there, but this strong decision is needed.

19

Mind is looking for awareness, but the aware mind does not look for anything

Question: In the preface to *I am That* it is said that Nisargadatta Maharaj received instructions from his Guru, who died shortly afterwards. It took him a further three years, he says, before he could really abide in the teachings.

Papaji: It may take time for the teachings to mature. Maturity must be there. Understanding can come instantaneously for some people, but with others there is a kind of haggling that comes from not fully agreeing to the truth the first time it is heard. Old habits of the mind might reassert themselves for a while. It may take time for the final settlement, the final agreement, to be enacted. It may even take a few lifetimes. Even after receiving the knowledge, it may still take a few more births. Some old attachments may be left for a while. However, in some cases it may not take time at all. It all depends on how the teaching is received, and, what's more, it has to be practised for the whole of one's life afterwards. That full abidance can take a long time. Then only can you abide in That. Otherwise, old habits will pull you back again and again.

In most cases people do not attain the perfect state. They obtain information about it by listening, but this kind of information is indirect knowledge. Then you have to abide by it, abide in it by reflecting on it again and again. How successful you are depends on you.

Question: You are telling us all to be without thought, not to stir a thought. I am reminded of the wonderful lines of Seng-Tsan, the third Zen patriarch who wrote: 'Stop talking and thinking and there is nothing you will not be able to know.'

Papaji: Yes, stop talking and stop thinking. That's the way to true knowledge.

Question: I have been reading about various Tibetan practices, and I have come across many descriptions of *deva* and god realms. There are practices whereby one can go to these realms and experience them for oneself. There are many levels of gods and spirits in this Tibetan hierarchy. I spoke to you once about all these different worlds and you said that they really did exist and that one could visit them. But at the same time you said that they were all a projection of the mind, and as such were nothing to do with freedom.

Papaji: If you think, the whole process of manifestation is there. Mind can construct anything, even all these realms of gods and spirits. Many seemingly impossible things can be constructed by the mind.

Question: I was in Bodh Gaya once, listening to a teacher say, 'Empty the mind. You must empty the mind.' He said this again and again. There was a very crazy monk there who kept saying that he had an empty mind. I asked this teacher if it was really true because this man was acting in a very bizarre and irrational way.

The teacher told me, 'This man was born with an empty mind, which means that he is naturally stupid. When you have something in your mind, and when you have the discrimination to throw it away and leave an empty mind, then this is wisdom, enlightenment. This is the difference. You must have the discriminating wisdom to discard what you see is there.'

Papaji: When the mind is naturally empty, how can it still be called 'mind'? Mind is mind only when thought is there. No thought is something else. In no thought there is not even the idea of an empty mind. While thought is still there, 'empty mind' is just another thought, another concept.

If I tell you to meditate but not think of a cat while you are meditating, what will happen? You will naturally sit there thinking of a cat because I have put this suggestion in your mind. If I say 'Empty the mind of all thought', you will have this idea of an empty mind inside you while you meditate. That too will become one of your thoughts, one of your concepts. It is better not to talk about states of mind, particularly ones that you think you have to reach, because ideas about these states will end up as extra thoughts in your mind.

It is better not to talk about the mind at all. Don't touch it or have thoughts about it because, if you do, they will just bite you. When you need to make use of it, then use it, but don't carry it around with you unnecessarily. Don't keep it in your pocket when you don't have to. When you are not using it, leave it alone.

Question: *[new questioner]* This morning I had a very strong sense that nothing has awareness. I realised that something in me was clinging to this idea that 'I' have awareness, or that 'I' had awareness at some point in the past. But as I looked at this idea, I realised that it wasn't true. My arm doesn't have awareness, my leg doesn't have awareness, my nerves, my muscles don't have awareness. Not even my brain or its thoughts have awareness. I came to the conclusion that nothing can 'have' awareness. Awareness just is.

Papaji: Mind is looking for awareness, but the aware mind does not look for anything. This teaching is still undescribed. That's what I think, anyway. It's untouched, unspoken, virgin, no one has arrived there, and no one has made a teaching of it. No one has even touched this teaching so far. This is my conclusion. Anyone can pick up a pebble here and there, go to the summit of a mountain and cry, 'I have found the diamond!' The true teaching is still undescribed, unexplained.

Question: Do you mean that the words that people use to describe the diamond are really only words that describe the pebble?

Papaji: What do you mean?

Question: That he who finds the diamond doesn't have the vocabulary to describe it properly. There are only words to describe the pebbles.

Papaji: Yes. When you talk, your talk can only be about the pebbles. The diamond needs no description. In fact, it cannot be described. It simply shines by its own light. It has its own lustre, its own luminosity. It is in no need of anyone's description. This is the diamond. Direct awareness of it with no mediating agent – no teacher, no *sutra*, no mind, no practice – is direct and true knowledge. For freedom you need this unmediated and indescribable awareness of what is true and real. All the other things – the teachings, the practices, and so on – are just maps that give indirect information about it. The map is not the reality; it is just a description or a picture on a piece of paper. You can have a lot of maps, a lot of information that gives you directions, and still have zero knowledge of what they all pertain to.

This knowledge is not far from you, so you don't really need a map to find it. Whatever you speak about, that object, that thing, is something that is separate from you. Even the word 'Self' is just an idea that you talk about. It is not the real thing. You only speak of things that are some distance from you. When it is too close to you, you can't see it and speak about it. What I am pointing to is nearer than your own breath, it is behind the retina through which you see. It is prior to the beginning of all thought. See it if you can. You have a desire for freedom, but what I am speaking of is prior to that desire. What teaching can reach there? A teaching about freedom will only be there after the desire for freedom has arisen.

Question: I want to ask about the maturing process that you talked about recently, and the fall that some people seem to experience after they have had a good experience. When I went back to England, I found many problems arising when I took the position, 'I am free; these problems can't touch me'.

That stance didn't seem to do me much good or solve any of the problems. In the end I felt I had to re-engage with the world, immerse myself with all these stories, work them through in the traditional way with the feeling, 'I must solve this problem'. Trying to create a safe space around myself by thinking, 'None of this can touch me', didn't seem to work. I decided that I was manifesting a state of 'unfreedom' by hiding from the everyday problems of the world. It seems to me that I had to fall from my state of detachment to get things done. In the end I came to the conclusion that when problems came up, I had to attend to them in the usual way. I decided that real freedom is not to deny them.

Papaji: When the time comes, you have to act. If you are on the battlefield, it is your job to lift up your gun and shoot. Lifting up garlands of roses will not do. If it is your dharma to fight, you must fight, and not run away or hide. But whatever your dharma is, you must not forget the root, the source. Whether you are meditating, praying or fighting, the source is the same. You must be aware of that source at all times and take dictation from it. It will make you do what you have to do, but if you are aware of this source that prompts the actions, there will never be a problem for you. Always be aware that there is dictation going on. A dictator is dictating to you. If you don't interfere and allow all these dictated actions to take place, you will never regret anything. You will know that you are simply doing what this higher power is making you do. What is going to happen is going to happen. You can't change it by deciding on either action or inaction. These choices are not available to you.

Question: *[new questioner]* A little while ago you mentioned that freedom is prior to the desire for freedom.

Papaji: Yes.

Question: Something struck me when you said this. The thought came up, 'How can there be separation between the desire for freedom and freedom itself?'

Papaji: Yes, I said that freedom itself is prior to the desire for freedom. If the desire for freedom arises, it means that you are no longer knowingly in freedom, that you have somehow left that pre-existing state and want to return to it. If that desire for freedom arises, then spend your whole life finding out where that desire has come from, where it originated. If you finally arrive at that place, that freedom, you will immediately understand that this freedom is something that you already knew; it is something that you always had. You will understand that this desire for freedom was a state in which you ignored or were not aware of what was already there.

When freedom is discovered, it is the natural, spontaneous return to your own Self-nature. When you arrive, you will immediately know and understand, 'I already knew this. This was here all the time, but I didn't pay attention to it.'

I recently told you the story of what happened to me when I was a child, when I was offered that mango lassi and couldn't drink it because I was plunged into a paralysing state of beauty and happiness. This happened to me long before I had any knowledge about freedom or any desire for it. When I returned to normal consciousness, there was this compelling urge to go back to that state, to experience it and to understand it. I didn't call it a desire for freedom in those days because I didn't have that concept. There was just an overwhelming urge to go back to that state.

'What is this happiness? What is this thing that is so beautiful, so loving, I have not seen anything equivalent to it in the world so far?'

This search obsessed me, compelled me to plunge myself into this beauty again and again. Though I regained the experience, I never 'understood' it. I could never explain it, and I could never talk about it. This is why I say sometimes that it is 'untouched', 'undescribed'. This urge to have it explained and talked about is still there, though, which is why I love to hear people trying to describe it.

I say to people, 'Come on! Describe it to me! Give me some hint. I want to listen as you try to express yourself. Come near and let me enjoy your description.'

No one has ever described it, but I still love listening to people try.

Question: Sometimes we have an experience and we don't even know until you tell us about it. Did this happen with you? Did somebody, Ramana Maharshi, confirm this experience for you? Did you also need to be told?

Papaji: It was not verbal, but the confirmation was there. In his presence I was absorbed in this same happiness and beauty that came to me spontaneously when I was a child. I recognised it to be the same state, and I recognised it to be my own Self. It was not a new thing that happened. It was a confirmation, a recognition of a truth I already somehow knew. But still, it has never been described; it has never been defined.

Different people talk about it in different ways. The Buddha called it emptiness, the void. That's not a true description either. It is really just another way of saying that it cannot be described. Ramana called it 'Arunachala', 'the unmoving mountain of light'. That's what Arunachala means. '*Achala*' means both 'stillness' and 'mountain', and '*aruna*' means 'light'. This is the wisdom that never moves. That is his description, his explanation, but this is still just a finger pointing at something that cannot be truly explained or described. I say 'happiness' and 'beauty' when I have to think of a word, but these are also just words that merely hint at something that is utterly indefinable.

20

The Guru is none other than your own Self

Question: What is the role of the Guru?

Papaji: A person approaches the Guru and says, 'I am suffering. I am tired of coming again and again into the womb of different species. I am burning. Please help me. Save me from this fire.'

The Guru is the one who can free you from this suffering. That is his role. The word Guru literally means 'dispeller of darkness'. He who dispels the darkness from the minds of the people who come to him, saying that they are bound, is the Guru. He who removes their sufferings and their doubts and helps them have the firm conviction that they are free is the Guru. This is his role.

Question: *[new questioner]* The role of the Guru doesn't really happen on an outer level, does it? The outer Guru is just there to remind us of what is inside us. Is this not so?

Papaji: The Guru speaks of the Self, and he speaks to the Self, not to the clothes you are wearing. He doesn't speak to the body, the senses or the mind. The Guru's role is to speak to the inner Self that is already free. People do not know this Self.

Question: I have the feeling that we dream the Guru who is outside us.

Papaji: Yes, the outer Guru, in your dream, tells you that he is within you. What else will he say? If you see him outside you, that means that you have projected his form in the dream that you are dreaming. That dream form of the Guru will then tell you that, in reality, he is within you as your own Self.

Question: Amazing!

Papaji: The Guru is none other than your own Self; your very own Self. Your own Self is your own Guru, and the real Guru always takes you back to your own Self, not to somewhere else. He withdraws the outgoing tendencies of the mind and puts them back within you.

Don't project outside to things that are external. Bring all these tendencies, wherever they go, back to the source, the Self. When they have all been brought back there, you will know your own Self. It is the outgoing tendencies that are keeping you occupied, so occupied you have no time to look at your own Self. When this mind is not going outwards, when it is not preoccupied with an object, a thought or a desire, the outgoing tendencies will withdraw and you will shine as your own Self. What else can shine in that state? You are always, always That.

Question: *[new questioner]* All questions here seem to have the same answer.

Papaji: When you are lost in the forest you have to ask many questions. In such circumstances you need a guide and a map.

Night is falling. How do you get out of the forest? How do you return home? If you are already in your home, you don't need a map or a guide. You have no problems in this situation.

Now though, you are out in the forest, wondering what to do. In a real forest your first priority is to find out where you are, because without that knowledge you cannot move in the right direction. In the forest of the mind, which is where all seekers are lost, the most important question is 'who' not 'where'. Who are you? And, earlier on, where did I come from? These are the problems you have to solve if you want to leave this particular forest. If you can't solve this problem by yourself, then seek someone who can help you to solve it.

Try to find your own Self by spending some time on this question. You have never asked this question before. You have spent your life asking 'What is this?' and 'What is that?' but you have never asked yourself the question 'Who am I?' In an entire lifespan no one spends even five minutes on this most important of questions. Five minutes is enough, quite enough. You can ask this question anytime, anywhere. There are no auspicious circumstances for this question: no holy spot is needed, no holy river, no particular place, no special environment. Just ask it wherever you are.

No one is serious about this. This is a question one has to solve now itself. It is not something that you postpone for later.

Everyone is trying, indirectly, to solve this problem by looking for happiness, love or beauty. The hunger for happiness is actually a hunger for the happiness of one's own Self, but people don't know or understand this, so they look for it in the wrong place.

'No, this is not what I want. I will try something else.' This goes on throughout life. One thing after another is picked up and rejected because no one knows the true place where real happiness can be found.

'Where should I search? Where can I find it?' The correct place to find happiness is not known, and so everyone continues to search in all the wrong places. It is akin to looking for one's glasses while one is actually wearing them. We forget or don't know that the Self which is being sought is the same Self that is doing the looking. The same power, the same consciousness, the same awareness that is enabling us to conduct these futile external searches is actually the target of our search.

No one questions 'What is this consciousness through which I am searching for consciousness?'

You need this consciousness for everything. You need this awareness for everything. What is this awareness that you need? No one takes notice of this or tries to find out what it is and where it comes from.

21

Dwelling on the enjoyment creates the desire to enjoy it again and again

Papaji: When objects are there, consciousness gets occupied. It disintegrates into separateness. It gets caught up in the perceived objects and loses awareness of the source of consciousness. In that fragmented state it is not aware of itself as consciousness, and it is not aware that it is being obstructed by associating with an object.

You cannot see an object without being conscious. It is through consciousness alone that objects are seen. You are conscious of seeing an object, but as the process of seeing goes on, you become attracted to the object, and then attached to it. These objects are then known as enjoyments of the senses because it is through the senses that these objects are registered in consciousness. The mind gets attached to enjoyment of the object and forgets its own source, which is consciousness or emptiness. When the object is removed, the mind returns back to space. When there are no objects, the inherent nature remains, as it is. The obstruction to this natural, inherent state is our attachment to objects. When this happens, this same unitary consciousness gets cut up, divided, limited. In this disintegrated state we feel that we are not aware. Consciousness is no longer being experienced as a unitary whole.

This process that continues indefinitely is called 'manifestation'. However, once you know that these objects are within consciousness, that they are not separate from it, you are not troubled by them. Consciousness is not affected by having objects appear in it. It is all the same to consciousness whether it is holding objects or not holding objects. If you identify with consciousness instead of the objects, there will be no trouble. You must learn this trick.

You can play with the objects and not hold them if you know that they are just appearances in consciousness, but this is not what happens in most cases. Most of the time there is the desire to enjoy, which is followed by the enjoyment itself, and that in turn is followed by the remembrance of it. This is where the trouble arises, not in the enjoyment itself, but in the remembrance of it afterwards. Contact with the enjoyment is over, but remembrance is still there. That residual remembrance sets up a desire for enjoyment of the same object again. And so it goes on indefinitely.

Dwelling on the enjoyment creates the desire to enjoy it again and again. This is what troubles you; this is what causes you suffering. When there is an absence of enjoyment, there is suffering because you still have the unfulfilled desire to go back to that enjoyment again. Let the objects come; enjoy them and then drop them. Once you have enjoyed them, drop them from your mind. They are no longer needed.

When you go to a restaurant, you eat, and then you walk out of the restaurant. You have satisfied your hunger, your need for food, so why do you need to think about the food and the enjoyment of it afterwards? Mentally revisiting the enjoyments sets up a desire for more of the same. Remembrance is troubling because it leaves footprints in the mind. When you dwell on enjoyments, the dwelling leaves footprints in the memory. This should not happen. It just creates desires and suffering in the mind.

Where have all these objects that you desire come from? They are within consciousness, and they are your own projection. In the ocean the waves and the eddies are just features of the ocean. They may have different names, different forms, but they are still ocean. The ocean has no dispute with any of these features, no desire to own or consume them. Let them appear; let them stay or disappear. What difference will it make to the ocean?

Once you know that all objects are within your own consciousness, that they are all you yourself, that they are all your own projection, there will be no trouble. With that attitude, with that perspective you can go ahead and enjoy. But don't think about the enjoyments afterwards. That will only leave footprints in the memory.

Once you have footprints in the memory, your activities will be motivated by desire and fear. These footprints will choose your activities on the basis of past experiences. Your thoughts about the past, your experiences of the past, will make you choose your future actions.

About twenty years ago I was speaking about fear in Barcelona. There was a professor there who came from San Sebastian. I made the statement, 'Fear always belongs to the past,' and he disagreed with me.

'No,' he said, 'it can also be in the present. It can even be of the future. Suppose, when this class is over, I drive home and see a policeman. Seeing this policeman in the present might cause me fear if I have done something wrong. This fear arises in the present moment, in the moment I first see the policeman. I know what the policeman might do to me, and that creates in me a fear of future events. That puts fear into the future realm as well.'

I disagreed with him. 'Fear arises in you at that moment because you have a past experience, a past knowledge of what a policeman can do to you. You know from your past experience that a policeman might decide to pull you over for some minor fault, for speeding, for not stopping at a light, and so on. So your fear comes from a past thought, a past memory.

'In the sleep state you are in the present with no thought of the past. There, in that state, there is no fear. As you enter this sleep state, all your memories of the past, all your accumulated fears, disappear. You cannot carry this fear with you into the sleep state because fear is thoughts about the past, and such thoughts have to be dropped before you can enter the state of sleep. In the present moment there is no fear. There is only fear when you take your mind into past thoughts, past experiences, and then use them to evaluate the merits of future courses of action.'

He understood the point I was trying to make. When you stay in the present moment, when you avoid the thoughts of the past, fear is not there.

In 1968 I was living in Rishikesh near a foreign couple. They were part of the first batch of hippies who were slowly invading the town. They had a child who could crawl but not walk. I was living near them. I was cooking on my veranda, and they used to come and eat with me. This child also used to crawl over to see what I was doing, and when she came I would give her some food. Once this child got hold of a scorpion in her hand.

I said, 'This is a scorpion. It can give a very poisonous and painful sting. I will take it away.'

The mother surprised me by saying, 'No, let it sting her. Only if it stings her will she know next time that this kind of animal stings and that she should leave it alone in future. This is how we learn.'

It was an interesting theory of child development, but I don't think the mother really knew how bad a scorpion sting could be, especially in a very small child. I took a pair of tongs and gently prised it out of the girl's hands.

This child was living in the present. She had no scorpion footprints in her memory that would make her afraid of scorpions. All fears come from the past, from associations with previous experiences, or from things we have heard or read. Without these associations, without these memories of the past, there can be no fear.

Question: How do we prevent the footprints from forming in the first place? Or how do we stop them from influencing us so much?

Papaji: The birds who fly in the air – do they leave any footprints?

Question: No.

Papaji: Fish live in water. Do they leave any footprints as they swim around? When you do something, just do it and move on. Don't remember what happened, don't remember what you have done, and don't think about what you have to do next. Have no thoughts about what might happen tomorrow. Forget about it completely.

A few days ago I told the story of the prostitute who was carried across a flooded river by a teacher, and how his disciple reacted to these events. The teacher dropped the story from his mind as soon as he put the woman down, but the disciple carried it in his head for miles afterwards. It is not the actions that leave footprints, or even the enjoyment of them. It is the thoughts about the actions – your reactions to them, positive or negative.

The master did the work and instantly forgot about the action. He was not touched by his action and not affected by it. He just did what needed to be done. A person needed to be helped; he helped her, and that was the end of the story for him. But the student carried the thoughts and the judgements about the incident in his head and left footprints there. These footprints make memories, they make judgements, they make desires for the future, and in the end they will make you reincarnate. This is the continuity of *samsara*, the never-ending cycle of birth and death. These footprints will keep you on the cycle of birth and death for millions of years.

All this is not inevitable. It is within your power to be free of this manifestation right now. Or you can just postpone it. If there is no footprint, how can you reincarnate? On what account? For what purpose? If you leave no footprints, no impressions, you are carrying nothing. When you have no baggage, what will happen to you? The baggage is the merit and the sin you have accumulated from actions and your thoughts about them. I will tell you what will happen. Nothing will happen. This will be the end of *samsara*. This is what I mean when I say, 'Carry nothing'.

Do good, be compassionate, if the circumstances arise in

which you can help people. But then forget about what you have done. Don't remember in the afternoon all the good things you did in the morning. Keep your memory and your mental reminiscing clean and empty. Shut your eyes to the past and help when you are in the right place to do it, but don't remember it afterwards. Don't accumulate footprints.

22

Don't stir a single thought

Question: This morning I woke up very early, about 3.30. I was thinking about my husband. Today is the third anniversary of our marriage. I showed you his photo once and asked if I should invite him to come to India. You said it might be easier for me if he did. I was thinking this morning that maybe I should call him and tell him to come. I went outside because it was cooler and saw a shooting star very close to the horizon. I have been thinking about this story quite a lot recently.

Papaji: Wherever you go you always carry something which is very dear to you. I told you once about a place where you can't carry anything with you.

Question: Yes, there is no need to in that place.

Papaji: *[laughing]* Yes, no need. You can't carry anyone there, and that includes someone who is closest and dearest to you. This place itself is the closest and nearest and dearest, the most eternal thing there is, but no one knows about it. No one ever knows about this relation. No religious book mentions it; no wise man talks about it. It is up to you to find it because no one speaks about it. They will only speak about what is already known. All relationships that are known to you can be spoken about, but what I am talking about is the relation on which all other relationships are based. This relation on which all relationships are based is still not discovered, even though it is the ground, the base, the foundation for all other relationships. This is a great mystery, and only a rare one, a fortunate one, will find it. Some rare gem of a person, some Kohinoor may find it, but it's not for everyone. Most people can't even think about it.

All centres, ashrams, communes, monasteries are full of sheep. There is only bleating there. There are no wise words. No one even talks about this thing we are talking about. Abandon all dharmas and return to your Self.

Question: There is an awareness in me of who I think I am. Most of the time my attention is centred there. Sometimes, though, this awareness seems to move away from this person, to something else that is just awareness. I feel a sense of loss when this happens. I feel like I am leaving someone I have known all my life. It's not a happy feeling. It's quite sad at times. Sometimes it even feels like I am dying.

Papaji: First of all, the centre of awareness is not moving anywhere. The centre of awareness never moves. The centre that you are talking about is the centre that is accepted by society as the real centre. It is the ego centre, the 'I', the centre from which proceeds the concept of ego, the idea that you are the body, and so on. When you proceed from this false centre to the true centre, awareness, everything falls away. Everything cracks and disintegrates. That is why you experience fear.

The castle of 'I' is built on the beach, out of sand. It has no firm rock foundation. It can collapse at any time or get washed away by the incoming tide. This is the ego-built castle, a temporary and unsound edifice on the beach. No one knows the true centre of awareness because who is there to know it? The 'who', the person, is just part of the sandcastle on the beach. There is no recording, no record of what true awareness is like because there is no one there to do the recording. Everything dissolves there, including fear. There is no possibility of having fear in that place. Fear is the experience of the ego 'I' reacting to its imminent dissolution. It is not the experience of true awareness. In awareness body concepts go, the senses go, the mind goes, the intellect goes, the ego goes. Everything collapses and you are free once and for all.

Question: I think my problem is that I am stuck somewhere between the two. I feel like I am in a space where I am abandoning the personal 'I', which is reacting with these feelings of fear, but I am not settled in the awareness where the 'I' and the fear would go completely. The feeling of some kind of presence is intense. A tide is coming in to wash away something that was there before, but it is not strong enough to complete the job. The true presence is not sensed clearly enough to give me the security of....

Papaji: You are talking about insecurity, the feeling of finding that you are not at home. You feel a need for security because you feel that you haven't reached home yet. You are always at home. You are not somewhere else, a place that you have to come home from. Now itself you are in the centre of true awareness. Now itself you are free of all subjects. You don't have to go anywhere; you don't have to return from anywhere; you don't have to become anything. You are already That. Start from where you are and stay where you are. Don't move from this place. Don't stir a single thought. Let no thought stir, or just look at this source. Just keep awake; keep alert; keep attentive; keep conscious.

23

No teaching has so far touched the truth

Question: I have been thinking about what you said a few days ago, when you were speaking about the practice of self-enquiry. How you have to find out where you are now, then ascertain your destination, and finally decide which route and which mode of transport to use to get there. When I look at myself, there doesn't seem to be any distance involved, and that means I don't know about the mode of travel. It's hard to work out a travel plan when no distance is involved.

Papaji: Everyone in the world has decided that he is in a particular location. That location is a fixed point. Then the religions come along and proclaim that there is another fixed location that you will arrive at when you die. Now you have two points. The point where you are, and the point where you have to travel to. There's some distance involved. Then the religions lay down the rules of the journey. They tell you what you must do or not do if you want to travel from where you are to where you think you need to be. They will also tell you that if you choose the wrong path, the wrong road to travel on, you will end up somewhere very unpleasant. They make you promises: 'If you do this, you will go to heaven when you die. If you don't, you will go to hell.'

You have looked at this situation and discovered for yourself that there is no distance between where you are right now and where you need to be. You have made an enquiry and discovered that no distance is involved.

Question: And because there is no distance, no vehicle is required either.

Papaji: No vehicle is required to travel because if there is no location, no desired destination separate from you, no distance is involved. So you have no distance, no vehicle and no location to think and worry about. When you know this, thought will not try to arise and go somewhere else in search of freedom. No method is required to get you to where you want to go. That idea is also finished. You are where you are, and you know there is nowhere else you need to be. Since you are not thinking of other, more desirable places, the contrast between this place and that place has also gone from your mind. These are relative ideas.

If you live in Lucknow, you think that that is your home and you think that cities in other countries are foreign places. When you don't have thoughts that somewhere else is foreign to you, then the concept of motherland and home also goes. The idea of location is always of one place relative to another. But location too is just a concept, an idea. Truly, everything is empty. There are no locations and no destinations. There is nothing for you to do because there is nowhere for you to move. This is very important and you must understand this. Through investigation you have thrown all these things away. All these impediments are no longer there. These are the concepts that have been rising and troubling you for the last thirty-five million years. Now, they are no more here. What do you have to do here? How do you meet this situation? This is very important.

Here, don't use a word that has been used before. Don't utter any words that foolish men before you have uttered. Foolish men use the tracks and are led like sheep. You don't even need to use a word at all. You can enjoy yourself without even speaking to your own Self.

When you retreat into the sleep state to experience the joy...

Question: I'm having difficulty bringing the enquiry into the dream state.

Papaji: The dream state?

Question: I find that I'm not engaging in enquiry in the dream state. Enquiry is not there when I am dreaming.

Papaji: This is the enquiry while dreaming.

Question: No, I mean the other dreaming. The dreaming that takes place during sleep.

Papaji: You are sleeping even now. What is the difference between dreaming while you are sleeping and dreaming while awake? Whenever you see a name and a form, this is a dream. In sleep, do you see any names, any forms? Is the concept of sleep present while you are asleep?

In sleep there are no names, no forms and no concepts. Within this sleep state a dream state will arise. Dreams can only arise when we are asleep. So, when we see names and forms, what is the basic underlying state?

Question: Basic state?

Papaji: We only have dreams while we are asleep. In the dream we see names and forms – mountains, rivers, and so on. When we see names and forms, which state are we in?

Question: The dream state.

Papaji: Yes, the dream state. To have a dream state we must have previously been asleep. Isn't this true? We start from the sleep state in which there are no names and no forms. Then the dream state manifests in which there appear to be names and forms. The dream state ends, sleep takes over again, and we are back in the state in which there are no names and no forms.

Now, in this so-called waking state you are seeing names and forms. They trouble you in just the same way that names and forms trouble you in dreams. To avoid them, to take a rest from them, we go back to sleep at night, to the place where names and forms don't arise. You can't play with these names and forms for more than eighteen hours without getting so exhausted, you have to lie down and go to sleep. Ultimately, we reject this state of names and forms and go to a state where we forget everything.

When you wake up from the waking dream to awareness of the Self, you find yourself in the place where there are no names and forms. You understand yourself to be the unmoving substratum on which all the transitory images, the names and forms, come and go. You understand yourself to be the screen on which all the names and forms are projected. When you are rooted in that place, that knowledge, names and forms will not cause you suffering any more. You have to identify yourself with the underlying screen, not with the transient images that appear and disappear on it. That screen is your own true nature. It has no location; it is at no distance from you; no vehicle is needed to transport you there. Do you understand?

If you fix a location that you want to travel to, then you have a distance that you need to cover, and once you have a distance, you then have to start thinking about what sort of vehicle you need to traverse the distance. This is not my way; this is not my teaching. In fact, I don't have a teaching at all. There is no teaching and there is no teacher who is telling you something.

If someone tells you something, don't accept it because no teaching has so far touched the truth. This much I will tell you. No one ever spoke the truth. No word has ever been coined to present it.

You have to wake up yourself; you have to see for yourself. The senses are not needed, nor are the eyes. The eyes cannot see it; the mind cannot understand it; the intellect cannot grasp it. None of these will accompany you. You have to be alone without these things. You have to proceed alone. None of the five elements will accompany you. You will go alone to meet this situation, but what it is, no one knows.

You can reject the whole of manifestation because this is something that can be rejected. The whole of manifestation – its beginning, its middle and its future end – can be removed from the mind. Erase it all. Next, if there is anything that might happen to you after life, after death, reject that as well. This too is possible because these things can be grasped by the mind. The mind can grasp manifestation and it can also grasp any idea that you might have about an after-life. The creator of these two can also be imagined and grasped. Reject that creator as well. So far you have rejected the creator, you have rejected all of his manifestation and you have rejected all ideas about a state that might exist after you die. Now, what is there left to reject? The rejection itself. That which has rejected all these things should also be rejected. Reject rejection itself. Then what will be left? There will be no concept of rejection.

Please understand me: when I say 'no concept of rejection', I don't mean acceptance. I am just speaking about what can be rejected. Go on rejecting everything that can be rejected, and when you have done that, reject rejection itself. Then face the situation.

There was once a teacher – I am not as strict as he was – who told his students, 'I have spoken. Beyond that no one has spoken. If you speak now, your head will fall.'

Question: I couldn't understand the last sentence. I think I missed the punch line.

Papaji: He meant, 'If you speak, I will cut your head off!'

Some teachers have been very kind to their disciples, giving knowledge with great love to their children. Some, though, have been very strong and forceful.

Some say, 'The path that you have to tread is like the edge of a sword. You have to be very careful, very attentive. Don't look this way or that. Two cannot walk abreast. This path is narrow and the edge of the sword is sharp, but on the other side is freedom. It is not far away. Just be vigilant as you walk.'

Others will say, 'It's as easy as rubbing a petal off a rose. It doesn't take that much time. It's just like taking a petal off a rose.'

The daughter of Kabir – she was seven years old – saw many people coming to visit her father every day. About five hundred people a day used to come and see him. Her name was Kamali.

She went to her father and said, 'So many people are coming to see you. They keep you busy all day, but I don't see any results. No one seems to be getting enlightened. Why do you waste your time with these people? You don't even take food at a proper time. Mother is there, the food is ready, but when we call, you just shout back, "Wait! Wait!" Sometimes you don't eat for the whole day because you are giving *satsang* all the time. These people come back day after day, but I can't see that any of them is being benefited.'

'No, Kamali,' replied Kabir, 'you are just a child. You don't understand these things. This is *satsang*.'

Kamali didn't believe her father. She decided to test all the people who came to see how serious they really were. The next day she sat outside the gate, sharpening a butcher's knife.

When the people approached her and asked her what she was doing she replied, 'Today my father is giving away freedom. It is Guru Purnima and he has decided that he will give away freedom to everyone who comes, but first he has asked me to check and see who is ready and who is not. He wants to know who has really come for freedom. So, if you will lie down here, with your head on this chopping block, I will chop off your head and show it to him. When I take the head in and show him the face, if he then decides that you have come here for freedom, he will give it to you.'

The first woman said, 'No, today we did not come here for *satsang*. We have a daughter we want to marry off. Someone was going to come today to have a look at her, so I came to get Kabir's blessings. Just touching the door will be blessing enough. I will touch the door and go.'

The next man said, 'I haven't come for *satsang*. I have a court case today. I just wanted his blessings so that the case would go well.'

The third person had a son who was about to be married. And so it went on all day. Everyone made an excuse and left. Kabir ended up sitting in the *satsang* hall by himself.

After some time he called his wife and said, 'No one is coming today. And I haven't seen Kamali either. Go and see what is happening. She may be doing some mischief outside. Call her in. Maybe she knows something about this.'

Kamali's mother found her on the road, still sharpening her knife, and brought her in to the *satsang* hall.

She immediately told Kabir, 'Father, I told you yesterday that no one comes here for freedom. I tested everyone today and discovered that what I said was true.'

'How did you test them?' asked Kabir.

'I said that you had asked me to interview everyone who wanted to come to *satsang* today. I said that you were giving everyone freedom today, but only to those who really wanted freedom, those who had come for nothing else. I asked them to lie down and told them that I would cut off the heads of all the people who had come for freedom. I said that I would show you the head, and if you agreed that they had come for freedom, you would give it to them. I showed them how sharp the knife was and told them that it wouldn't hurt when I did the cutting. I said that I could behead them with one chop, so that they wouldn't feel anything. Nobody accepted the deal. They all claimed they had come here for some other reason, not for freedom.

'You are wasting your time talking to all these people every day. Speak to me. Speak to my brother. Speak to us and give us *satsang*. Don't waste your time with these other people.'

[*A short pause*]

Here the doors are closed, and you are inside. You have arrived here. Now, here, there will be a fire, only fire, and this fire will burn all the tendencies that have been stored. That is, if there are any left. There will be a fire, a fire of knowledge. Everything will then be very clear.

24

Give up all relationships

Question: You say that thoughts arise out of 'I am'. That must mean that when I am not, all thoughts will cease. Complete thoughtlessness must be the state 'I am not'.

Papaji: Even this must go. Even this thought must go.

Question: You sometimes say that the last wall, the last obstacle or obstruction, is ecstasy. Right? So then, in order to be free, we have to let go of the last wall, ecstasy. Right? So the wall is ecstasy. Is that falling away by itself, or in awareness do I have to have a desire to be free of that?

Papaji: Free of?

Question: Ecstasy, bliss.

Papaji: In ecstasy you are lost. You don't have a choice to give it up or keep it. When a man is completely drunk, how can the desire arise, 'I want to give up drunkenness'? He is not aware of anything. He is just drunk. Completely drunk. In ecstasy you have even less control than in drunkenness. You don't know anything.

I was in Barcelona a few years ago. One of my talks was attended by a man who was not a member of the yoga institute where I was giving my talks, so no one there knew who he was. He came up to me while I was giving *satsang*, prostrated and proclaimed 'I am God! I am God!' Then he left.

He was found eighty miles away, later that night, dancing on the highway, shouting 'I am God! I am God!' The police arrested him, found his address from his wallet, and told his wife to come and collect him with two other people.

They told her, 'He is completely out of control. He is not able to drive by himself. Bring two people so that you can take care of him.'

His wife had to go and fetch him at two o'clock in the morning.

Question: I am sure you are not talking about that kind of ecstasy. You don't mean that kind of ecstasy.

Papaji: You're right. This is not real ecstasy; it is just a meeting. For me, real ecstasy is something like a peaceful stability, a stability of peace from where there is no return. That should be ecstasy. Generally, though, I don't use that word. I don't use the word 'ecstasy'.

Question: I find in myself a joy of awareness that knows itself to be unconnected or related with anything and....

Papaji: Being not related with anything is still a relationship. You are still maintaining a relationship with those things you claim you are not related to. You are still maintaining relationships. When you say that you have no relations, or even no ex-relations, you are still using a word that positions yourself in relationship to something else.

A man divorces his wife and says, 'She's my ex-wife'. Isn't that what they say? 'He's my ex-husband', or, 'She's my ex-wife'. This is what you are saying. 'I used to have a relationship with things but now I don't.' This is still a relationship.

Question: I'm not sure I understand this. Can you clarify what you are saying?

Papaji: *[long pause before replying]* Give up all relationships. Give up all your awareness of things that are known, seen, smelt, felt or heard. You have seen the result of maintaining these awarenesses, these relationships. Everything that you can speak about is encompassed in these things. These are your relationships. Let us proceed to that relationship that no one knows, that relationship which cannot be described, sensed, seen, or processed by any faculty of the mind.

Question: It feels like the joy of giving that receives itself. It feels like the joy of giving oneself that is being received by itself. Awareness that is not related to anything.

Papaji: What is giving? What is giving to that thing that doesn't fall within the scope of those things we just spoke about? It is unseen, unsmelled, untouched, unfelt, unheard. What are you going to give to it? Nothing. You have nothing to give. And if you have nothing to give, what do you have to receive?

Question: *[new questioner]* I think I feel that I expect something to come out of this talking, but it feels like everything has already been said in so many different ways. But the talking still goes on.

Papaji: No, it has been ended. On many occasions it has been ended. Do you find any word to describe this? I have been working on this but so far I have been unsuccessful. In my eighty years I have tried with two or three people. They arrived at this situation that you have arrived at in three days here. I'm very happy with you. This is the place. This is the time to describe. Say a word. After forgetting everything and arriving in this situation, I ask you this question.

Know who is meeting this situation, who is forgetting everything that has happened up till this moment. Forgetting everything. Thirty-five million years of burdens burnt and altogether destroyed in front of something that is not seen. I want some description of it. I have tried with a few people so far but they were not able to say anything. It is not referred to in any scripture; it has not been mentioned by any person. It has not been given out by the words that I have used many times. What

I say is a very shallow description of truth. I say, 'enlightenment', 'emancipation', 'liberation', '*moksha*', but none of these things fit. These descriptions, these words are no good. You have good vision. If you can say something, describe something, then use some better word.

Can you be satisfied with the words that you have heard already? If these words were good enough, then people would have become enlightened by reading the scriptures. But they have not given any help so far. Man cannot speak when he is face to face with the indescribable, the untouchable, the unseekable. You are face to face now. This is direct seeing. Everything else that you have seen before has been indirect seeing. You have been seeing through the mind, through the physical body, through your knowledge, your intellect, and by using these media you have been knowing things indirectly. This is the time for direct vision. This is the time for you to see directly: face to face, eye to eye, retina to retina.

I want this description from you, a description from the place where nothing is mediated and filtered through something else. I don't want something that comes from some in-between knowledge. You don't need any agency because no one is there any more. You can't make use of your mind because it is not there. Now is the time to make a description, but no one comes forward to do it, including myself. I don't find any word myself. I can't find one. You are a young man. Can you give me that one word?

Question: You want one?

Papaji: Just by being in that state you are describing it very well, but I want a word. I want to be satisfied with the description. I want something that can be spoken. I want something that can be said. Now, you are seeing it face to face. I am satisfied with that. But now you must either speak of something that can be described, or say something that cannot be described. There is nothing apt, is there? The symptoms can be seen and talked about, but not the original cause.

Question: What?

Papaji: Symptoms. A person may smile, and I may know from that smile that the person is face to face with this knowing. The smile can be understood, but nothing touches or reaches the cause of it. It is so calm, no ripple of anything is there. It is nude even of nudity. Do you understand? Nude of nudity. One can say that it is a lake without a ripple, but not even calmness is there. Such is the state of silence. It's like this. Who can ever describe it?

[Long pause]

25

Nobody believes me when I say, 'You are already in this state, this place'

Question: *[the same man who asked the final question of the last section, but speaking the next day]* When I look, anything I would say about it would be a lie because it's so empty.

Papaji: *[laughs quietly and then keeps quiet for some time]* You have nothing to talk about, so I will talk with your friend. You have to speak. What are you going to speak about?

Question: There's nothing I can say.

Papaji: If that is so, I have nothing more to tell you. When the mind is quiet, why disturb it? With most people the mind never gets quiet, or if it does, it only happens very rarely. I go on advising, speaking to the people who come, but their minds mostly don't get quiet. It's only in very rare cases. In those rare cases when it does get quiet, it doesn't want to speak. That's also one of the tendencies of the mind. When it is truly quiet, it doesn't like to speak, and it doesn't even like to hear anything. It doesn't matter, though. Silence is a tremendous language that you can speak with. In fact, in silence you can speak better than through any other language. It is very close to something that you are trying to know through silence, and not through words.

Yesterday I told you how beautiful it would be if you could describe this thing. I would like to hear about it. I would like to hear how the indescribable can be described or brought into some formulation of words. This work has not yet been done. All other things have been done, but this work still remains to be accomplished. It's still unsaid. I wish it could be done, but so far it hasn't happened.

I have seen the statements of all the wise people, but somehow I don't agree with any of them. That's why I am looking for a better statement. With you, it is very fresh right now. It's not too late. In the freshness of this experience, say something about it. It's not too late. Since you are there, you can describe it for me. It's not past and it's not future, so you can describe it here and now. You said it's very empty. That word has already been used, but it is not a good one because what you have seen is not empty. This is not an appropriate word. You have borrowed this word from the dictionary because this is the nearest word that you can think of. You have stolen this word, but it is not the right one. This is not it. Definitely not it. You see something else. What is it?

I am asking you this question. I do not talk to many people like this. I asked a professor many years ago, and I also asked one other man. You are the third. Only three people. It is not worth asking ordinary people this question because they do not have the experience that I am asking them to describe. I will not ask a blind man to describe an elephant. He will catch hold of the tail and give a ridiculous description. It is not for the blind man to give a description like this. It is for the man who is wide awake. Only the wide-awake man can speak about this. This is called 'the natural state'. You see, you are not in meditation right now. Nor are you out of meditation. This is something else. This is a state which is neither meditation, nor any other common mental state.

Question: It's everywhere.

Papaji: *[laughing]* 'This is everywhere!' 'This is everywhere!' This is the language to use. You have found another word, but when you say it, it's a new kind of language. You didn't need to meditate or go on a retreat to discover this! It's everywhere. Some man, some monk, wrote to me recently, 'We are in a three-year retreat'. You don't have to meditate or go into a retreat to discover this because it's everywhere. It doesn't leave you; nor can you leave it anywhere. This is your own state, your natural state. This is what you are. You are never out of it.

Question: Because it's so... 'everywhere', everything I say is inadequate, not enough....

Papaji: Yes, not enough.

Question: It's like an empty field. Everything is arising in it, but I can't say anything about it. I mean I can, but it's just words in the wind. It's just...

[Long pause]

Papaji: Activity is going on, but you yourself are inactive. Do you see this? The ground, the foundation, is inactivity. You have never been active. You are untouched by activities. This is called 'emptiness'. This is inactivity. The ground, the foundation on which all this activity is taking place, is inactivity. This is a wonderful experience.

Could there be any way to understand this experience? You have experienced it, so what is your answer? Can there be any way to have this experience? Is there any way for an ordinary man, for everybody, to get into this experience?

Question: They are all in it. They are already in it.

Papaji: *[after laughing a lot]* Excellent! Very good! Very good! There is no better statement than what you have just said. That's what I say as well, but nobody believes me. These people who all disbelieve me tell me that they have to do something to attain this state. They all think they have to meditate to reach it or get into it. Nobody believes me when I say, 'You are already in this state, this place'.

I say, 'You are already free. You don't have to do anything.' But nobody believes me.

Question: No. I wouldn't have believed it either if you had told me.

Papaji: *[laughs even louder and harder than before and then says]* So, you are all right then?

Question: *[new questioner]* So you're saying that we don't have to practise? Are you saying that there is no work involved? And no hindrances? Is that what made you laugh?

Papaji: These hindrances are all self-imposed. There is no external power or authority imposing bondage on you. You see a dark, wet line on the road; you think it is a snake, and immediately fear arises in you. You don't want to proceed on your way because of this fear of the snake. A cow was passing and she urinated on the road as she was walking, making a wiggly line on the ground. You look at it in the evening half-light and come to the conclusion that a snake is in front of you. Fear, a self-imposed hindrance, arises, and you are afraid to walk any further. Who created all this trouble for you? There's no snake, so you can't blame it on the snake. Your fear is not the fault of the cow. She has to urinate somewhere. She didn't do it in that spot at that time just to make you afraid. The only hindrance here is your mistaken belief that there is something dangerous in front of you.

Likewise, in your everyday life your hindrance is the concept 'I am bound', or 'I am a sinner and my sins will make me go to hell'. You have been told these things, or you have read them in books and believed them. They are not your experiences; they are just your beliefs. You give reality to things that are just in your imagination. You are living in your imagination, believing concepts that are not true and suffering as a result. Stop thinking. That's my remedy. If you are not thinking, then you are not imagining things that are not true. That's all you have to do. Don't think and see what remains.

Question: But surely, don't we have to work at not thinking?

Papaji: Let us see. Try it for yourself right now. Don't think. Don't give rise to a thought and let us see what happens. Try it. Look for a single thought. What is your first thought?

Question: Am I right? About not-thinking being work?

Papaji: No, we are talking about something else now. What is the first thought on which all other thoughts depend?

Question: I don't know. I don't know.

Papaji: It is the 'I'-thought. When a man is alive he has relations: wife, sons, in-laws, and so on. When this same man is dead, he no longer has any relations. While you are alive, all these relations exist in relationship to this 'I'-thought. 'I have a wife; I have sons; I have in-laws.' When that 'I'-thought is there, everything else is there along with it: this world and all the relationships you have in it. I am asking you to find out what this 'I'-thought is. Find out where it rises from. If you can find the solution to this, you will be safe. You will have solved the problem of thinking and the imaginary problems that it brings into being.

If you don't address this problem you will end up following the other sheep of the world. You will follow the sheep in front of you, and all of you will be herded around by the shepherd who is following you with a big stick. Every flock of sheep is herded by a shepherd. If you stay as a sheep, you will need a shepherd to tell you what to do and where to go.

Question: Tim *[the person Papaji was addressing]* used to be a sheep farmer *[laughter]*.

Question: *[Tim speaking]* I've got twenty-five years of hindrances *[laughter]*.

Papaji: Good. He knows, then. If he knows how to take care of sheep, he knows that they need a shepherd. They walk one behind another, and they need someone to herd them in a particular direction. But you have never seen a herd of lions being herded by a shepherd. The lion makes its own way, makes its own route. It follows no one, and no one tells it where it should and should not go. To find freedom you have to stop being a sheep. You have to stop doing and believing what everyone else does.

Question: *[new questioner]* Then this freedom is reality. Reality is this freedom.

Papaji: Yes.

Question: But we have been hypnotised to believe that it is not real. Isn't that correct? Maybe the function of a Master is to dehypnotise us so that we can find the freedom again. All we have to do is sit here and be dehypnotised. Is that correct?

Papaji: Yes. If someone has hypnotised you into believing that you are a donkey, you need someone else to come along and show you who you really are. If someone holds a mirror in front of you and says, 'Look, this is who you really are', you may be able to give up your strong belief that you are a donkey. What you really are never changes. It is what you believe yourself to be that changes. And what you believe yourself to be depends on the company you keep, and the things they tell you. If you associate with people who continuously tell you that you are a donkey, and if you have no other source of information, then you will grow up believing that you are a donkey.

Everyone is naturally the same. Everyone is naturally free. If one is not free now, where will freedom come from in the future? It is not worthwhile trying to achieve something that you don't already have, because if you don't have it now it means that your attainment will be limited by time. What you attain in time, sooner or later you will lose in time. Any attainment that comes after some time is not natural, not abiding, not permanent. So I tell you, 'Don't aspire for anything that is not with you here and now'.

This concept, 'I am bound', is not a true concept. This is not your true experience; it is something you have borrowed from your priests, from your society. All these people have told you that you are bound and that you have to work hard to attain freedom. I say that you don't need to practise at all. You are a man, aren't you? What would you say if I told you that you had to practise to become a man? You would just laugh at me. In just the same way, you are already free. You don't have to do any spiritual practices to become free.

Question: Don't we need some kind of discipline?

Papaji: Discipline? You are already disciplined *[laughter]*. You have been disciplined very well as you have moved from species to species. Among them all, man is a very disciplined being. The human being is a very disciplined animal.

How many donkeys are there? How many sheep are there? How many other species are there? We humans are just six billion in number. How many other animals are there? Look at the ants, the mosquitoes, the plant life, the marine life. We are vastly outnumbered by the other forms of life. And amongst the human beings, how many are just undiscriminating animals who have merely learned to walk on two legs instead of four? If discrimination and self-awareness have not come with your ability to walk on two legs, then you are no better off than the other animals.

In how many people does the question 'Who am I?' arise? In how many does the question 'What is this "I" and where does it come from?' arise? A small handful of people out of all the billions in the world. And among those in whom this question arises, how many actually find the correct answer? How many have crossed this ocean of *samsara*? Have you seen any? Have you heard of any? You will find that very, very few accomplish this.

When this question is asked, our minds go back two thousand six hundred years, to the Buddha, to find an example. When we search the whole of our history for a few examples, we begin to realise how rare it is. You can't find many who have accomplished this. It is such a rare phenomenon. Just one man who was a prince. A thought came to him, 'I want to be free'. A prince is sleeping with his queen, and a thought comes to him, 'Who am I?' He went out of the palace and was successful in his quest to find the answer to this question. Because he was successful, we still honour him today. There are statues of him and monasteries dedicated to the pursuit of his teachings all over the world, just because he was so successful in this quest. He found the answer to this question two thousand six hundred years ago, but still this man is living. We don't even know our own ancestors who lived less than a hundred years ago but we remember and honour this man. His name will live forever because of what he accomplished.

His is the true example of how to live a life on earth. This is the kind of life that everybody should live. This is the best form of compassion. The best form of service that you can do for the world is to know yourself. It will be enough. Wherever you are, the world will be benefited. It doesn't matter where or how you live. Even if you just keep quiet, that will be enough.

Question: This is our true heritage.

Papaji: Heritage? There's no heritage.

Question: Heritage means, what we are born for, what we are born to do.

Papaji: Ah, yes. This inheritance is your birthright. You have accumulated enough merit to become a human being. That itself is a great accomplishment. You have achieved this after going through how many species? For millions of years you have revolved from species to species without knowing who you are and why it is all happening. Now you have attained this rare birth as a human being, a birth in which you can ask and find out who you are. What's even better is that the thought 'I want freedom' has arisen within you. This is a very, very rare combination. Don't waste it.

It's not hard; it's not difficult; you don't have to do any practice to win this freedom.

One man, Steven was his name, came to my house while I was still living in Narhi [central Lucknow]. It was the afternoon, the time when I used to go out for a walk. I invited him to come with me.

As we were walking along, he asked me his first question:

'What is *sahaja*?' *Sahaja* means the natural state. He had heard of this natural state and wanted to know what it was and how it could be attained.

I told him, 'This is the natural state. Look around you. There is a traffic island. On one side is the post office, and over there are a restaurant, a hospital and the zoo. Many people are sitting here. Cars and buses are moving around; people are travelling to and fro. This is the *sahaja* state.'

That's all I said, but he suddenly got very excited and started exclaiming, 'I got it! I got it! I got it!' He didn't ask anything else. At that time, for this man, that was the right answer.

What is *sahaja*? This is *sahaja*. Where you are right now is *sahaja*. You cover it up with thoughts about good and bad, about what you need to do and what you don't need to do. You introduce confusion, and part of this confusion is the idea that you need to do something to attain this natural state. Wherever you are, wherever you go, you cannot leave this state behind. You cannot keep it in your house and go out without it. It has always been with you, and it will always be with you. It is the easiest thing to get because you don't have to practise for it. It's natural; it's already there.

26

The primary mistake everyone makes is to seek happiness from transactions that involve the senses

Question: Can people who suffer intensely really be cured?

Papaji: Suffering comes from old problems, from shocks people have had in life. People go all over the place to get rid of these problems: religious centres, yoga centres, therapy centres, and so on. That's what I saw when I was in the West – people running from centre to centre to get rid of their problems. I have seen these centres all over Europe. Everyone was going to them to get rid of their problems, to get help for things such as broken relationships, and so on. However, they were all looking in the wrong direction. Freedom, liberation, ends suffering, and not these assorted therapies. That's why I say that it is very rare to give rise to the thought of freedom. It's very rare. The people who go to these centres are running away from their problems; they are not facing them head on. They run away by dressing up in different clothes, doing yoga and meditation, and so on. If you speak to these people and ask them why they are attending these centres, they will tell you why they have come, and the reason is usually to get rid of some problem or other. They will not say, 'I am here to attain freedom'. It's very rare to find a person like this – very, very rare.

Question: Do these sufferings come through wrong identification, through association with the 'I'?

Papaji: Yes, it's all wrong identification. You might say that suffering comes from bad luck, or from mistakes made in the past, but the primary cause is association and identification with the body and its senses. The primary mistake everyone makes is to seek happiness from transactions that involve the senses. Once you make this error, you get kicked from one transaction to another, from one relationship to another. People who do this get lost and often get into serious trouble. Some of them have come to me with their stories. They come with stories of broken relationships, and one man even came with some cyanide in his pocket, saying that he was keeping it to commit suicide with. I have seen many such cases.

One of these was a man I met in Switzerland. He heard about me and asked if he could join my meditation sessions. I told him he was welcome to come. After some time he slowly began to tell me his story. He was a maths professor from Paris who had left his family.

'My wife ran off with one of my students, taking my six-month-old son with her. I can't bear the suffering this has caused me. I have come here to end my life, but so far I have not been able to muster the courage to do it. Perhaps if I stay here long enough with you, I will get the courage to do it.'

Then he went on to list all the preparations he had made for his suicide. He had some property and insurance policies which he wanted his wife to benefit from after his death. Since he was planning to end his life, he had done the necessary paperwork to ensure that she received all the money from them when he died.

I listened to his story but then I told him, 'You are a foolish man. Come back to India with me. I am going to Paris first. Come with me to Paris and then we will travel to India together. Don't commit suicide. Come with me and I will show you another way to get happy, one that is not dependent on relationships. I will show you a better wife, one you have never ever seen before, one who will not behave like this, and one who will never run away from you.'

He agreed to my proposal, but then he said, 'I have no money to come to India. However, I still have my car. I will sell it and get some money.'

He put an advertisement in the local newspaper and the following day the first potential buyer came to have a look at it.

'Take it for a trial drive,' said the professor. 'Try it out for a day and see if you like it.'

'How much do you want for it?'

'You can have it for half price.'

'That's not a fair price,' said the man who had come to look at it.

The maths professor misunderstood him. 'Look at the mileage,' he said. 'There's hardly any at all. I have only been using it to drive from my apartment to my university.'

'No, no. I mean you are undercharging me. This car is worth far more than half the new price. It has hardly been used. Why are you selling it so cheaply?'

'I want to go to India with my new Master, and this is the only asset I have that can provide me with the means to accompany him. I need this money to follow him.'

The man liked the story. 'That is a good reason, and I like what you are planning to do. Going to India like this is a very beautiful thing to do. I will pay you the full price of the car because it is as good as a new car. Now you can go to India with your Master.'

He came with me and we spent about a year together in India. When I saw that he had got over his problems I told him, 'You can go back to Europe now. You are a professor of mathematics. It will be easy for you to get a new job. Get another wife if you want to. You will have no problems now.'

People get into these states of acute suffering and don't know how to handle them. I have seen many such cases, not just one or two. These people had been to ashrams or other centres, but hadn't changed or improved. True change will only come when you truly understand that happiness and love do not come from transactions with outside things.

Let us say that you fall in love with someone and that someone is in London. You need to go to London because your beloved is in London. You need to travel to get there, and to pay for the travel you need money. But what would happen if your beloved was so near to you, she was nearer and closer to you than your own breath? If you start running or moving in any way, you will be running away from her, not towards her. When you run, you are escaping from the presence of your beloved, not moving closer to her. Whenever you seek something else, something other than this beloved who is closer than your breath, your seeking takes you away from her. This is always the case. If you want freedom, you have to learn to stop running. You have to learn to stay and be where you are. This freedom is not sold in the vegetable market, or anywhere else.

You have to understand that freedom is within you and not in objects that are separate from you. Then, having ascertained its location, you have to decide, 'When do I want it?' This is a big decision, one that you have been putting off for millions and millions of years. Make that decision. Make that decision now.

Question: What is that decision?

Papaji: *[addressing another man from New Zealand]* You wrote to me about making this decision, and wrote very well. You wrote to me about the origin of this decision, and how you had postponed making it. You finally decided, 'This is my own Self'. It was a very beautiful letter, even though it contained very few words. I asked you to write something, and this is what you came up with. Words like these come from the source itself. I wanted you to write from the place where the words originated, and this is what you came up with. All words, all activities of the intellect come from this source.

Self, Self-realisation, enlightenment, truth, freedom – all these things that we talk about – what are they, and where are they? Spend some time on this question and find out the answer for yourself. We started with the idea of distance: where you are now and how far do you need to go to reach your goal. This is a very short job. It is your *sutra*. It is the beginning and the end, and the whole path is contained within it. There is no distance and no location, and that means there is no way either. When you know and understand this, all is finished. Everything will be finished. No distance will have been travelled.

You told me, 'I can't describe it,' but later on I pushed you to describe it. It is a description, but at the same time it is not your description.

Question: I was very sick when I wrote that.

Papaji: It's not 'your' description. 'You' wrote no description. You told me yourself, 'I can't describe'. Your *sutra* was 'Beginning to end'. That was all you needed. Everything is contained and covered in these three words. There is no use in looking in books to find the solution to this. You have to find for yourself that the beginning and the end are the same place.

[The term 'sutras' is often used as a generic term for the scriptures, but in this context a sutra *denotes a great spiritual truth or practice that has been condensed into a brief phrase.]*

Question: *[new questioner]* Is suffering needed to break the infatuation with the illusion? Do we need to suffer first in order to be inspired to transcend it by going back to the source?

Papaji: What is suffering? 'I am not at the source' is suffering. That's all. 'I am not at home right now' is suffering.

Imagine you are sleeping very nicely and comfortably in a five-star hotel. You have had a good dinner and have gone to sleep. The doors are closed. In your sleep you start to dream. In your dream you find that you have gone abroad and that you are being attacked by robbers. You are surrounded by them and in your dream you know that they are going to kill you. That's your situation. You are in a terrible mess and you are screaming 'Help! Help! Help!' because you really believe that you are about to die. Who is going to help you in this situation? Who?

You are really in a five-star hotel, surrounded by many people.

Inside that room you have a phone that could connect you in a few seconds to the manager or to the security staff. You are in a completely safe environment, and yet you are suffering acutely on account of your own imagined dream creation. You are not at your source. You have moved away from it by identifying with a dream body, and that alone was enough to cause you all this suffering.

The idea 'I am the body' takes you out of your source, and once you move from that place, suffering, never-ending suffering, is inevitable. Suffering always begins from the 'I am the body' idea. Who has this idea? The body doesn't say, 'I am the body'. Ask it yourself and see what it has to say for itself. Start from the foot. The foot doesn't say 'I am the body'. It doesn't even say 'I am the foot'. It has nothing at all to say on this matter. You are the one who declares 'I am the body'.

This attachment to the idea that you are a body arises from spurious imagination. Imagination made you suffer when you were in a dream body, safe in a hotel, and imagination makes you suffer when you decide, erroneously, that you are the body in the waking state. Every time you imagine something that is not true, you have to suffer the consequences. It is like the snake and the rope story. When you imagine that the rope is a snake, you suffer fear, but when you know the truth that it is just a rope, there is no suffering at all. Believing in imaginary things is your own choice, your own decision. That means that you can choose not to believe in them as well. You have to decide yourself whether to believe in imaginary things and concepts or not.

I am not putting pressure on you to do this, but I will say that at some point you will have to make this decision. At some point you will have to do it. It's a very gentle process. I am speaking of your own source, your own house. Your Lord is very generous, very patient. You can come home, home to your Lord and home to your own Self, whenever you want to. There is no pressure. You will be welcome whenever you choose to return. For now you can play outside, if that is what you want to do. But when you make that final decision to come home, you will be made very, very welcome.

I was reading your letter in which you wrote that 'many years of search are over, millions of years'. I can tell you how these millions of years will be accounted for from the standpoint of reality. I told you a few days ago how I had once seen all my past lives, but I will tell the story again in more detail because it is very relevant to what I am saying.

I was once on the bank of the Ganga, just sitting there, when I saw the whole history of my manifestation, how I had passed from the beginning, moving from life to life in different species. There were all kinds of marine lives, not just fish – many kinds of marine animals. There were lives as a rock, lives as plants, lives as animals, including those sea animals, and then there were many human lives. There were even lives on different planets where I had a different kind of body and different kinds of thoughts. While this was going on, I knew that I had been each of these bodies, but I also knew that I was also this body that was sitting next to the Ganga. I saw all these lives as I sat there by the Ganga, and as I saw them it seemed as if I was experiencing the full life span of each of the creatures involved. I cannot explain this, but if I want to, I can still see what I saw then. There have been other occasions when I have seen and known my more recent human lives.

At the end of this long series of incarnations I saw an image of my Master, Ramana Maharshi. He stood before me, and as he stood there, the sequence of births came to an end. Now, what is strange about all this is that while I was re-experiencing all these lives at full length – millions of years of them – the amount of time that passed on the bank of the Ganga was only a fraction of a second.

When you come home to the Self you will immediately understand that all the time that seemed to pass while you were experiencing your countless incarnations was not real. It will seem like an instant of time, and when you come home and know this directly, you will know this secret and you will laugh. It looks like a long time when you are experiencing it, but when it ends, you will know that it was just an expanded imagination that all took place in an instant of time.

Prior to this experience by the Ganga I had not asked or talked to anyone about this business of incarnations being compressed into a single instant. I didn't discuss it with anyone afterwards either. I had not read about anything like this in any of the books I had read, so I kept quiet about it. Then, a few years later, when I was in Paris, I read a Buddhist text in which it was mentioned that the Buddha had also had this experience. Actually, the book was read to me. It was in French and someone I knew there read it out to me, translating as he went. Hearing this similar account somehow satisfied me.

I can now say from my own direct experience that all phenomena take place in just an instant of time. This is the secret that is revealed to you when you step out of time. The same thing happens at night. In a dream it might appear that an enormous amount of time is passing, but when you wake up, you realise that only a few minutes or seconds have passed since you were last awake. You can spend a whole lifespan in a dream, and suffer a whole lifetime of agonies there.

When you finally come home to the Self, you will know who and what you really are, you will know the true nature of the illusory manifestation that engrossed you for so long, and when you transcend it, you will know what true freedom is. In that final resting place you will know that this is where you really were all along. You will know that you suffered pointlessly by choosing to believe that you were something and somewhere else. You will know that you knew this all along, but chose to ignore it. You are ignoring it now because you don't believe what I am saying. You are believing your imagination instead. You will not believe that this is your birthright, that it's always here, and that it is always what you are. Nobody believes this, so everyone carries on making efforts to reach this place where they are already resting. There are different methods and different ways, but they all boost and sustain the imagination that makes you believe that you are something other than what you really are.

Question: The state I wrote about seems to be one of quiet contentment. There was no urge to run outside and make contact with people or anything else. It's hard to explain. I didn't actually want to do anything at all.

Papaji: This is the time, this is the moment for you to enjoy. Enjoy as much as you can, and then do whatever you want to. Enjoy! Enjoy!

Question: Enjoy or die?

Papaji: Enjoy! This is enjoyment!

Question: First you told me I must die, and now you are saying that I must enjoy.

Papaji: They are the same thing; they are not different. You have no need to control the mind. Do you feel that you have to control your mind?

Question: I don't know how any more. I just don't know how.

Papaji: *[laughing]* Very good! People get lost trying to control the mind by *pranayama* and meditation. This is a very correct view, a very correct view. How simple it is!

I knew a high school student in Bombay. She used to come with her mother to see me in Bombay. I think she must have been about eighteen or nineteen at the time.

Once she told me, 'I use the mind when it is needed, otherwise I leave it alone. When I don't need the mind, I don't engage with any of its thoughts. I go to school, study, eat and sleep, but I don't need my mind for any of these things. However, it's still there if I need it for anything.'

That's the right attitude. The mind can be a useful tool, but don't let it run or ruin your life.

27

No one has so far described it, and no one ever will

Question: The three states of waking, dreaming and sleeping, are they part of the illusion? And if so, what about *turiya*, the fourth state in which they appear? Is that also an illusion? Does this *turiya* come from somewhere?

Papaji: There is some other indescribable state. *Turiya* still exists in relation to these three other states that you reject. It has a relationship with this rejection. Do you understand what I am saying? Since it has a relationship with these rejected states, it is state itself, and as such, it deserves to be rejected as well. Beyond them all is *turiyatita* [beyond the fourth]. That, nobody understands.

Turiya can still be grasped in some way by the mind. In sleep there is still some residual awareness that enables you to say, when you wake up, 'I slept well. I had a good sleep last night.' That knowledge, that awareness, comes from a subtle contact with the fourth state, the *turiya* in which the three states of waking, dreaming and sleeping appear and disappear. From the fourth state one can revert to one of the three states – the next waking state, for example.

There is something utterly beyond these four states that you spend your time moving through. Something beyond, a place where there are no changing states or processes at all. That's the original substratum, the foundation of all, beyond all concepts. It is not a state like the other four because it is beyond all states.

The fourth state, *turiya*, can still be a concept; it can still be something that you understand and grasp with the mind. The mind can grasp the idea of something that underlies the three other states and which subsists as an awareness during deep sleep, but it can have no idea or concept of what lies beyond or behind that residual awareness.

A sharp intellect can grasp many things, and it can experience many things, but it cannot touch or understand this *turiyatita*. People have experiences. The intellect grasps them and calls them 'enlightenment'. Most people make this mistake; they confuse a clear intellectual understanding with the true experience of that original state in which no understanding is possible. The true experience has nothing to do with understanding. *Turiyatita* is an absolutely virgin experience. No one has so far described it, and no one ever will. All the *sutras* are silent about it. No one has ever spoken of it.

Question: What is the difference between the realisation of a *bhakta* and the realisation of a *jnani*?

Papaji: In *bhakti* there is always some persistent concept of duality. The idea of devotion to a divine personal God maintains the element of duality. When this duality is maintained, it will transport you to the realms of the gods after you die. There are many descriptions of these heavenly worlds, but they are all still mental. They are concepts, creations of the mind. Devotees, even some great saints, believe in these concepts and go to a heaven that accords with their concepts. These people do not aspire for true freedom in this life because they have been conditioned to believe in heavenly realms such as Vaikunta that they will go to when they die. The power of the mind creates these *lokas* [worlds], and after physical death it goes there to enjoy them. There are many different worlds that one can go to after one dies, but they are all creations of the mind. You can spend millions of years in such places, enjoying yourself all the time, but that doesn't mean they are real. The freedom that I speak of liberates you from the necessity of reappearing in any of these worlds. This freedom is not spoken of there.

Question: So people who go to these realms eventually have to reincarnate again? They have to come back to earth and have more lives here?

Papaji: It is very difficult for the desire for freedom to arise in a place where there is no apparent suffering, where all is happiness and pleasure, where no aging is taking place. In these divine *lokas* everything is very fine and very beautiful. The people there think, 'This is enough for us. What more do we need?' This is why it is so rare for the desire for freedom to arise in such places. The great *bhakti* saints – Tukaram, Namdev, Tulsidas, and so on – all aspired to go to a heavenly realm when they died. They wanted to stay permanently with the divine through their devotion to that divine. Devotees who have this intense devotion to God will go to a divine *loka* and stay there for thousands of years, but sooner or later they will have to return here if they want true freedom.

Question: What about Meerabai? Was she like this? Didn't she change in the end?

Papaji: She changed her attitude and outlook in the end, and so did several other saints.

Meerabai was a former queen and a mystic poet. She renounced her royal privileges and went to live in the forest. She became so famous, the emperor of India came to hear about her and wanted to see her.

He asked his prime minister to arrange a meeting, but the prime minister told him, 'She will not see you if you go as an emperor. She has already rejected all the trappings of royalty and has gone to live in Vrindavan. She is living there like a beggar, singing ecstatic songs to God. She has a divine madness. Sometimes she lives in a tree, sometimes she travels, and sometime she just sings to God. I have a suggestion, though. We can go there in disguise. You could come with me in the dress of my servant.'

The king agreed to this proposal and they both set off to look for Meera in the forests of Vrindavan. After a long search they found her. As they approached they saw that she was in a state of ecstasy with her eyes closed. They sat there for an hour, waiting for her to come out of this state. When she finally opened her eyes and looked in their direction, the emperor realised that he had never seen such an inner beauty before. She was glowing with purity, and he felt this inner beauty radiating out of her. The peace that was flowing out of her body made the emperor very happy indeed. Now, when a king is happy, it is his nature to give out a reward to whoever has caused him to be happy. He forgot that he was supposed to be a servant. His hand automatically went under his robe, and he pulled out a diamond necklace which he offered to Meera. Meera, who had once been a queen herself, knew that only the emperor could possess such a necklace.

'I have thrown away all stones such as these,' she said. 'I can't accept them.'

The emperor prostrated before her and left.

This is how she spent her life, not caring for anything, living in the forest and subsisting on whatever food came her way.

I have read one thing though, one thing that made me think that she eventually gave up her devotion to her personal God. There is a poem she wrote which says, 'At last I have found a bed, a bed on which my beloved has spread himself. Now I am going to sleep.'

I will tell you more about this poem in a few minutes. First though, I have to explain about her background. She had spent her whole life loving Krishna. Her devotion dated back to when she was seven years old. She saw a marriage procession going down the street, and she asked her mother what was going on. In India the bridegroom goes on horseback to the house of his bride. This was the procession that she had just seen.

Her mother said, 'He is the groom. He is on his way to get married.'

Meera than asked, 'Who is my groom?' and her mother replied 'Krishna'.

In that moment her love for Krishna was kindled, and for the rest of her life she loved no one else.

Now, going back to that poem, she uses the word '*nirgun*' there. *Nirgun* means formless. She says that her beloved is *nirgun*, and that the bed is *nirgun* as well. She says, 'Now I am going to share a bed with the formless and there will no longer be any separation'.

This is what she said, and I think that this is the end of the story. This is called freedom. Reading this, I thought that this was where her *bhakti* ended.

Other saints have written similar ideas in their poems. I have read a verse by Tukaram that indicated that the same thing happened to him, but it is not as clear as this verse of Meerabai.

The story of Kabir is also interesting. He started off as a Ram *bhakta*, primarily because his Guru was a Ram *bhakta*. His Guru, Ramananda, was a brahmin who would not accept anyone who was not a brahmin as a disciple. Kabir, who was not a brahmin, was convinced that Ramananda was the only man who was qualified to be his Guru, and he was determined to get *diksha* [initiation] from him. However, to get the initiation he desired, he had to trick Ramananda into giving it to him.

Ramananda used to come to the *ghats* in Varanasi to have a bath in the early morning, when it was still dark. Kabir decided that he would lie down on the steps on Ramananda's route and hope that Ramananda would accidentally step on him. He would take this accidental touch to be his initiation. Kabir's plan worked and Ramananda stepped on him in the dark the next morning. When Ramananda stepped on this unexpected object beneath his feet, he spontaneously said 'Ram, Ram'. Kabir took that to be an initiation to chant the name of Ram. From that moment on, the name of Ram was always on his lips and in his mind.

Kabir was a weaver by profession. Sometimes the threads on his loom would break and he would have to stop the weaving to make repairs. He noticed that this repair work demanded so much concentration, his flow of Ram *japa* would temporarily stop or slow down. He appealed to Ram to help him with this problem.

Ram physically appeared before him and said, 'You carry on with your *japa*, and I will take care of the repairs and the weaving'.

And that's what happened. When the threads or the fabric of his work broke and needed repairs, Kabir would just ignore them and carry on with his *japa*. Ram would do his weaving and repair work while Kabir would continue with his *japa*. A point was reached when Kabir was doing the *japa* automatically, twenty-four hours a day. When you reach this stage, the name begins to chant itself without any volition from the chanter, and it continues as an undercurrent in all the three states of waking, dreaming and sleeping.

Despite having this background, there are several instances in Kabir's poems where he indicates that he transcended his dualistic devotion to Ram and attained the final, liberating experience that was beyond this dualistic relationship.

In one verse he says, 'Kabir says that it is good that he has forgotten the name of Ram. It was a ghost that was hanging on me all my life. Now I am free. Now I am free. I have returned to my nature. I am now as I was.'

Now, this seemed quite clear to me, but Kabir's poems are written in an old dialect that I can't read very well. When I was in Varanasi with some foreigners, I went to the Kabir Math there to see if they had any experts who could shed any new light on these intriguing lines. I knew they were all *bhaktas* there, but I thought there might be someone who could give me an honest explanation of what the original words meant.

The head priest was very old. He looked as if he was in his nineties. When I spoke to him about this problematic verse, he said he didn't even know the lines I was referring to, but he did tell me that there was a *sastri*, a pandit, who was in the *math*. He thought that this man could probably help me. A scholar from Benares Hindu University was also there, collecting and researching Kabir material for a book that he was going to bring out in Hindi.

I spoke to both the pandit and the university scholar about

these lines, but it soon became clear that they wanted to interpret them in a dualistic way. Neither would accept that Kabir had transcended his Ram *bhakti* and left his mantra behind. The meaning was clear to me, but they tried to cover it up with a dualistic interpretation. Even the foreigners, who were from Australia, could see that they were twisting the words to suit their own particular preferred philosophy. They complained to these scholars and had a bit of an argument about their interpretations.

Ultimately one has to arrive at the Self and abide there in a non-dualistic way. There cannot be two selves, one who worships and another who is worshipped. You can call the Self 'Ram' if you want to. If it serves your purpose and gets you closer to the Self, you can give it any name you like. Even 'Self' is just a name. It is not the reality of what the name indicates. This final place has no name of its own. You cannot think about it, and you cannot feel it in any way. It is beyond thought and feeling.

28

Find the thoughtlessness that is there between thoughts

Papaji: *[flipping through one of his old diaries in which some addresses had been written]* This page came from a man who had read about me in an old Urdu article that had been published in Punjab. It had been printed years before, but on the strength of it he came to Ramanasramam looking for me. They gave him my address, and he eventually caught up with me. This language is Persian and I will translate what it says: 'In this class of love there is a very strange rule. He who has done his work is not allowed to go home.'

Don't you understand? In an ordinary school, when you have completed your work, the teacher tells you that you can go home. In this school of love, divine love, when you have mastered the subject, you have to stay. For the rest of your life you will never be allowed to leave. This is what happens in the class of love where true love is taught.

Question: You will never want to leave.

Papaji: You will be involved more and more, and you will never be free to leave and go back to where you came from. Very nice.

[Turning to someone else] Are you working on your meditation? On what do you have to meditate? Meditate on that which is beyond any kind of perception, or even imagination. Meditate

on that which is beyond both perception and imagination.

Question: When imagination comes in, what does one do?

Papaji: That's what I am saying. Meditate on that which is beyond imagination. Liberate the mind from clinging to any perception or imagination.

Question: Yes, I think I understand what you are saying. The past does come in. Then what happens?

Papaji: OK, the past is coming. While you are meditating, the past is coming. It will come in the form of a thought, won't it? One thought will come, followed by another, and then a whole train of thought will follow. Pick up that one thought, the first one, when it comes. I am telling you not to meditate on imagination, but this imagination is still coming. When that thought comes, just look at it and tell me what happens to it.

Question: It goes away.

Papaji: So that's a simple solution. And then?

Question: Another thought replaces it.

Papaji: I asked you to look at this thought that appeared in front of you, and I asked you what happened when you looked. You said it disappeared. Then, you say, another thought takes its place. Now, between the disappearance of the first thought and the appearance of the second there must be some gap, some space. Look at this empty space. The first thought has stopped and the second has not yet arrived. Look at this space. Be quick! Do it now! Don't waste time! Be quick and tell me what is there.

Question: There's nothing.

Papaji: It's finished. Look again. The previous thought has gone. Look at where it went. Look at that disappearance. You have to do it. Do it again and again and you have won the game. Do this properly and the other thoughts will not come. These thoughts

189

are sheep. They will not come out and bleat while they know that the butcher is there.

Question: What's the difference between doing this and suppressing thoughts?

Papaji: This is not suppressing.

Question: But what is the difference between suppressing and nothingness?

Papaji: I am not allowing you to suppress. Suppression is for yogis. That is not the way that I teach. I am teaching you to accept whatever comes. If a thought comes, accept it. Look at the process. A thought arises inside you. Accept it. Now this thought has to disappear to give room for other thoughts to come. Let it go. Don't try to hold onto it, and don't try to suppress it. Make use of the letting go. As you watch it disappear, be aware of the thoughtlessness that replaces it when it disappears. Give some time to this. Find the thoughtlessness that is there between thoughts. This thoughtlessness is not suppression; it is your nature. When you follow the path of suppression, you get strangled in thought. I am not telling you to do this at all. Thoughts come and thoughts go. When thoughts go, in the gap before the next one arises, you are truly yourself. It is not suppression. It is returning to your own Self.

Question: So in this method one is not to try to find out who or what is doing the thinking?

Papaji: I am saying, if thoughts come, let them come. Whatever they are, let them come.

Question: It doesn't matter if they come, or what they are like?

Papaji: Whatever they are, let them come. They have come to play with you. It doesn't matter what they are. Let them come and play. If you play soccer or tennis, you just play. You run around for a while, enjoying the movement of the ball, and then it's over.

Nobody stays on the tennis court or the soccer pitch when the game is over. Everyone goes home. The winner goes home and the loser goes home. The game is over and everyone disperses.

Everyone has to return to emptiness. This is the place of rest, and this is your real nature. Just don't forget it. These things are here to enjoy. Enjoy them, and then go home. Who tells you not to enjoy them? But don't let them get their enjoyment out of you. You can enjoy them, but don't let them enjoy you.

Question: Do you suggest that in ordinary life people such as myself should have a period each day for this kind of meditation?

Papaji: One should always be meditating. With each breath and in each moment, meditate.

Question: When I am walking, sitting...

Papaji: Yes. Whatever is happening: sitting, living, dying. Now you must ask the next obvious question – 'Why?' I will answer it for you before you ask. 'This is your nature. This is your nature.' That's why I am saying that in each moment, each second, meditation should be going on. It's your natural state. You are naturally meditating all the time, but your problem is, you deny it.

Question: Why?

Papaji: When you look at the 'I', you are in meditation. When you are not looking at the 'I', you are denying that you are meditating. Who is denying? It is the 'I' that you are not looking at which is doing the denying. Hold onto this 'I' so that it can neither deny nor accept. When is 'I' not 'I'?

Question: When it causes no problems to me. There is no 'I' when it causes me no problem.

Papaji: 'I' is there all the time. This 'I' is your real nature. You don't have to meditate to return to 'I'. You are 'I' itself.

Question: But it's not the Self when it's causing suffering?

Papaji: The Self doesn't cause suffering. It is the ego that causes suffering. 'I am so and so.' When the ego decides it is 'someone', suffering starts. When you are 'I' alone, there is no suffering. 'I' becomes 'Tim' and suffering begins. You wake up in the morning. Who wakes up? Tim wakes up. The first breath of the morning will wake up Tim. Then, all manifestation will appear and simultaneously with it suffering will arise. Let 'I' stay by itself and you will not suffer. Suffering is always related to other things, other circumstances that belong to the past. Suffering is connected with the past.

Let us go back to the beginning of our conversation. One thought has disappeared and the other has not yet come. If you look at and stay in that gap between the thoughts, what kind of suffering can there be? No suffering can enter there. No suffering can be experienced there. Just look at it. We suffer because we don't pay attention to this.

29

This is a fathomless ocean, a fathomless ocean

Question: Freedom is a desireless state, but I have sometimes heard you say that there is sometimes a desire to realise the freedom more fully once it has been experienced. So, this state is not completely without desire.

Papaji: Ah, that's a good subject. Not one that we can discuss, but still, it is a good subject. It is too sacred to be discussed, but I still like it.

[Pause]

I'm searching for some words. Allow me a few moments to search for some words.

[Another long pause]

You are right. Desire is there. Always, always, there is this constant desire. After freedom it still persists.

Freedom enables you to erase manifestation from the mind. In that moment you enter the unmanifest. From the unmanifest this desire arises. It is an impulse to seek beyond. This is a fathomless ocean, a fathomless ocean. It is beyond all concepts. It is consciousness itself and no one has ever measured its depth. Even in emptiness, even in this state of what one might call 'unmanifestation' some impulse arises to go beyond even this 'unmanifestation', beyond this freedom.

When you win freedom, what you have won is freedom from bondage, or rather, freedom from the concept of bondage, since bondage is wholly imaginary. Someone imagines he is bound, thinks he is in the thrall of *samsara*, of endless births and deaths, and so within him arises this desire for freedom. Freedom doesn't destroy bondage, which has no real existence, it just destroys the concept of bondage. Bondage was a concept, and while you still believed in it, freedom from bondage was the other concept that was associated with it. Freedom is freedom from both concepts. However, it is not enough to free oneself from this concept that is the cycle of *samsara*. In some rare cases a desire will arise to go beyond this freedom itself. Is this what your question is? Is this your question? Are you asking about how to jump beyond freedom?

Question: I don't know, Papaji. I think my question is coming from a more simple place. It's just that….

Papaji: Yes, it is this simple place that I am talking about. There is nothing to do there. Its nature is spontaneous. There may be some effort where you are now because you are holding onto some concept, and that needs effort. You may be holding onto 'freedom', worrying that you may lose it if you don't safeguard it properly. You may be thinking, 'I must not do this', or 'I should not proceed in that way because if I do I may lose this freedom'. In this state you are involved in fear and thought. However, when you return to your natural state there is no fear of loss, no idea of further gain. That's the spontaneous state that is termed '*sahaja sthiti*'. '*Sahaja*' means 'natural' and '*sthiti*' means 'state'.

Your desire for freedom may win you freedom, but once that freedom has been won, 'you' are out of the picture. When there is no person left, there is also no one who can have a desire. So, when this desire arises within this state of freedom, this desire that wants to take you even further, it is not a personal desire. You are not involved in it. It arises from within, from within itself.

It is a revelation within itself, for itself, to itself. You can call it a 'revelation', but I can't really think of a good word for this. In that revelation everything will be revealed. You will discover the hidden secrets. This desire will win you the secret and show you what it is.

Question: *[new questioner]* I am new here. Do you have any advice on how I can make the best use of this precious moment in time?

Papaji: Not giving rise to the question is making the best use of this time. Leave this 'precious moment' alone. Don't let anything arise in it. It is so immaculate, it should not be tainted by any kind of imposition. It should not be 'this way' or 'that way'. It's so immaculate, so pure, so chaste, nothing can trespass on it. Leave it alone.

It is your own Self. It is not a stranger. This is your own being, your own Self. If you want some advice, I will give it to you: dive into it. You have to dive into it, and merge in it once and for all. Right now the advisor and the advised are speaking on the bank of the river. Let go of both of them, and jump into the river. A stern, sincere and honest desire is enough to do this.

Question: Stern?

Papaji: S-T-E-R-N. Don't you use this word in New Zealand?

Question: Yes, yes, very much *[laughter]*, but we don't like the idea much. Does 'stern' mean 'in a disciplined way'?

Papaji: When you want to get this thing, have a stern desire to attain it. What discipline do you need? Throw away all the disciplines. Disciplines are the opposite of what I am talking about. Go inside and win the hand of the bride. Don't listen to anyone else. All these other things are in your mind. Cancel all your other programmes. This is the stern desire you must have. Have it once. That's all you need. Have it once in any incarnation. You have already spent thirty-five million years just to reach the point where you are now giving rise to this question. That's enough! More than enough! You have attained a human birth, which is the auspicious birth for this desire to arise. You were born in good circumstances, in a country which allowed you to have this desire. There are many places, many countries where you are not allowed to have this desire. In some places they will stone you if you talk about things like this. There are parts of the world where it is prohibited to stand up in public and say 'I want freedom!' There are countries that don't allow this, and there are religions that don't allow it either. You are lucky. You come from an independent country, from a society that allows you to think like this. Your parents have allowed it, and you yourself have given yourself permission to follow this desire. What an auspicious conjunction of events has brought you here! You have a mountain of merits. You don't need anything else. Enough!

This desire for freedom will only come when you have a mountain of merits. When you have won this mountain, then and only then will this desire arise. Then, when this desire arises, keep quiet and watch. That's all. Put it into practice. When this desire arises, wait, watch and keep alert. That's all you have to do. See for yourself and give me the result. Don't disturb yourself. Wait a few seconds. Just a few seconds and watch. That's all you need to do.

Freedom is clear of all moralities and disciplines. These belong to the religions that promise you heaven or hell and make you live in fear. If you don't abide by the rules, you go to hell. If you do, you go to heaven. And what kind of heaven is being promised? Just enjoyment – wine, women, and so on. These are the promises they try to make you believe.

30

Your acts of concentration and meditation leave footprints

Question: I come from a Buddhist background. Would you call the teachings of the Buddha a religion?

Papaji: Buddhism really means 'enlightenment'.

Question: So you think it has been corrupted in some way?

Papaji: I think so. The Buddha himself taught enlightenment. He worked for many years to get it, following many disciplines. In the end he found it by himself, after rejecting all the disciplines. He went to all the places where disciplines were enjoined, and one by one he rejected them all. 'This is not the way. This is not what I am looking for.' He moved on, rejecting everything he came across. In the end he just sat down under a tree and found it by himself. What observances did he follow there? He just had a sincere desire for freedom, nothing more. If you want to, you can call this a discipline. I just call it a strong desire for freedom.

Don't let the past disturb the present. Look at this present moment. Be in it without any thought of the past intruding.

Question: Let the past go?

Papaji: We talked about this yesterday. I said, 'Look at a thought, any thought that appears before you, and tell me what happens'.

Thoughts come from the past. Let a thought come from the past. Look at it and it will disappear. You yourself said this happened when you tried it. When the past disappears, the disappearance stays. Now look at the disappearance.

Question: Thank you.

Papaji: That's all you need to do. It's simple work. A thought comes. Look at it. Look at the last thought that came. You did this and then said that it disappeared. The thought came, stayed for a while, you looked at it, and it disappeared. That much was very clear. Now what is it that remains? The disappearance is there because you can no longer see the thought. Thought disappeared and emptiness is there. Now you have to look at the emptiness.

An object was there, a thought object. You looked at it and it left. Fine. It has gone. Now there is the absence of the object. Look at the absence. Look at the emptiness itself. The next thought is not coming because just emptiness is there.

Question: There is just a momentary awareness.

Papaji: OK, you can call it 'momentary'. I like this word 'momentary'. It's very good. Now, there is momentary awareness. Just awareness. We'll deal with this awareness. A thought has disappeared, emptiness has disappeared, and awareness is just there. Awareness is there now.

Question: Then another thought comes in.

Papaji: No! No! Now we will have to start again, right from the beginning. Let's not repeat this endlessly. A thought came, you looked at the thought, it disappeared, and you looked at the disappearance. Then you said there was a 'momentary awareness'. Now we will work from this momentary awareness. How can any other thought come when this awareness is there?

Question: I could say, 'By constant identification', but I don't really know.

Papaji: You say, 'I don't know'. There cannot be any other knower, a knower of awareness. There cannot be any other awareness to know that awareness. One awareness is enough. Is awareness witnessed by another awareness? I don't think that this is reasonable. To see the sun, do you need another sun? Do you need to hold up a lit candle to see where the sun is? You don't need to because this sun is light itself. To see something else you need the light of the sun or some artificial light, but the sun itself doesn't need to be illumined by some other light. It is light itself. Awareness is the same. You don't need anything else to be aware of awareness. Awareness is itself aware. There is nothing else that can be aware of awareness.

Question: No effort is needed to be aware?

Papaji: What kind of effort do you need to be aware?

Question: Don't I have to concentrate on it, to put my attention on it in some way?

Papaji: Concentration is needed when you need to know something that is imaginary. When you need to imagine something, then you have to concentrate. Right now, I am sitting in front of you. Your eyes are looking at me. You can see me directly through these eyes without any effort or concentration. Do you need to make any great effort of concentration to see me? Just look at me. How much effort does that need?

Question: Yes, I see.

Papaji: How much concentration are you utilising when you look at me? How much?

Question: There is a concentration that comes from awareness.

Papaji: No. Look at me. I am now looking at this object, my glasses. How much concentration do I need just to look at these glasses?

Question: You need a desire to look at the glasses, an intention. Some thought has to happen before this looking happens.

Papaji: My intention to look at the glasses is no longer there. Now there is just awareness, Now there are just eyes looking at the glasses. My eyes are there, and they are looking at things. What meditation do I need to look without any desire? What meditation? What concentration? If you want to imagine something that you want to see, then you will need some concentration. You will have to close your eyes and put all your mental energy into an image of the thing you are concentrating on. But for direct seeing, you don't need any of this. You just look.

This awareness doesn't even need to be seen. You don't even need to point your eyes in that direction. This awareness is there even prior to the act of seeing. In fact, if you want to see, that awareness is needed to activate the eyes and make them register objects. You need awareness even to look through the eyes because this looking is an activity of the mind and the senses. There is an interaction between the mind and the senses, between the 'I' and the object. Some small subtle effort is needed for this, but to be simply aware, no effort at all is needed.

You say that you need to concentrate a little to know or find this awareness. You are thinking, 'I will know this awareness through concentrating on it'. If you want to concentrate on this thing called awareness, then awareness itself is what you will use to do the focusing. The awareness will activate the mind and point it in a particular direction, towards the object you are meditating on.

You think, 'I am executing all the activities in the world', but the truth is, it is this awareness that is sustaining all this activity. Once you have understood that all this is going on in awareness, and is sustained by it, you are free of all the activities in this world. It may look as if you are doing things, but you are not doing, and you know it. You know that it is this awareness that is doing everything.

When you know that it is awareness and not 'you' which

performs all the activities, there will be no footprints left in your memory. You will accumulate no more *prarabdha*; there will be no more karma to produce another birth. This is how you end *samsara*.

Your acts of concentration and meditation leave footprints. You make memories with them, and these memories are *samsara*. You will accumulate karma, and this karma will result in your being reborn. It is a never-ending cycle, and it is all your creation. It can be checked at any time if you are aware because in that awareness everything will burn like fire.

You have to return back to who you really are. If you go back to 'I am awareness', everything collapses, the whole game of manifestation and *samsara* collapses. When this happens, this is called freedom. I therefore say that you don't have to make any effort to attain it. It's there all the time, supporting everything that you do or say.

Those who have a sharp understanding, a very sharp understanding, may get it. Some will understand, and some never will. Some will understand in an instant, in the time it takes to snap a finger. It will be a moment that is out of time, not even a sixtieth part of a second. The awareness is always there, but who is going to see it? No time is needed for this. Why should time be needed to know awareness? Some may see it in an instant; some may take years; some may take a whole lifetime; and some have been trying for thirty-five million years. Some instantly see and understand just by hearing a word from the teacher. One word from the teacher and all is over. I don't know how this happens and what it depends on. That's why I don't fix any preconditions. I don't give you moral rules. That's for the religions to do. I say, 'No disciplines'. I say, 'No yoga'. There is nowhere that you need to go. You don't need churches, pilgrimages or dips in holy waters. None of these things is going to help you. You may go to the Himalayas. You may go to any shrine. You may go to any god. But none of these things is going to help you. I am very sure about this. You have to face your own Self.

If you want to ignore this, you can go instead to see four-headed Brahma in the heavens, but he can't do anything to help you because he himself is bound. He himself is waiting for liberation. All the gods are waiting for their own liberation. The best god, the best place, the best church, the best temple – all of these things are very close to you. The difficulty arises because they are much too near to see. Because they are so close, you don't pay attention. It's too easy for you. You want it to be a problem. You want some difficulty in your search, but what you are looking for is there all the time. It is hiding behind your breath. Look at it now. Where is the breath situated? How many miles away from you is your own breath? It is hiding behind the retina. Just turn inside and look behind the retina and see that place that gives light to the eyes, gives them the power to see. No one ever talks about this. No one has told you this before. There is a place behind the retina from where the retina gets the power to see the whole of manifestation. That's all you need to know. Just look there. Not by yoga, not by *yagnas*, not by prayers, not by charities, not by pilgrimages, not by holy dips can you ever attain it. This place I am speaking of is the holiest of the holies. Having one bath in it is quite enough. And what is that bath? This very holy bath is when thought is absent and no longer pollutes. Have a bath in this Ganga, in this holy water, this place where thought does not enter.

Question: *[new questioner]* What did you learn from the Buddha? What did he teach you?

Papaji: He didn't teach me anything. I just read about him in a history book. I was in the eighth class, maybe thirteen years old. I saw a picture of him and immediately fell in love with it. I had never seen such a beautiful person. It was the beauty that caught me. It was not a traditional beauty because the picture was of the Buddha when he was starving himself. He was a skin-covered skeleton, so thin I could count all the bones. This was my concept of beauty at the time, and this is what attracted me.

I thought to myself, 'This man is very handsome. This man is very beautiful,' but I had no idea what he was doing. I had no idea why he was sitting cross-legged with all his bones protruding. It seemed that his body was dead.

I loved this picture so much, I decided I would try to become like this man who was depicted in it. Since I had no idea what he was doing or why he was doing it, the only way I could imitate him was to become as thin as he was. I stopped eating at home. I would take food from my mother, go out onto the street with it and feed it to the dogs. I wanted to become thin like this man I had fallen in love with. I managed to do this for two or three months, all the time getting thinner and thinner. When my classmates noticed that my bones were starting to stick out, like the man in the photo, they gave me the nickname 'Buddha' because they too had seen this picture in our history book.

Once I had become thin, I looked for new ways to imitate the Buddha. I saw that he was sitting cross-legged, with his eyes closed, so I started doing that as well. I had no idea what meditation was. I had not learned anything about meditation or concentration or liberation. I had never come across any of these concepts. I just started to sit cross-legged, with my eyes closed, without understanding what the Buddha had been doing.

After that I decided I should change my clothes in order to look more like the Buddha. Since he was wearing a robe, I had to have a robe. I stole one of my mother's saris, hid it in some papers, and wore it in the street when no one was looking. By this time I had learned a little more about the Buddha's lifestyle. I knew that he used to beg for his food and preach in public, so I started to do this as well. I used to put on my mother's sari, go to the clock tower in Lyalpur, which is where all the public meetings took place, and give lectures there.

One of my neighbours spotted me and told my mother what I had been doing. My mother had had no idea what I had been up to until this neighbour came and told her. When she found out, I had to give back the sari and stop all these imitation-Buddha activities.

Where did all these desires and activities come from? Nobody told me anything about the Buddha. How did such thoughts arise in me? I wasn't practising any discipline. All these things came naturally, by themselves. There was no desire to attain anything by doing all these things. Even that desire was absent. I just fell in love with this man. That's all.

31

Investigating and analysing your beliefs will not help you unless you choose as the subject for your examination the ego that has all these beliefs

Question: Is it ever useful to deal with specific beliefs and feelings? To look at them and analyse them, as opposed to asking 'Who believes this?' or, 'Who is thinking this?' Is it ever actually useful to deal with specific beliefs?

Papaji: Your beliefs are all contingent on the 'I am the doer' idea. So long as that is there, you will have beliefs and feelings. This doer is the ego. The ego is the entity that says, 'I am doing this; I am thinking this; I am believing that'.

The first belief that arises is the 'I am the body' idea. It's just a belief, an idea. No one thinks or believes 'I am awareness'. No one speaks like this. Everyone says 'I am the body' instead. Everything starts from this body idea. When you say 'I', you are always referring to this body and not to the awareness. When you say, 'I have done that; I am doing this; I will do that', you are referring to the activities of the body. And when you think, 'This is my relationship', or 'This is someone I am related to', again, this is something that you think and believe in because you assume that you are the body. All the ideas you have about yourself and the world have, as their root, this conviction that

205

you are a body, or inside a body. Once this belief is established, if it goes unchallenged, you will start to live and discriminate with this false idea as your foundation. This is ignorance. It is this ignorance that you want to use as the basis for your investigations into these 'specific beliefs' that you are talking about.

All these identifications, and all the things that go with them, are for ignorant people. All the books and all the *sutras* are for ignorant people, not for the wise. Discipline is for these same ignorant people. Once you have recognised who you are, once you have made the correct identification, 'I am awareness; I am not the garments it wears,' then everything else will go. It will just collapse. Once you know, 'I am not the T-shirt or any other garment that I wear', you will know 'I am awareness'. But if instead you become a body, you have to suffer.

This false identification has massive and painful consequences. When 'I am the body' is the basis for your thoughts and actions, manifestation arises, and while it is there, it will become your reality. Hell will be there; heaven will be there; the gods will be there; religions will be there. All these things will be true and real to you for as long as you think that you are the body.

Investigating and analysing your beliefs will not help you unless you choose as the subject for your examination the ego that has all these beliefs. Look at this ego. Don't allow it to make a whole universe for you. Instead of thinking, 'I am this body', tell yourself 'I am consciousness'. You have to make a choice between the two. You have to choose where you are going to live your life from: from the ego or from consciousness.

Consciousness is needed to do all the things that you do in life, but you are ignorant of this. You think the doer, the ego, is in charge and that it carries out all the actions that you decide to do. This is ignorance. It is an identification with all the pictures that appear on the screen, and not with the underlying screen onto which all the pictures are projected. You are seeing a picture that is projected on the screen and you are saying, 'This is me. This is who I am.' The screen itself, consciousness, is the underlying support of all the pictures that appear on it. You are that screen, and not all the images that appear and disappear on it. The screen is absolutely untouched and unaffected by all the images that appear upon it. You are identifying with one of these pictures by saying 'This image is me', and once you do this, you suffer whenever that picture gets involved in some drama.

Wars are going on; romances are going on; dances are going on. All these things are projected onto the screen. If you think you are a body – one of these flickering images on the screen – you will identify with all the things that this screen-body is going through, but when you know that you are the screen, the awareness that is untouched by all the pictures that appear within it, you will not suffer any more.

The light that is this awareness is not affected by any of these pictures. They can be there or they can be absent. It makes no difference to the awareness. It is untouched by the actions of these images, and it is equally untouched if they are not there at all. We may meditate, but the light is not affected by this. We may speak, but the light is not affected. We may sleep, but the light is not affected. This light, this consciousness, is there all the time. It is the animating force that makes the images appear and which also causes them to interact with each other, but you are not aware of this because you have this stubborn conviction, 'I am the body that is engaging in all these things. I am the person who decides what this body will do.'

We see each other through the light of the sun, but we are so busy looking at each other, and interacting with each other, we forget that this is only possible because the sun is there. In the same way, awareness is there all the time as the background against which this whole drama of manifestation takes place. We make use of it, but we never bother to find out what it is, or where it comes from. Instead of finding out what this awareness is, and what our relationship with it is, we misappropriate it and attribute all the actions that the body performs to some imaginary 'I' that we claim lives inside a body.

When you allow this invented 'I' to take charge of your life, you will be responsible for all the actions that the body performs, and you will have to harvest the consequences of all the deeds that you imagine that you are performing. Everything will be on your own shoulders, and it will be a great burden that you carry with you from life to life. But if you know and understand that it is this light, this awareness, that is animating you, and that it is this light which is really performing all your actions, then you no longer have any personal responsibility for the actions that the body is doing. Just be the instrument for this consciousness to do its work through. Let your body act according to its dictates. Know that you are just an instrument. If you live in consciousness, as consciousness, without claiming anything – such as a body – as 'mine', you will live a very free life. You will be freedom itself. You will live very well, very happily, knowing that you are the underlying consciousness, and not any of the petty dramas that manifest within it. Suffering may be there; happiness may be there. As they come to you or leave you, you will not be bothered or elated because you will know and live in the truth that is the underlying consciousness.

[There was then a discussion between Papaji and several people in the room about a foreign woman who was in Lucknow and who was suffering from some sort of mental disorder. She seemed to be alternating between rambling incoherently and bouts of depression. He asked Surendra, his son, to visit her to check up on her condition.]

Papaji: I don't think it is a serious problem. Some problem has come to her mind. When I spoke to her she was speaking about many different unconnected things.

Question: Sometimes she seems to be aware of what is going on around her, but at other times she is not.

Papaji: Yes, she was rambling. Her mind was in many different places.

Question: Sometimes she seems to know very well what she is talking about. She knows that something odd has happened to her mind. She thinks clearly for a while, but then her face changes and she is no longer aware of what state she is in.

Papaji: I saw many cases like this in Europe. When something like this happens, I generally advise people to go to the beach. Unwanted thoughts are demanding attention, and the simplest solution is often a change of scenery in which new impressions crowd out the old thoughts. These people become obsessed with old thoughts; they cannot forget them.

[Speaking to Surendra:] Take her to the hospital, the civil hospital. You know lots of people there. You can arrange to have her treated there, if she needs it.

[Speaking to everyone else:] I knew a thirteen-year-old girl who got into a state like this. Her brother used to come to my *satsangs*, so he asked me for help.

'She's in the mental hospital. I can bring her here, though. She is not locked up.'

I told him, 'If she is not behaving aggressively, you can bring her to *satsang*, but I don't want her to disrupt proceedings here'.

Her brother said, 'Well, at times she does get very excited and aggressive. I can't guarantee that she will behave herself if she comes.'

'In that case,' I replied, 'bring her before the *satsang* starts. I will meet with her in private.'

The girl was brought to me and my first impression was that she was a healthy young girl.

She spoke good English, but she was in a very agitated state. The first thing she did when she saw me was to shout, 'That guy cheated me! That guy cheated me!'

I immediately understood what was going on. She was just obsessed with a boy who had ended a relationship with her.

I told the brother, 'She doesn't belong in a hospital. Take her out for long walks along the beach. Try and find this boy she is angry with and get him to talk to her. The mechanisms of her brain have become overloaded because she can't deal with or process all these thoughts she is having about this boy.'

The brother knew who the boy was, but he had already found

himself a new girlfriend. The brother persuaded him to come and visit, without the new girlfriend, and after a few minutes the raging energy in the girl's brain started to subside. She recognised him, and the shock of seeing him again jolted her out of her state.

I met someone else who had a problem like this when I went to New York. What's that place you go to from New York through a tunnel under the river?

Question: New Jersey?

Papaji: Yes, that's the place. He was a big, strong, healthy nineteen year old. I met him at a gym where he was doing chest expansions with big weights. I knew his parents. At that time he was in a healthy condition, both physically and mentally, but about a year later he got involved in a relationship drama and committed suicide by jumping into the river. His parents wrote and told me.

Sometimes these youthful obsessions are focused on better objects or goals. I met a girl in Rishikesh who had left home while she was still at school and come to India to win enlightenment.

She had told her parents, 'I am going to India to get enlightened. I need to go now because as soon as I finish school, you will want to send me off to university. I will take a year off, and when I come back I will go back to school.' She was only sixteen years old but she had travelled all the way from the West to India by herself because she had this strong desire to get enlightened. How many people have the desire and the courage to do something like that while they are still at school?

She was staying at the Lakshman Jhula Hotel, but once she got to know me, she used to come and sit with me all day. How does something like this happen? It's old *samskaras*, habits and inclinations left over from some other life. Why else would a girl so young give up her life in the West and come to India?

32

This is the ultimate and final truth: there is no bondage, no liberation, and no one even aspiring for liberation

Question: I want to talk about memory. You speak sometimes about the imprints, the footprints that are left in the mind by the things that we store there. These footprints, you say, are what cause us to react and behave the way we do. Is there nothing we can do about what we do or don't store in our memory? Let me give an example. I walk down the street and I see a man selling tea by the side of the road. I notice him, and that impression is stored in my brain. It is there if I need to access that particular memory again. If I maintain full awareness of myself, does that mean that such events will not be recorded in my memory, that they will not leave a footprint there?

Papaji: Some things will go into the memory and some will not. Whatever makes it into your memory will leave an impression. This is the footprint I was talking about. All these footprints will collectively determine your future actions and reactions. Your body will come into existence as a result of all the footprints you have accumulated in past lives. These footprints will give you a script, a destiny to fulfil. Your body has to take birth to experience certain events that are determined by this massive collection of footprints you have accumulated. That momentum is there and it cannot be stopped. You yourself are responsible for all your

211

actions and thoughts, and it is these actions and thoughts that will determine your future actions and thoughts. And while you are experiencing the events that are the direct result of all the past footprints you have accumulated, you are making and storing up new footprints that will add themselves to your collection. These in turn will have to be experienced in the future, in a new body. And so it goes on, endlessly.

It is said that there are three kinds of karma. The first is the whole store of karma that you have accumulated in all the previous incarnations. Some of this huge store causes a form to manifest, a form that will experience some of those past footprints in a particular incarnation. The destiny of that one particular life is the second kind of karma. It is only a tiny fraction of the total amount, so as you go through life, you are only working your way through a very small amount of this pending karma. And while you are working off this small portion of your karma, you are accumulating more footprints, more impressions that will go into the warehouse of your unexperienced karma, impressions that will cause yet more births in the future. These new footprints are the third kind of karma. They are the new items that you are adding to your already existing warehouse of footprints.

Now, your original question was, 'Can I cancel out the impression of a man who sells tea by the side of the road by maintaining full awareness?'

When you get this full awareness, this knowledge, this enlightenment, a fire is lit. This awareness becomes a fire and this fire burns up the whole store of footprints that you are keeping in your memory. All the millions of *samskaras* which are stored in the warehouse, just waiting to manifest and cause us more trouble, are burned up and destroyed. Without this full awareness, this true knowledge, each of these *samskaras* has to fructify, but the moment that the full awareness comes, they are all burnt to ashes. That great bonfire includes the whole of your future, the whole of your past.

The liberated person will move through life without accumulating any new footprints. The bonfire has destroyed his old stock, and his enlightenment will prevent any new ones from sticking to him. For him, past and future have both ceased. The actions of such a being are no longer motivated by ideas of future rewards. He will not perform actions, thinking, 'If I do this, this will happen'. Actions will still take place, but there will be no sense that there is a person who is performing these actions. There will be no particular interest in what is being done, and no attachment to it.

The karma that brought you to your final birth, that gave you a body with a particular script, will keep the body engaged in all the activities that it is destined to perform, but there will be no identification with the body, no planning, no scheming, no idea that there are things that should be done or not done. You will live through it all like a dream character in a dream. You will understand how the whole process came into existence – how these footprints caused you endless births and endless suffering – you will know that they have ended for good, and you will also know that they can never start again.

You will also understand and know directly that there never was a creator of this world. No creator of it, and no creation either. This is the absolute truth. If you want to come to that place where footprints no longer stick to you, you have to arrive in this place where you know directly that there is no creator and no creation. There you will know that no one has ever been bound, no one has ever been liberated, and no one has ever even been an aspirant for truth. I will repeat this again because this is the ultimate and final truth: there is no bondage, no liberation, and no one even aspiring for liberation.

Question: It sounds very simple: just living in the present moment. In this present moment can I actually erase all the footprints, all the memories of the past that I have created?

Papaji: I will tell you a story. There was once a man who wanted freedom. He wanted to be initiated into some path that would lead him to truth, so he asked around and was told, 'You have to go to this Guru. He will help you.'

He went to the Guru, but this Guru said, 'You have to go to this particular god'.

He went to that god but was told, 'You have to go to an even higher god'.

Like this, he was passed through several deities until he finally ended up with the highest god.

He told this deity, 'I have been sent from Guru to god, from god to god, and now I have ended up with you. Everyone is sending me somewhere else. You are my last hope. Please initiate me into freedom.'

This highest god said, 'Go and have a bath in the Ganga, first thing in the morning. The first person you see when you get out of the river will be your Guru.'

The man took his bath and when he emerged from the river, the first person he saw was a bird catcher who was spreading a net in an attempt to snare a parrot.

He walked towards the man, thinking, 'This is my Guru', but as he approached the hunter said, 'Wait! Don't come any closer! The bird is about to enter the net!'

This man didn't listen to the instruction. As he walked up to the hunter, the bird he was trying to trap flew away.

The bird catcher was very angry. 'I told you not to come any closer. What are you doing here? Why have you come?'

'I am looking for a Guru who can help me attain liberation,' he said. 'I went to the highest god and he told me that the first person I would see after getting out of the river would be my Guru. You are that person. I want you to be my Guru. I want you to initiate me by giving me a mantra.'

The bird catcher, still angry, shouted back, 'What's a Guru? What's initiation? What's a mantra? What's liberation? I don't know anything about these things. I am just a bird catcher, and you are ruining my business! That's all I know! Go away and leave me alone!'

The man thought, 'There must be some mistake here. I have come to the wrong man. I had better go back to that last god and get better instructions.'

He went back to the god who immediately asked him, 'Did you find the Guru I sent you to?'

'I found a man who was catching birds, who knew nothing about enlightenment. He wasn't a Guru at all. He was just a hunter who chased me away because I was interfering with his activities.'

'Stop! Stop!' exclaimed the god. 'You can't criticise Gurus like this. I will have to curse you for this. For speaking ill of the Guru I sent you to, you will now have to undergo an extra cycle of birth and death. Then, and only then, will you get liberation. There are 8.4 million species and you will have to have a birth in each of these species before you have a human birth and attain liberation.'

The man was now very desperate and very unhappy.

He thought, 'I started off wanting liberation, wanting freedom from all future births. I was given the run-around by all these gods, and now I have been cursed to have another full cycle of birth and death. That bird catcher may have been a real Guru. The gods can't help me any more. All they do is curse me. I have to go back to the bird catcher and ask him to help me.'

He went back to the river bank and found the same man there, still trying to catch birds.

'I came to you this morning, but you shouted at me and sent me away. You told me you were not a Guru, that you knew nothing about liberation, and I believed you. I went back to the god who sent me and told him that you were just an ignorant hunter. For that criticism he has sentenced me to have another 8.4 million births, each one in a different body.'

The bird catcher listened, but still showed no signs of having any spiritual knowledge.

'What are these 8.4 million species? I have never heard of ideas like this before.'

They were on the bank of the river, so the man tried to give the bird catcher some idea of what 8.4 million might mean by showing him all the grains of sand that were on the shore. Then he showed him the insects that were crawling around.

'That's a beetle; that's an ant. Each of those different creatures is a species. I have to live in 8.4 million of them again before I can attain enlightenment. The highest of the gods has cursed me, so this curse has to take effect. However, I now recognise that you are my Guru, and that means that you alone can save me from this horrible fate. I prostrate to you and ask you to free me from this curse.'

The bird catcher laughed and said, 'Freedom is very easy. Let these gods do whatever they want to do. This supreme god, this godhead, is the creator of all this manifestation. He is responsible for all of it. If you want to live in his world, you have to subject yourself to his rules, his incarnations and his curses. But you can get out of this manifestation and live in a place where he can't touch you. I can pass you through all this manifestation in an instant. Just write down what the god has condemned you to.'

The man wrote the curse in the sand and the bird catcher ran his hand along it and wiped it all out.

'Now you are finished,' he said. 'You are liberated. Now you can be truly happy.'

What did he do, and how did he do it? He made the man write down '8.4 million births' in the sand and then wiped it out. The 8.4 million births was just an idea he had in his mind, nothing more. By wiping it out with a physical gesture, he convinced the man that the rebirths were just a concept that had no ultimate validity. The man also had the idea that there was a supreme god who had cursed him to experience 8.4 million births, but the Guru wiped out that god-idea as well. The millions of births and the gods who condemn you to them are just ideas in your mind. They are very strongly held beliefs and they exercise such a hold over you, you will have to experience them repeatedly until you finally stop believing them. This bird catcher simply wiped out the idea in the man's mind that he had to undergo all these births, and when that idea went, his cycle of births and deaths came to an end.

This can happen. Don't think that it is just a story. The idea that there are all these different species and that you have to work your way through all of them is just an idea that can be erased. The footprints can be erased, and the one who thinks he is the performer of actions can be erased as well.

'I am the doer' is the idea that keeps you busy and preoccupied. You are always doing things, thinking 'I am doing this', or thinking about what you are going to do next. You might think that you are helping others with all your various activities, but so long as you indulge in this persistent idea of doership, you are not helping yourself, or anyone else. If you want freedom, you will need to devote a small portion of your time and your attention to your own Self, and to do that properly, you will have to give up this 'I am the doer' idea. You work for others, you keep others in your heart, you think about others, you live your life through relationships with other people. Why not instead devote just a little of your time and attention to your own Self? In a whole life span no one spends even five minutes with full, undistracted attention on that Self. Spend just five minutes on your own Self, with no other thoughts trespassing on your attention.

You meditate and a thought comes that distracts you. What is this thought? It is a piece of your past, an attachment that you have stored up in your memory. If the attachment was not there, the thought would not pop up and grab your attention.

Question: *[new questioner]* You told us a story not long ago about how you reacted when you saw Buddha in a book. Is that attachment? Is that the sort of thing you are talking about?

Papaji: When you have attachment, when you associate with some thought or image, when your attention goes out to a particular idea or form, you acquire something of the object you are associating with. The '*sang*' in *satsang* means 'association'. You can associate with truth, *sat*, and let that association rub off on you, or you can associate with garbage and let it run and ruin your life. When you associate with your own Self, when you talk only of that Self and think only of that Self, you are in *satsang*. All the rest is '*asang*', bad association. Don't associate with people or ideas that are *asang*. Keep your thoughts on the Self, wherever you are. This is the number one *satsang*. In all the worlds of gods and people there is nothing that can match or equal this *satsang*.

Your senses don't want you to be in *satsang*. They will always be trying to divert your attention somewhere else. Don't feed them by giving them your attention. Your interest in them sustains their activities. Withdraw your interest and they can have no hold on you. Stay focused within.

If you need more help, and if your luck has not failed you, you might find someone you can be in *satsang* with, someone who embodies that *sat*, that truth. You may or you may not. There is no guarantee in this. If you think you have found such a being, be very careful. Don't trust the impression your senses give you, for these impressions are not reliable. If you think you have found a good teacher, a good place to have that *satsang*, then you are entitled to test that teacher until you are satisfied that he is the genuine article. In the same way that you test the purity of gold before you commit to buying it, test a potential teacher very carefully. Then, if you are satisfied with your choice, stay there and have *satsang* with that person. If you can't find such a being, then it is better for you to stay alone. Freedom can wait for another life, but entrusting an unqualified and foolish teacher with your spiritual wellbeing can destroy your prospects for much, much longer. You will die without attaining that freedom, and afterwards you will wander off into births where *satsang* will not be available for you. If you cannot find a genuine teacher to commit yourself to, it is much better to stay alone. *Sat* means 'truth', and 'truth' means the Self. You will never get led astray by putting your attention on the Self. It's always best to depend on your own Self. That way you will never get lost.

Question: *[new questioner]* If I give up all attachments, all the imprints in my memory, that means I have to lose the love I have for my friends and my family. They will still be there, in front of me, but I somehow won't care for them any more. You are speaking of a state in which one cannot entertain thoughts of the past friendship any more, a state in which nothing that interested or moved me before will ever interest or move me again.

Papaji: We come to this life with a *prarabdha*, a destiny that we have to fulfil. There are certain people we have to live and interact with. These interactions are inescapable. However, the relationships that we are destined for can be conducted without having them affect us. If they affect us, touch us, or move us in some way, we create new karma for ourselves, karma that will bring us back to this world again and again.

Everyone comes to this world with a script of activities that is determined by past-life events, past-life relationships, past-life desires and aversions. Some arrive in this birth with a very strong desire for freedom as well. When this freedom is attained, the body will continue, and it will continue to experience the consequences of all past-life attachments and desires. The Self of the liberated being will experience no karma at all, but the body will still have to complete its span on this earth with a script that is determined by all its earlier associations and attachments. Ramana Maharshi had cancer; Ramakrishna had cancer; Yogananda had cancer. The body will continue to experience the fruits of past actions and reactions, but the realised being will not be bothered by any of this. He will know that he is not the body that is sick and in pain, or the person who is animating the body. He can watch the body complete its *prarabdha* in a detached way.

Those who win freedom in this life will not be reborn again. This means that all the pending physical karma has to be crammed into one last incarnation. That's why enlightened beings sometimes end up with very diseased bodies. All the outstanding karmas will jump onto their bodies from all directions.

Question: *[new questioner]* Going back to the earlier question, would you say that the footprints that caused you to have an attachment to the Buddha were beneficial in your case?

Papaji: I cannot say. I really cannot say. This was just something that sprang up inside me. I don't know where it came from. No one had ever spoken to me about the Buddha. I just read about him in a history book. Many other things were there in that book, but they didn't interest me at the time. There were lives in that book that other people might have thought were just as beautiful. I merely saw the Buddha sitting there in that picture and fell in love with him.

Question: You must have seen many terrible things in your life.

Papaji: Yes.

Question: You still remember them. If you can still see them, why don't they carry you into the past, to places where attachments form?

Papaji: The enlightened man is not like a rock. Memory is still there, but he has no attachments to events that are stored there. When a memory surfaces, he doesn't run after it. It doesn't produce a desire in him, or an aversion. Memory doesn't carry him to new places, to places that make new karma. Memories, and attachments to them, pull you into new births where you have to experience these attachments.

There was once a king in ancient India who had ruled his kingdom for many years. One day he approached his wife and said, 'My hair is going grey. I have other priorities to attend to. I am going to leave you, leave the kingdom, leave the government of this country and go to the forest where I want to meditate and get enlightened. I want to search for the Self. You have ministers here who can help you to run the kingdom. Please don't follow me.'

He went to the forest, built himself a simple hut and started to meditate there. While he was living there a hunter shot a pregnant deer. The deer died, but the baby deer came out and was still alive. The king, now a *sannyasin*, came across this crying baby deer and took pity on it. He took it home and looked after it by feeding it milk in his hut. The former king completely fell in love with his new pet. He had left his queen but instead of meditating on the Self, he fell in love with a deer. This is a story of footprints – how they form, and how they make future karma for you. This man had two strong passions: his desire to do *tapas* to attain enlightenment, and his strong love for his pet deer.

As he lay dying his final thought was about his pet deer: 'If I die, some tiger will come and eat the deer.'

This is compassion, but it is also attachment. In his next life he was born as a deer, but because he had done a lot of meditation in his last life, he had earned enough merit to be born as a deer in the ashram of a *rishi* who was called Bharat. He spent his life in that ashram, living the life of a *sadhu* there. He didn't mix with the other animals. Instead, he sat with the other *sadhus* and listened as they chanted portions of the scriptures.

This is how rebirths happen. This king had a desire to meditate and a strong attachment to a deer. In his next life he became a deer who had the company of *sadhus* who were meditating in the forest.

[A few seconds of silence followed]

Somebody asked me a question recently: 'How do I avoid falling from freedom?' I can give a different answer now: 'If you don't make any new footprints, you cannot fall.' Keep your whole focus on that Self. This is the work you have to do. After some time it becomes automatic.

I read a letter from a French girl recently. She also spoke about this. She said, 'There's nothing else to do now except this work'.

> *Master, my own Self, I feel very deeply that at present for Nicole there is only one thing to do in order to accomplish whatever arises in a day. Not to forget to see myself as the one and only being-principle in all that I touch, I see, I feel, and especially to live life myself as the unique principle itself, seeing itself in what I still call others; and if forgetfulness arises, not to forget that forgetfulness is also the being-principle because other than that nothing exists. The being-principle, emptiness, silence, now are the same. There*

is no difference between them. With my profound respect and my sincere love, Nicole.

Question: *[new questioner]* Does the desire for freedom leave footprints? And are these footprints good ones? Will they take us to circumstances where we can do something about our desire for freedom?

Papaji: The one who has made a decision to win freedom has no feet to leave footprints. Who is the one who has decided to win freedom? This is something that has to be decided. Who is going to win this freedom?

Question: It's our choice.

Papaji: Yes, maybe this is your thought, but this thought will not leave any footprint. Somehow, this thought of freedom just jumped out of the memory. By sheer luck it jumped up and grabbed your attention, but it will leave no footprint behind. It rises and waits for the answering call from the other side, from freedom itself. Let this thought rise. It is not really a thought; it is freedom itself calling you home. You can call it a thought, though, if you want to. Let this thought rise because it is a blessed thought. Let it rise and then wait for the echo from the other side. Listen to the echo of this thought because that echo is freedom itself.

33

When you have lost the concept of duality, of two, oneness also goes

[Most of the satsangs that have been reproduced in this book have been taken from a series of audio tapes that were recorded in 1991. One tape is missing from this sequence. Papaji's initial remarks in the dialogue that follows appear to be a continuation of a conversation that began on the missing tape. From the way that the tape begins, it seems that Papaji has been trying, unsuccessfully, to make a visitor describe an experience he had had in Papaji's presence.]

Papaji: I don't agree with any of the descriptions of reality that I have heard. Many words have been used to describe it, but I can't accept any of them as being accurate. People say 'emptiness' or 'the void' or 'fullness' or any number of other terms. I have been trying for a long time to find some word, some expression, that describes it, but I have failed. When I see someone who has just woken up to that state, I usually ask them to describe it, to tell me what it is like. I always hope that someone will say something that satisfies me, but nothing I am told ever does.

You have not spoken to me before, except for a few words now and then. This has happened to other people as well. Some people come, directly experience what I am talking about, or pointing to, even though I have never had any one-to-one conversation with them. They just heard one or two words and that was enough. Afterwards, I tried with these people as well. Sometimes I have spent days with them, mostly just sitting quietly. We just enjoy each other's presence. The love, the beauty, the understanding, the enjoyment is there, but it is not something that either of us can speak about. I am asking you to speak because I can see that you are seeing,

Question: There's nothing I can do.

Papaji: I know. That's why I am asking you this question. I am asking you this question but I am not expecting an answer. It doesn't matter. I am very happy with you, very happy. But it doesn't matter.

[Papaji laughs, after which there is a long pause.]

Clear all your doubts. Clear everything.

Question: *[new questioner]* I find it interesting that I have no doubts now. Doubt used to be my major stumbling block.

Papaji: It's very good to have doubts, to wonder what is going on.

Question: Yet I have had no doubts for the last five days.

Papaji: I repeat: it is good to have doubts.

Question: Yes, I understand what you are saying. That it's good to have doubts so that you can remove them.

Papaji: Doubt must be there initially. There must be this doubt that stands between you and freedom. Some people have no doubts at all. These people are in complete darkness. In sheer ignorance there is no doubt at all, but there is no benefit in being in that state. If you are completely content to remain in your ignorance, doubts will never arise. Doubts will only come when you have glimpsed the possibility of getting out of it.

Question: That's why I asked the question. I thought I was having too easy a ride. I was not worrying about anything, and for a while it was fun, but now I am beginning to wonder whether I am stuck in this state. Whether I need to have more questions, more doubts, in order to move on to something else.

Papaji: Always have doubts, and then get your doubts cleared. Doubts are hurdles that have to be cleared. Doubts are impediments. They place themselves between you and freedom. In the completely ignorant mind there is no doubt. Such a person is quite content with the level of ignorance that is being experienced. The first step to freedom is to have some doubts, to question whether your ignorance is something that you really want to live with. When this doubt arises, approach someone who can help you to remove the doubt.

Question: I had so many doubts in the past. You know that because I brought many of them here. But what I am saying is that for the last five days none of these standard doubts has arisen in my mind. A lot of my doubts centred on things I had read in the scriptures, things that didn't really make sense to me. Now, after hearing you for a few days I feel that I am leaving behind the scriptures. I feel I have somehow let go of them. Abandoning the scriptures and my associated ideas of what the dharma is, and should be, is somehow a great relief. These ideas don't bother me any more.

Papaji: Excellent!

Question: There were no more doubts about these ideas. They just didn't appear any more.

Papaji: This is very clear. Just go on sailing.

Question: Now I am fine, but when I go home I don't know whether I will be just as content to have no thoughts about these matters. *[Laughs]*

Papaji: This mention of 'dharma' reminds me. Where is that little text that someone sent me? There is something in there about doubts.

[Someone found the text, a translation of Seng-Tsan's Verses on the Faith Mind, *translated by Richard Clarke, and gave it to Papaji. Seng-Tsan was the third Zen Patriarch of China. Papaji read out the*

text in full, pausing occasionally to make comments on what he was reading. He also repeated some of the lines. The portions of the text that he read out twice are underlined:]

The great way is not difficult
for those who are unattached to preferences.
When love and hate are both absent,
everything becomes clear and undisguised.
Make the smallest distinction, however,
and heaven and earth are set infinitely apart.
If you wish to see the truth,
then hold no opinions for or against anything.
<u>To set up what you like against what you dislike
is the disease of the mind.</u>
<u>When the deep meaning of things is not understood,
the mind's essential peace is disturbed to no avail.</u>
The way is perfect like vast space
where nothing is lacking and nothing is in excess.
Indeed, it is due to our choosing to accept or reject
that we do not see the true nature of things.
Live neither in the entanglements of outer things
nor in inner feelings of emptiness.
Be serene in the oneness of things
and such erroneous views will disappear by themselves.
When you try to stop activity to achieve passivity,
your very effort fills you with activity.
As long as you remain in one extreme or the other,
you will never know oneness.
Those who do not live in the single way
fail in both activity and passivity, assertion and denial.
To deny the reality of things is to miss their reality.
To assert the emptiness of things is to miss their reality.
<u>The more you talk and think about it,
the further astray you wander from truth.</u>
Stop talking and thinking
and there is nothing you will not be able to know.

> To return to the root is to find the meaning,
> but to pursue appearances is to miss the source.
> At the moment of inner enlightenment
> there is a going beyond appearance…

[Papaji, chuckling, exclaimed, 'Yes! Wonderful!' before continuing with an emphatic repetition:]

> At the moment of inner enlightenment
> there is a going beyond appearance and emptiness.
> The changes that appear to occur in the empty world
> we call real only because of our ignorance.
> Do not search for the truth.
> Only cease to cherish opinions.
> Do not remain in the dualistic state.
> Avoid such pursuits carefully.
> If there is even a trace of this and that, of right and wrong,
> the mind-essence will be lost in confusion.
> Although all dualities come from the one,
> do not be attached even to this one.

Papaji: *[turning to the last questioner]* You have to understand this line.

Question: That is quite difficult for me to understand.

Papaji: Yes, that's why I stopped there. It says, 'Do not be attached even to this one'. I will explain this because he is not being completely clear here. When you have detached yourself from duality, that means that at one time you accepted duality as being valid. The accepting and the not accepting are both conclusions. When you have rejected duality, what remains is the one. That's true, isn't it? All dualities, all ideas of duality, come from the oneness, and when duality is discarded, what remains is the oneness. Then he says, 'Do not be attached even to this one'. Up to here you have obviously understood, but now I have to explain what this line means. He is telling you not to be attached to the 'one' as a concept. 'One' and 'two' are two concepts that are related to each other. Is it possible to speak of two unless you have the concept of one? You can't, can you?

Question: No, I can honestly say that I can't.

Papaji: Two is one plus one. When you see it like this, the oneness has entered the duality, at least in your concept of what is going on. Two always has a relationship with one when one is still a concept. But when duality is lost, where is the one? Where is it?

Question: In the two? Back in the two? I don't really know.

Papaji: When you have lost the concept of duality, of two, oneness also goes.

Question: Right.

Papaji: When you are one, when you are alone in the oneness, you don't count yourself as 'one' because there is no two for you to be in a relationship with. One can only exist as one if there is a two for it to be in a relationship with. When two doesn't exist at all, one cannot exist either.

What happens when we sleep? We reject everyone. Many people came to see you while you were awake. Perhaps you were at a wedding, your own wedding, where you were socialising with many friends and relatives. One by one everyone leaves and says 'goodbye'. Now you are left with your bride. There are just the two of you left and it is time for you to go to sleep. You are both there, in the same bed, in the same room. The two goes when you say goodnight to your new wife, and the moment you enter deep sleep, the one goes as well. You enter a place where neither one nor two can exist. When the one goes, when it disappears, everything else goes with it. Ideas of one and two cannot rise or exist there.

You can't even think of one unless you speak and think of something that is other than that one. When you return to the Self, duality goes, and the one goes along with it. The Self is not something that can be counted in units of one or two. Neither one nor two is there. This is what this Zen master is trying to tell you. You have to reject the idea of one as well as two.

> Although all dualities come from the one,
> do not be attached even to this one.

I told you earlier that you had to go on rejecting everything that could be rejected. This one is one of the things you have to reject. Reject everything as 'not me': 'I am not the many; I am not my parents; I am not my brothers; I am not my son.' Then you are reduced to the possibility of your being the one. Reject that as well. When you say to yourself, 'I am not the mind, not the body, not the ego, not the intellect,' and so on, add 'I am not the one'. Reject that as well and then rest in the quietness of what remains and see what reveals itself to you.

> When the mind exists undisturbed in the way,
> nothing in the world can offend,
> and when a thing can no longer offend,
> it ceases to exist in the old way.

'It ceases to exist in the old way.' The mountain will be a different mountain. The tree will be a different tree. The man will be a different man. Things will be the same, but the way you view them will be different.

> When no discriminating thoughts arise,
> the old mind ceases to exist.
> When thought objects vanish,
> the thinking subject vanishes,
> as when the mind vanishes, objects vanish.

'When thought objects vanish.' This is where you start your enquiry, with objects of thought. When you say, 'I am the body', the body is your thought object. Start from that place. 'I am Tim'. When this thought vanishes, the 'I' who thought he was Tim also vanishes. When the mind that has objects of thought vanishes, the objects themselves vanish. Consider what happens when you go to sleep. Mind vanishes, and all the objects it was previously perceiving vanish.

> Things are objects because of the subject [mind].
> The mind [subject] is such because of things [objects].

Things are only objects because of the subject that perceives them. Mind is what it is because of the things that it perceives. The mind is the subject because of the objects it sees. They both appear and disappear together. Neither can exist without the other.

> Understand the relativity of these two
> and the basic reality, the unity of emptiness.
> In this emptiness the two are indistinguishable,
> and each contains in itself the whole world.
> If you do not discriminate between coarse and fine,
> you will not be tempted to prejudice and opinion.
> To live in the great way is neither easy nor difficult,
> but those with limited views are fearful and irresolute.
> The faster they hurry, the slower they go,
> and clinging [attachment] cannot be limited.
> Even to be attached to the idea of enlightenment is to go astray.

Ah ha! Very nice! 'Even to be attached to the idea of enlightenment is to go astray.' *[Laughs for some time]* We were speaking earlier of meditation and ideas and decisions. This is the dharma! This is the dharma!

> Just let things be in their own way
> and there will be neither coming nor going.
> Obey the nature of things, your own nature,
> and you will walk freely and undisturbed.
> When thought is in bondage, the truth is hidden,
> for everything is murky and unclear,

and the burdensome practice of judging
brings annoyance and weariness.
What benefit can be derived from distinctions and
    separations?
<u>If you wish to move in the one way,</u>
<u>do not dislike even the world of senses and ideas.</u>
Indeed, to accept them fully
is identical with true enlightenment.
The wise man strives to no goals,
but the foolish man fetters himself.
There's one dharma, not many.
Distinctions arise from the clinging needs of the ignorant.
To seek mind with the mind is the greatest of all mistakes.
Rest and unrest derive from illusion.
With enlightenment there is no liking and disliking.
All dualities come from ignorant inference.
They are like dreams or flowers in air:
foolish to try to grasp them.
Gain and loss, right and wrong,
such thoughts must finally be abolished at once.
If the eye never sleeps, all dreams will naturally cease.
If the mind makes no discriminations,
the ten thousand things are as they are, of single essence.
To understand the mystery of this one-essence
is to be released from all entanglements.
<u>When all things are seen equally,</u>
<u>the timeless self-essence is reached.</u>
No comparisons or analogies are possible
in this causeless, relationless state.

[Papaji laughed before repeating the last statement:] No comparisons or analogies are possible in this causeless, relationless state.

Consider movement stationary and the stationary in
    motion.
Both movement and rest disappear.

231

> When such dualities cease to exist...

Oho! This is the thing I was just talking about. I was trying to explain it to you, but he explains it himself in the next line.

> When such dualities cease to exist,
> oneness itself cannot exist.

He did it! He explained this himself. I thought he was not going to say this, so I explained it myself earlier. This is very good, very nice. I am reading this for the first time. If I had known he was going to say this himself, I wouldn't have stopped earlier.

Question: Really! You have never come across these words before? They are quite famous.

Papaji: Yes, I'm reading them for the first time, thinking about them without any support from anything or anywhere else. It's very nice. No, better than that: it's excellent!

> To this ultimate finality no law or description applies.

No laws operate in that place, no revelation is valid. Nothing applies there. What is this situation? This is what you have to know and experience.

> For the unified mind in accord with the way
> all self-centred striving ceases.
> Doubts and irresolutions vanish,
> and life in true faith is possible.
> <u>With a single stroke</u> we are freed from bondage.
> Nothing clings to us and we hold to nothing.
> All is empty, clear, self-illuminating,
> with no exertion of the mind's power.
> Here thought, feeling, knowledge and imagination are of
>   no value.
> In this world of suchness
> there is neither self nor other-than-self.

> To come directly into harmony with this reality
> just simply say when doubts arise, 'Not two'.
> In this 'not two' nothing is separate,
> nothing is excluded.
> No matter when or where,
> enlightenment means entering this truth,
> <u>and this truth is beyond extension or diminution in time
> or space.</u>
> In it a single thought is ten thousand years.

[Laughing again] This is what we talk about here. This is the space we speak of here. 'A single thought is ten thousand years.'

> Emptiness here, emptiness there,
> but the infinite universe stands
> always before your eyes,
> infinitely large and infinitely small:
> no difference, for definitions have vanished
> and no boundaries are seen.
> So too with being and non-being.
> <u>Don't waste time in doubts and arguments
> that have nothing to do with enlightenment.</u>

[The Richard Clarke translation that Papaji was reading from actually says 'nothing to do with this' but Papaji somehow read it as 'enlightenment' and then repeated the two lines again, with the same final word.]

> One thing, all things:
> move among and intermingle
> without distinction.
> To live in this realisation
> is to be without anxiety about non-perfection.
> To live in this faith is the road to non duality
> because the non-dual is one with the trusting mind.
> Words!

> The way is beyond language,
> for in it there is
> no yesterday,
> no tomorrow,
> no today.

Papaji: Did you like this?

Question: Yes, it was very beautiful.

Papaji: Yes, very beautiful. What a teaching! You won't hear a better teaching than this. As you listen to this, you can't cling to anything. That's the beauty of it. You can't cling to any sentence, any word, any teaching to give you freedom.

34

This place where the 'I' vanishes is wisdom

Question: Today I am besieged by doubt. Huge, vast doubts. Everywhere I look I see doubts.

Papaji: Doubts are related to what you are doing, or what you think you should be doing. You imagine you are climbing some great and dangerous mountain. In this imagination you see sharp, steep rocks, glaciers and ice, and so on. You imagine these things and then you imagine skidding, falling and dying. But I am telling you that you have climbed the mountain. You have done all the hard work. You are standing on a plateau that is only a few easy steps away from the summit. You are face to face with that presence which you have climbed the mountain to meet. There is nothing more that you need to do. Nothing more is needed now.

Question: How can I overcome this doubt without making some effort?

Papaji: All the effort you are making is taking place in your imagination. You imagined that you had to scale a summit, so you put in lots of imaginary effort to get there. You were so fixated by the imaginary scenario, you didn't realise that you were already on the plateau at the top of the mountain. There was nowhere else for you to climb, but in your imagination you thought you were on a steep slope, and that you were in danger of falling off it. Say to yourself, 'I am face to face with the presence'. Leave your efforts alone. Leave everything. The efforts are an obstacle.

Question: I can't see myself being in this place you tell me about. From where I am right now, all I see is the imagination.

Papaji: You have to become the seer. Not the individual person who sees imaginary objects and struggles, but that seer through which everything else is seen. You are that seer already. You don't need to make any effort to reach that place, that perspective, because that is where you are right now. You are just imagining that this is not true.

Question: Yesterday you spoke about your own experiences. You said that the experience, the realisation, came first, and the understanding of it came later.

Papaji: Yes, the experience came first, but I had no context to put it in, no way of explaining to myself what had happened. I could say that understanding came later, but even that is not strictly true. The experience is still there, but I have never really understood it.

Question: My experience seems to be the reverse. There seems to have been some sort of understanding, and then that was followed by an experience

Papaji: 'Reverse' also means 'to go backwards'. You left yourself to get an understanding, and then you reversed; went back along the route you had travelled to get the experience. Leaving the Self to get an understanding and returning to it to claim the experience never happened at all, except in your imagination. You didn't go anywhere. You just made a dream journey. You can dream you go to New York, and in that dream you can travel back to wherever your bed is, but when you wake up you immediately know that you never really took a journey. You slept in your room the whole time, without moving anywhere at all.

While you are dreaming about effort and *sadhana*, while you are pretending to do all these things, the Self is not doing anything at all. Self is Self, and it never moves anywhere or does anything. It never makes any effort, and it never goes out and comes back to itself. All these things go on in your imagination. The non-Self can never become the Self. The non-Self is the person who runs around looking for the Self, and imagines that he is having a tough time trying to reach his goal. Not through any amount of effort will the non-Self ever become the Self. The Self requires no effort to remain as it is. It just is.

Question: Yes, I can see that. I find that it requires an effort on my part to remain vigilant, to watch the rising thoughts. If I don't maintain that effort, that vigilance, I become seduced by the contents of the mind and forget the presence.

Papaji: Presence is what you are. Presence is the Self. Self is what you are, and you do not need to be vigilant to be what you are. You are already that. If you feel that you are not the Self, if you feel this, then you have to be vigilant when thoughts arise because those thoughts will take you away from the Self. They take you into the imaginary world of the non-Self. There, you have to start thinking about how to return home. If you choose this route, you will need to maintain some sort of vigilance to see how this thought of the non-Self arises. It rises from somewhere. If you can find that somewhere, the thought of non-Self will go back there and disappear.

Question: That was what I was getting confused about yesterday. I understood that I had become more and more seduced by the contents of the mind. I didn't want to use effort to solve this problem, yet at the same time I find that some effort is required in order to maintain vigilance. I want to be aware of the rising thoughts that take me away from the present so that I can stop associating with them and remain in the present. But the more I purposely chose to not use effort, the more I was seduced by the contents of the mind.

Papaji: For the concept of effort to arise in the mind, there must be a thought about it. Isn't that true? There is a thought that arises, that says to you, 'I need to make an effort'. Only after this thought has arisen will you decide to make some effort or ignore this thought. But even that is not the first thought, the primary thought. For the thought 'I need to make an effort' to arise, there must be an 'I' that has that thought. That 'I' is itself a thought. So, the first thought that arises is this 'I', which later decides whether you are going to make some effort or not.

This 'I'-thought is there. Let us see where it comes from. This situation has come up several times in the last few days. We have all been sitting here; someone has raised a question like this, and I have recommended as an answer that the questioner finds out and returns to that place where the 'I' first emerges. This is not something new that I am prescribing today. I have asked you all to work on this problem: to find out where that 'I' comes from, to follow it back to its originating point. I tell you all to do this because if you can find that point, that place in yourself where the 'I'-thought emerges, that 'I'-thought will disappear.

When that primary 'I'-thought goes back to its source and disappears, everything disappears along with it. In that moment you are the 'present' that you were talking about. You are then the Self. When you stay in that place and know it for yourself, that is the Self. That is freedom. From there, where do you have to go? What do you have to achieve? This place where the 'I' vanishes is wisdom. It is indescribable. No one has ever truly described what it is. In that place you won't need any effort. What possible effort can you make there?

This is the place where effort has not arisen even as a thought to be considered. Why should you let all these thoughts arise, thoughts that will compel you to choices and actions, thoughts that will keep you away from the Self?

What happens when you choose to leave that place? The 'I'-thought arises; the senses start collecting information and feeding it to the 'I'-thought. Then you start making choices about the perceptions and ideas that the 'I' is associating with. This whole process just propels you into trouble. Why do you need to let all this happen? Abide in that place where there is no thought of effort or non-effort, the place where even the thought 'I' has not risen. It's all quiet there. It is so quiet, words are an obstruction. When we speak, words arise and obstruct that silent flow of Self. The spontaneous flow of wisdom is obstructed by these words.

Question: Mind seems to have a momentum of its own. We can all agree with what you say, but that doesn't stop our minds from being persistently busy.

Papaji: Mind is the past. If you are present, you will not see the mind at all. In 'present' you can't see the mind at all. This 'present' has no valid description. It is just there if you don't look at the past.

Question: Mind wants to deal with things on its own terms. It likes to have a problem that it can figure out through thoughts and actions.

Papaji: This is the kind of talk that takes place before the honeymoon happens. Forget all these thoughts. Leave them all behind. When you enter the honeymoon chamber, everyone else has left. You go in there alone. Leave the world of words behind you and go in to meet your bride. Talk is over now. Face your bride. No one else is there.

35

Give up the mind's conviction that this is something that you 'do'

Question: I have a copy of that lovely poem by the third Zen Patriarch of China. Jim gave it to me. But there is one paragraph that I don't understand.

Papaji: This is the same one I read recently?

Question: Yes, the same one. This is the portion I don't understand. *[He shows the lines to Papaji, who read them out.]*

Papaji: Indeed, it is due to our choosing to accept or reject that we do not see the true nature of things.

This is the section you don't understand? Just these lines?

Question: I really don't understand what they mean.

Papaji: Let us say that you have a choice to accept something or reject it. You will accept it if you like it and reject it if you hate it. These are the two things that might happen.

Now, imagine that you are asleep, fast asleep in your bed. A beautiful, desirable woman comes into the room and sits on your bed. You don't see her as desirable; you don't desire her because you are fast asleep. She gets up and leaves. While she was there, you didn't accept her and you didn't reject her. She made no impression on you at all because your mind was not registering her and making choices about whether she was desirable or not.

Next, a man walks in who wants to quarrel with you. He is angry with you and he has come to have a fight. He sees you sleeping on the bed, waits awhile for you to wake up, and then goes away, thinking, 'I will come back and tell him what I think of him when he wakes up'.

You have neither accepted this man nor rejected him. The thoughts 'I will accept him' or 'I will reject him' couldn't arise in you because your mind was not there. You were fast asleep.

If you can keep your mind out of the way when you wake up, you can live the same way there as well. Someone comes and says, 'Oh, you're a very fine man!' Hear those words without having the mind jump up and be happy about them. And if the same person says, 'I hate you!', have the same non-reaction. I am not talking about a state in which you choose to ignore the insult, but still feel hurt and offended. I am talking about the state where the mind is not there to take delivery of the insult and react to it. If you can stay in that place, that state, you will be smiling when the compliments come and smiling when the insults come.

This is the state of waking sleep. It is like sleep in so far as the mind is absent, but there is a wakefulness there because you can still see the world and deal with it.

The moon is there in the sky. I can scream at it, or I can spit at it. I can worship it by throwing flowers at it and singing its praises. How is the moon affected by my actions? Not at all. It just carries on shining. We may behave well, or we may behave badly. We may quarrel or we may meditate. How is the moonlight affected by any of this? It is the same with emptiness. We are sitting in emptiness. Within these four walls there is emptiness. We may be meditating, or we may be doing something else. Whatever we are doing or not doing, the emptiness is not affected in any way. Our presence or our absence makes no difference to this emptiness, this space that exists within these four walls.

You are that emptiness in which all things appear and disappear. You are not any of them. Their activities and inactivities do not touch you. Their presence or their absence makes no difference to what you are. Always you are empty.

Question: When you put it that way, I completely understand.

Papaji: Nothing has ever entered there. Nothing can ever enter there. I am talking about a place where not even the thought 'I' can exist. An 'I' is needed to accept or reject. Until there is an existing 'I'-thought, there can be no acceptance and no rejection. This is the place where the 'I' cannot reside, not even as a first thought.

This 'I' is the source of not only the mind, it is also the source of the world and the creator of it. In that place, that state wherein the 'I' cannot exist, there is no creation and no creator. The created beings who make choices about accepting and rejecting are not there, and can never be there. The creator and his creation arise after the emergence of the 'I'. If the 'I' does not manifest, neither does the creator.

It is said, 'In the beginning was the word and the word was God'. That word, that name, comes out of this emptiness I am talking about. The emptiness of the Self exists prior to both. It is very silent there. Very silent.

Question: Can I ask a very practical question about this? A cobra suddenly jumps out in front of me in a place where I cannot run away. I am stuck in a corner with no possibility of flight. There's a split second in which I have options: I can kill it, ignore it, or let it kill me. Being philosophical about this doesn't solve the problem. I have a very real choice in that moment. What is this verse saying about situations like this? Do I just have to stand quietly and await developments? Am I not allowed to make a choice between living and dying?

Papaji: In a situation like this you don't make a choice that comes from rational consideration. You don't stand there thinking, 'If I do nothing, it will kill me'. Or, 'I must attack it before it attacks me'. In such circumstances a spontaneous action will come.

Question: Yes, I see what you mean.

Papaji: This intermediary thinking process that takes place between thought and action is absolutely foolish. It belongs to *samsara*, to karma. People in *samsara* think and then they act. And then they worry about what they have done afterwards. If you live in the Self, you act and forget. No thought prompts the action, and no thoughts analyse and judge the action after it has been completed. This is the difference. Act and forget. Kiss and forget. Slap and forget. This can only happen when you know your true nature.

To know the true nature of things, you must first know your own true nature. Knowing one's true nature is very simple. You just say to yourself, 'I am not the shirt'. Find out what is the real you, and what are merely the transient things that you own and associate with.

What is my true nature? It is not something that I can discard, something that comes and goes, something I cover myself up with. I can throw away the shirt and buy another one, so I know the shirt is not me. Underneath the shirt is my skin. If I experience a bad burn, I can have a skin graft and replace it. So I am not the skin either. I can have a bad accident that results in my hand being amputated. It may hurt for a while, but my true nature has not changed during the experience. It has not lost a hand, the body has.

We say, 'My house, my car, my wife, my body,' and so on. They are all possessions or relationships that come and go. They associate with you for a while and then they leave you. They are not permanent and enduring. They are not your true nature, that which never changes and which never comes and goes. Your true nature cannot be traded in for a new one when you get bored with it. It is not your possession; it is what you are.

Everything and everyone have to be abandoned at some point. All possessions and all relationships will leave you. No matter how much love you have for a person, how attached to that person you are, that person, that relationship, will go one day because it is not who you are. Who you are never goes, never leaves. A king of India built the Taj Mahal to enshrine his love for his dead wife. She was the love of his life, but the relationship ended and left him.

So what is your true nature? It is 'I am'. Not 'I am this' or 'I am that'. Not the 'I' that owns a house or has a relationship with a wife. Just 'I am', with nothing attached to it, or identified with it.

We were talking about the 'I'-thought earlier. This 'I'-thought is the first thought, the thought that causes the world and the creator of it to jump into existence. This 'I'-thought is not your real nature because it is always attached to something. It is always claiming 'I am this' or 'I am that'. It is not your real nature because it is not permanent. It rises, plays for a while, and then vanishes. If you want to know what your true nature is, you will have to go to that place where the 'I' rises. Go to the place where it takes birth. What is the source of this great fountain, this energy that rushes up and displays itself as the mind, the world and God? Go there and see for yourself. I cannot describe it and I cannot take you there. But if you arrive at this place where the 'I'-thought disappears, you will find out what you really are, what your true nature is. Always you are that. When you abide in that place without an 'I', what will you accept and what will you reject?

When you know that truth, you know that any other perspective is false. We can argue about what is true and what is false, but when you get to this place, you will know for yourself.

Question: My mind….

Papaji: 'My mind'! You are back in relationships again.

Question: I call it my mind. What else can I do? I see this thing I call my mind and watch it with disgust. It is like watching someone run into a living room and defecate. I feel that this mind runs into the living room of 'presence' and defecates there, and I am embarrassed and disgusted because I seem to have no control over it at all. I know what's going on. I watch it, but I can't stop it.

Papaji: These are all old habits manifesting themselves. Old habits are the past, a graveyard of dead thoughts and impressions. Everyone is living in a graveyard that is made up of all their old habits.

Question: Let's go back to the cobra. The cobra jumps up; an instant decision is made, whatever it might be. Does that decision leave an imprint on the mind?

Papaji: That kind of action is just a reaction. It is an automatic response – kill it or run away – that doesn't come from any thought processes. You take spontaneous dictation at times like this, and the body responds accordingly. This kind of reaction is not going to land in your mind and stick there.

When I was young, still in the Punjab, I saw a mother who had a baby that was in a cradle. A snake had crawled into the cradle and curled itself up there next to the baby. It was winter and it may have felt that it had found a warm place to sleep. The child was kicking its legs in the spontaneous way that babies do, but the snake didn't seem to be bothered by it. The mother was afraid to approach the cradle in case she startled the snake into a reaction. Since her husband was at work, she called in some of the neighbours.

We all watched the scene for a while and eventually it was decided that the snake and the baby would be left alone. The snake had been there for almost an hour and hadn't showed any hostile intentions. We all left quietly and the baby was left alone by the snake. The baby never felt that the snake was an enemy, a danger that needed a quick reaction of some sort. He neither accepted nor rejected the snake because he didn't have a mind that could do either. He just carried on doing what he normally did: lying there and kicking occasionally.

I remember another incident like this. There was a very young girl from Norway who used to meditate on the banks of the Ganga. This was a long time ago. She lived like a *sadhu* and even used to go begging for her food. Some of the local Indian families used to fill her begging bowl when she went on her rounds. A retired couple used to feed her most of the time. I used to take her fruits once in a while, because when you live on begged food, you don't usually get a very healthy diet. One day, when I went to see her, she was meditating by the river with her eyes closed. A big snake, maybe six feet long, had crawled over her and part of it was resting on her hand. I decided not to disturb her because I knew that the snake might react if she suddenly jumped up. This girl used to meditate for hours at a time. Sometimes she would sit for four hours without moving. I watched her sit with her eyes closed for about an hour, unaware of what was going on. At the end of that time, the snake stirred itself and slowly crawled away. She carried on meditating. She hadn't been aware that the snake had come, and she hadn't been aware that it had left.

When she finally opened her eyes, I gave her the fruits and told her what had happened. She had no idea that a snake had been sitting on her. At first she didn't believe me, but then I showed her the line that the snake had left. She had been sitting on a sandy beach, and the snake had left a clear trail when it came and left.

Anyway, to go back to your question, when you have an encounter like this, the response comes instantly and automatically. Where these instant reactions come from, I do not know. They just come. And when they do, such reactions don't stick to you.

Question: I am surprised that you say that you don't know where such decisions come from. Don't enlightened people know where their reactions come from? Would not someone like the Buddha know where such decisions came from?

Papaji: I don't know. But I don't think he would have left his wife if he had sat by her bed and considered the matter with his mind. She was a beautiful woman and he was in love with her. Some impulse arose from within, and in response he just got up and left. This kind of impulse is so strong. When it happens, you don't know where it comes from. You don't think about it, you just obey it.

> Live neither in the entanglements of outer things
> nor in inner feelings of emptiness.

This is *samsara* and nirvana. Don't be attached either to forms or to the emptiness that underlies them. Entanglements with outer things means getting caught up in things that have forms. At the same time be careful that you don't get attached to ideas about emptiness. Don't accept or reject either of them.

> Be serene in the oneness of things,
> and such erroneous views will disappear by themselves.

If you behave like this, everything will take care of itself. Most people, when they try to stop activity or work, are still working because 'When you try to stop activity and achieve passivity, your very effort fills you with activity'.

Question: *[new questioner]* In themselves there is nothing unskilled about either activity or passivity. It's the effort involved in them that taints them.

Papaji: Now you are making an effort to uphold or reject some theory.

Question: That's true, but I am talking like this because of a small thing that happened this morning. I woke up very early. It seemed like a beautiful day, and at first I just lay in my bed enjoying it. Then I made a resolve to sit in meditation for half an hour because that is something I have been told I should do. After five minutes it didn't really seem to be worthwhile, so I went for an early morning walk in the Botanical Gardens instead. The resolve disappeared, but I was still very quiet and peaceful. Is it not this choice to make an effort that causes the trouble?

Papaji: Yes.

[Long pause]

Anyway, all this is beyond language.

[Another long pause]

Let us suppose that you are proceeding from here, from where you are right now, to a destination, a goal. You have come to this place; it's as far as you can go. In front of you is this vastness, this emptiness. You can call it 'presence' if you want to. You can call it anything you like. You have brought your mind with you to this place, and as your mind contemplates this vastness, it keeps up its old habits of describing and understanding. It wants to see this vastness as an object it can describe and understand. This is how the mind functions; it needs outside objects to see, outside objects that can validate its understanding. The effort is still there, and this effort attempts to feed the mind with this thing called 'understanding'. This experience, though, is not complete. In fact, the real experience is not there at all. All you have is a mind that is maintaining itself, maintaining its dualistic view. This is the nature of the mind: it organises all the information it receives in such a way that it can come to the conclusion that its world view of a perceiver and a perceived is the only valid one.

You have to stop contemplating this emptiness, this vastness, from outside, because while you are outside it, it will just be another idea that keeps the mind busy. Step into this emptiness, without thinking about it in any way. How? Give up the mind's conviction that this is something that you 'do'. You can't lift a foot and walk into it because there are no physical dimensions there. You can't do it by an act of will, by deciding to do it, because while such thoughts are active, you are in the mind and not in emptiness. You have been cheated by the imagination of the mind which thinks that this is a problem that can be solved by thinking or doing. Imagination has to end. It has to end at this point where you first contemplate the vastness in front of you. Everything you see, hear, feel, think, and taste is just your imagination playing with itself. It has to end here, and it has to end for good. All *samsara*, billions of years of past and future imagination, this everlasting imagination of the mind, is just taking place in an instant. All *samsara* is just an expanded moment of imagination that ends up making us believe that the millions of years of experiences we go through are real. This is the ultimate truth that you have to come to by stopping this imagination that makes you dream of worlds and lives and efforts geared towards liberation.

Question: I'm painfully aware that what you say is true. I can understand that all this is sustained by my habit of thinking, choosing, deciding, understanding, and so on. But knowing this doesn't flick the 'off' switch in my head. I make decisions, and I know that I make decisions, but I am not even sure who is making these decisions. That's how ignorant I am of what is going on inside me.

Papaji: You don't take any decisions at all. You just think you do. You think your mind is taking all these decisions, but that idea is also part of your imagination. Something else is compelling you to do the things that you do, but you are not aware of it. You will not be aware of it while you engage in the thought process. You need to find that place of no thought, no imagination, the place of no effort. Find it, and there will be no return. Instantly it will happen, but it won't happen while you are thinking, or trying not to think. Without thinking or understanding, you have to find this place of no thought, and stay there.

36

Drop the idea that you are on a route to a destination

Papaji: *[speaking to someone in front of him]* Here you are, standing in front of emptiness. You have arrived at the last place, the last piece of land that you can put your foot on. You can't lift up your foot and plant it any nearer. It's all emptiness around you now. What can effort do for you now? Physical movement will not help you. Mental effort and imagination will not help you. Relegate imagination to the past. It's over. Let it be. You are here, and everything in front of you is just emptiness. What is to be done now?

Question: No judgement, no energy, no effort.

Papaji: Yes, it's the end of all this.

Question: 'Just fall into the emptiness.' I want to do it, but there is still a residual doubt that it can happen to me.

Papaji: That will hold you back. You are still making an effort to hold on to doubt. This doubt belongs to the past.

Question: *[new questioner]* It's like making an effort to hold onto a cliff instead of letting go and dropping.

Papaji: Don't involve thought or effort or imagination in this decision to drop. Let it happen by itself, without the thinking process.

Question: It sounds simple.

Papaji: It *is* simple. It only gets complicated when you start to think about it and wonder how you can accomplish it.

Question: When one reaches this edge, this place where one can't take another step, should one continue with the enquiry at this point?

Papaji: No. Drop the idea that you are on a route to a destination.

Question: No destination?

Papaji: Nothing at all. Have no relationship to anything at all. Don't touch any kind of relationship.

When you don't touch any relationship, you will find yourself in a place that people have used many words to describe, without success. I will add some good ones. 'Amazement' is one of them. You feel 'ridiculous'. That's another one that people don't use. You suddenly understand how stupid you have been, how wilfully blind, and your past stupidity suddenly seems very ridiculous. 'Dumbfounded' is another word that I like because you are suddenly aware that it is nothing like what you thought it might be.

Question: When I return home, I have to write a report for my university on how I spent my time here. *[Everyone in the room laughs]*

Papaji: His university let him come here for five months, but he has to tell them what he has done with his time when he goes home.

One other man wanted to come and see me about fifteen years ago. He was a maths professor, and he asked his university for a month's leave to come to India to see me, but the application was refused.

This man was determined to come so he said, 'If you don't give me permission I will resign and go anyway. You are not going to stop me by refusing this application.'

When his university realised that it couldn't keep him at work, it gave him a one year leave of absence. He was apparently a brilliant mathematician and his university didn't want to let him go. It gave him a bit of work to do, but he told me it was something he could do in a couple of hours. That was a good exchange for a year in India.

Your university has also given you time to come here. You will have to write something to prove you have not wasted your time. Start with the joy of being ridiculous. *[Everyone laughs again]* You can write a very good book if you start from this place.

37

The power that you are absorbed in looks after you

Question: There seem to be two ways of reacting in the world. One is spontaneous, and the other is acting through the mind.

Papaji: You are always acting independently of the mind, but your thoughts make you think otherwise. It is just an old habit to think that the mind decides what you do. Actions will go on whether you think about them or not. You don't need a mind to work or perform actions; you just think you do. When the mind is not present, work is done efficiently; very efficiently. I can cite my own experiences on this subject, and I have to cite them because not many other people seem to talk about this subject. I will tell you a story that comes from my own experience. It is not something I have picked up second-hand.

It took place in 1954. I was loading up a ship with manganese ore that was destined for Amsterdam. It was what is called 'offshore loading', which means that the transfer of the ore did not take place in the port. I took a boat out to the ship and spent the whole day with the captain of the ship. When the ship had been loaded to everyone's satisfaction, the hatches were closed. I received a certificate of delivery from the captain and a bank draft from the purchaser. I wanted to go back to my headquarters in Bangalore to deliver the draft in person, but it was already 11 p.m. at night and the distance from the port of Mangalore to Bangalore was over 300 miles. It was not an easy drive either. The first section was a difficult and slow mountain road that had many dangerous curves.

Since my company wanted the money urgently, I decided to drive through the night and then have a short nap on the other side of the mountains. I had had a hard day, and I knew that if I slept on the Mangalore side of the mountains, I would wake up late and not get to Bangalore until very late in the day. This mountain road had eleven hairpin bends, and it rose from sea level to over 5,000 feet before descending to the plains on the other side. There was a well-known coffee house on the other side of the hill that all the truck drivers used to use. There was nowhere else to stop on the way. Landslides were common, and there were even elephants that would occasionally wander onto the road and block the traffic. It was a narrow road with a steep drop on one side. If an elephant appeared in front of you, you needed to keep your distance and wait for it to wander off. If you annoyed one of these elephants and made it charge you, there was nowhere to run away to.

The most difficult section of the road was about ten miles long, and one needed to be very alert to navigate it safely, especially in the middle of the night. What happened? I fell asleep at the wheel, even before I reached this dangerous section, and when I woke up, I was off the mountains, and well on the way to Bangalore. I calculated that I must have driven about 50 km while I was asleep, navigating many tight bends on the way. When I woke up on the Bangalore road, I felt completely refreshed. I knew I had had a very good night's sleep. Once I woke up, I realised that I didn't need any more rest or sleep. Being completely refreshed, I was able to drive all the way to Bangalore without taking another break. Who was driving this car while the body slept in it? Even today I still ponder this question, this mystery. Something was looking after me, making the unconscious body do the right things at the right time. There was no mind and no body involved, no one who thought, 'I must be careful as I drive round this bend'.

I can tell you another story, not as extreme as this one, but it is still interesting. I arrived in Lucknow in 1947 from the Punjab. I was working because I had to support all the relatives who had come with me from what is now Pakistan. I occasionally used to get absorbed in states in which I wasn't really aware of what was going on outside me. I would walk around and get things done, without ever being really aware of what the body was doing. I wasn't even noticing what was happening around me, but it didn't matter. Something was looking after me, keeping the body safe and making it do what it had to do.

The same thing used to happen while I was working in Madras. I would walk from Mylapore to Mount Road, and even though I tried to pay attention to the traffic, I would find that outer awareness would disappear. I would find myself at my destination with no memory of crossing several roads.

I did have one accident though, and that was in Lucknow around 1948. I was walking from Lalbagh to the Post Office at Hazratganj when I was knocked down by a car that speeded past. In those days there were still prewar cars on the road that had running boards, those flat pieces of metal that used to stick out on the sides so that people could stand on them and ride on the outside of the car. I was hit by an old Ford that hit me from behind so hard, the running board detached itself and came off. When I realised what had happened to me, I saw it lying next to me on the road. Prior to the accident I had been in one of these states of absorption I was telling you about, so I don't remember anything about the accident myself. I was given all the details afterwards by the people who crowded around my felled body in the street. It was a hit-and-run job, they said, and all the people assumed that I must have been badly injured because I had been hit hard by a speeding car. I stood up, though, completely unharmed. There was a tear in my pants, but when I rolled up the leg to see what the damage was underneath, there was just a small graze. The spectators all wanted to take me off to the nearest police station to make a report, but, since I had not been injured, I ignored all their suggestions.

These have been my experiences. Not only can you live and

work without a mind, you can also live and work without any awareness of the outside world at all. Who will take care of you? The power that you are absorbed in looks after you. It gives dictation, and the body obeys its instructions. This is a way of living that you have to experience by yourself. It is not something that you can practise.

Some time back we had a discussion about the reactions one has when a snake suddenly appears. When you are in this state, you will not have to think about what to do, or ask others for advice. The right response will come spontaneously and automatically. There will be no doubts or thoughts at all.

Question: When you were working in the mines, there must have been lots of things that you had to think about. Appointments, accounts, papers to go through, and so on. How do you manage a job like this if you don't think or plan or organise your time?

Papaji: *[laughing]* It's like driving that car in the night. Something makes you do the right thing at the right time, even if you are not aware of what you are doing or why you are doing it. I have had many experiences like this.

Question: *[new questioner]* We had a discussion like this some time ago. Actually, it was a long time ago. You mentioned three different kinds of reactions. This car incident – being hit by a car while being unaware of either the vehicle or the body – was one of the three types you mentioned. I was hit by a rickshaw in the bazaar some time ago. I got up, turned round and my instant reaction was anger because I wasn't in the middle of the road. I was in a place where the rickshaw shouldn't have been. Then, without really thinking about it, the anger subsided. I realised there was no point in getting angry, so the anger just subsided and disappeared. That was the second type of reaction. There was a third type of response in which you get really angry with the person who has hurt you and respond by shouting at him or even hitting him. These were the three types you talked about.

Papaji: Yes, I remember talking about that. In one case there is no one to react. In the second there is a brief reaction, after which you return to your normal state, and in the third, you lose control of your emotions. Being hit by the car comes into the first category.

Question: I know it's not the same thing, but many years ago, when I used to be a heavy drinker, I occasionally used to black out – have periods when I knew nothing at all. Though I would have no memory of these states later, I could safely drive a car in them, and later have no recollection of having done this. These states can last for an hour or more. You can do complicated things well. People who watch you doing them have no idea that you are drunk, and afterwards you have no memory of having performed any of these actions.

I read somewhere that people who get into these states, through drugs or alcohol, are making a kind of secret appeal to the Self to take them over and be responsible for their actions. It's not actually a conscious desire for drunken oblivion, but an unconscious desire to reconnect with the Self that takes you over when you can no longer take care of yourself. I don't suppose you would agree with this.

Papaji: No, you can't reach the Self through these methods. These are states in which the unconscious mind can look after you, but they are still subtle states of mind.

The mind can have extraordinary powers, but they are still in the mental realm. I was living and working in Bombay in 1932. One of my neighbours came to see me and said, 'My cousin has come from Saurashtra. He is only sixteen years old, and there is a prediction that he will only live to be eighteen. His case has been taken up by one of the Maharajas of the princely states in that area because he has remarkable powers. He is taking him to London at his own expense.'

'What's so special about him?' I asked.

'You can ask him any question you like, and he will give you the correct reply. The right answer automatically comes to him and he says it. And if you write something and put it in your pocket, he can tell you what is on the piece of paper, even if he has never seen it before. You can come and see him and test him if you don't believe me.'

I have always been interested in cases like this, but at the same time I tend to be very sceptical. I like to test such people to make sure that they are not cheating.

I thought to myself, 'This boy is from Saurashtra. I will put a Persian poem in my pocket, in the original Persian script, and see what he makes of it.'

I went along to see him. There were many people crowding around him, thinking that they could get answers to future events.

'My wife is pregnant. Will it be a boy or a girl?'

'I made a business deal last week. Will I show a good profit from it?'

My neighbours were soaking up his words, and believing every one of them.

When there was a break in the questioning, I asked, 'I have a paper in my pocket. Can you read what is written on it?'

Without hesitation, the boy recited the Persian poem, a language he didn't know, and he did it with a good Persian accent.

I asked him, 'How did you learn to do this?'

He said, 'I didn't learn. Nobody taught me. I just found out I could do these things. I don't know where the words come from. People ask me things, the words come out of my mouth, and they are always the right ones.'

These are mental tricks, *siddhis* that either come naturally or can be acquired by effort. They are not a consequence of the no-mind state that I was talking about.

Question: I didn't know you read Persian. When did you learn?

Papaji: It was a compulsory subject at school. In the Punjab there are strong cultural ties to Persia. To get a job in the government, you had to pass exams in both Urdu and Persian, so everyone was taught these subjects at school. I liked Persian, so I kept it up after I left school. I had a Persian poetry book with me in

Bombay because I liked reading Persian poetry. Swamiji [Swami Ramanananda] still sometimes sends me Persian poems from Tiruvannamalai.

Question: Do you still read stuff like this? Do you still have the time and the inclination to read poetry?

Papaji: I don't have so much time nowadays, and I didn't really have much time then either. I was very busy earning a living.

Question: Maybe it was your good luck that you didn't have time for reading. You didn't have time to fill your mind with ideas.

Papaji: I was born in a place where there was little or no literature about freedom. I came from a cultured, well-read family, but books on this subject were simply not available. We were a small brahmin enclave in a predominantly Muslim area. The only religious talk was about Islam and mosques. We didn't even have many Hindu rituals. I think this was good because I might otherwise have got lost in books and rituals. Nobody ever told me, 'You must do this practice or that practice'. That background was not there.

Question: *[from the man who had to write about his visit]* Which part of India was that?

Papaji: A part of the Punjab that is now in Pakistan.

[Pause]

Words can take you away from the Self if you get caught up in them, but if you follow them back to where they originated, they can also take you back to the Self. You see something written on a page. Before it was written it was a word in someone's mind. For that word to have emerged, there must have been a prior thought of it. From where has this word been taken? From where has it been stolen? From silence. Why not go back to the silence, the ocean of silence from where all words have to emerge? The formulation of words in the mind is actually an impediment to an experience of this silence. The silence is there all the time, but when a word forms, you are obstructing the flow of this inner silence. There is a silent flow that is going on between us, but if you utter a word, you will lose the contact with that flow. Listen, and be watchful. That's all you have to do.

Can you write about this in your report? This is a true teaching, a true understanding, but what can you write about it? Anything you add to this, any words that you use to describe it, are a falsity. They will be false; not the truth. Even the word 'silence' is false. Just keep silence; don't talk about it.

All obstructions, all manifestation, arise from 'I'. Fear, everything that appears in front of you, past, present and future, all these things come from this one word 'I'. It has to come from somewhere. Why not go to that place yourself and see what is there? Find where this word 'I' comes from and all will be over. Everyone can do this, but no one can help you. No efforts will take you there, and no one can tell you what it is. You don't need anything to find that place.

Question: Why are we sitting here if we don't need help?

Papaji: To hear what I am saying. No one has told you this before. Why are you sitting here? To hear me say, 'Don't sit "there", sit "here"'. This is why you come: to find out how to sit 'here' and not 'there'.

Question: *[new questioner]* It's fun being here. It beats being anywhere else.

Papaji: You have come here to be here. You have come here and nowhere else. Who else will tell you this? Everyone else will tell you, 'Go there! Go there! Go there!' A teacher who tells you to do something or go somewhere doesn't deserve to be a teacher. If he tells you to do something, to make some effort that will produce results sometime in the future, he is not a true teacher at all. What shall we call him? He is a preacher. The teacher, if we want to use that word at all, is sitting in silent truth. We speak about truth by being in that silence. Silence is your teacher, here, now, within you. If you want a teacher, this is the teacher. If you want *satsang*, this is *satsang*. Where else will you go for *satsang*? Come 'here'. 'Here' means silence. Not even a single thought should stir in this silence. This is *satsang*, association with your own Self. True *sanga* is to remain as you are. If you can do this, this is *satsang*.

Question: *[new questioner]* It's here.

Papaji: Association with the Self is alone *satsang*. Nothing else deserves the name. See for yourself. When you are with the Self, there is no one to cheat you, no one to mislead you. There is no misleading, no cheating, no speaking, nothing but truth itself. That place where there is no duality at all is called *satsang*. Going anywhere else except 'here' will not help you. Try it and see. Go to the gods, and they will try to fool you.

They will say, 'Worship me, and I will give you what you want'.

These are the promises of the gods. Why should you listen to them and do their bidding? Why don't you have this *satsang* instead? When is the time when you are not having *satsang*? Tell me! When is the time when you are not having *satsang*?

Question: There's no time. There's no time that is not *satsang*.

Papaji: *[laughing]* Here you are! This is *satsang*! *Satsang* must always be there, continuously, otherwise it's not *satsang*.

Question: *[apparently having the satsang experience that Papaji had been speaking of]* You're right. It's 'ridiculous'.

Papaji: *[laughing]* He is very beautiful!

Question: So are you.

Papaji: This is *satsang*! This is *satsang*! I want to kiss you. He's in a very nice state. Let me see your face. This is a face I can kiss.

Question: *[laughing]* It's not going to work.

38

Mind is the transactions that take place between the subject and the objects you retrieve from the past

Papaji: *[reading out a letter]*

> *I am thirty-two years old and luckily married to a man I love. I have a still unfulfilled dream to be a writer. This is the second letter that I have written to you. The first was just to find out myself, but I want to know this from you. I realise that my life has a momentum that is already determined by circumstances, by the history of my family, place and time, where I was born, and so on. It has been lived much more within the western understanding of things. I have understood from this western understanding that there is no space for freedom at all because here one is constantly subject to society's laws. I realise that all this is 'not me', even though part of me is good both at understanding these laws and dealing with the circumstances that one usually calls 'reality'. Though my life has been built upon them, from somewhere else I hear a voice that has*

nothing to do with this life and these circumstances. It is as if a spirit from outside has chosen me and wants to use me for some purpose. This purpose is to find and communicate truth.

This 'something' comes to people. As she says, it picks people when they are ready to listen to what it has to say. Everyone has some background. You can see this very clearly from this letter.

In my everyday language I can say I want to become a writer and communicate my message, the content of which I can only vaguely define. It gains shape when the spirit leads me, but my circumstances are such that the part of me that lives with the real world occupies most of the time. It feels as if it is afraid to let go and let something else in. My wish is to connect myself with this spirit, which I feel is my own source, but which at the same time is a universal source. I want to make it the force that leads my life and uses its capacities to bring its voice into the world. What do I have to do? I ask myself, but then a voice speaks to me: 'I am here. I am here. I can tell you what you have to do. You only have to remain in touch with me. I want to speak through you. That is why I am here.'

This woman doesn't know what she is writing, but she is translating the experience very well.

[The voice says:] 'I have no name. I have no form. I have no message. I am. I am truth. I am truth itself. I am and am not. I have no voice. I have no language, but I talk. I appear here and now, but I exist beyond space, beyond time. I cannot be understood, but you will understand me if you will look right now into the eyes of Poonjaji. If you look right now into the eyes of Poonjaji you will know that I am within both of you.'

This is what happened to me when I wrote my first letter to you. The moment I asked a question, the answer was there. My mind was suddenly empty, instantly filled with shining consciousness, total awareness, liberating non-attachment. I remained in this state for many hours. It vanished gradually over a period of several days.

The experience described in my first letter is still in the background of my everyday consciousness. I want to get access to it again and again. I feel an encounter with you could be the next step on my way. I would love to visit you for about a week in the beginning of December. Dear Poonjaji, I'm looking forward to your answer and send you my best wishes.

Question: I can see that everything I think and perceive has some element of mind. You are asking me to drop the mind. I want what you want, but it's not happening to me. You have set up this teaching inside me, and sometimes I feel I am about to burst with it. And all the time I feel I just want to go home to the Self.

Papaji: You are at home.

Question: The mind appreciates the truth of that statement, but the knowledge of being 'home' doesn't arise in me.

Papaji: Yes. This appreciation will only take place when you do really know that you are home. The mind will celebrate its own death. It will no more be the mind. There will be a real celebration when you are reborn into your own home.

Question: I'm waiting for that step to happen. Meanwhile, I find that whatever comes up inside me is still mind. It is the mind appreciating ideas about the Self, or looking for the Self, or describing itself to itself.

Papaji: Yes. Mind is mind when it clings to any object, any object from the past. Mind is the transactions that take place between the subject and the objects you retrieve from the past. However, there is a place within you where that transaction doesn't take place. That is the place of celebration.

You live in the mind, in its thoughts. Because your world is circumscribed by the mind, and because you can't think or know anything that lies beyond the mind, you don't even have a word for what is prior to all this mental activity.

Mind takes you back to the past through the senses that are always clinging to affairs of the past. Everything you see is a creation of the mind, and mind is always in the past. In the present moment, where time does not exist, mind does not exist either. Find where mind comes from, watch it disappear in that place, and you will discover that time disappears along with it. The disappearance of the mind is not something that you should be worried about. You will manage very well without it. In that place I am speaking of, the word 'mind' won't exist, and nor will any other word. You don't need words to be yourself, to speak to yourself. When the words arise, they take you away from the Self. Words are always an obstruction, a barrier, a hindrance to your own silence. When you enjoy yourself in your true home, no word enters to describe it or interfere with it. It is a continuous flow, uninterrupted by words or time.

This is a place of transcendence. No one speaks of it. Words don't apply to it or describe it. The Buddhists have a nice word in their dictionary that points towards it. Have you heard of '*tathata*'? Usually it is translated as 'suchness'. Something that just is as it is. If you want to use a word at all, you can use a word like this. One that doesn't put new concepts in your mind; one that just points or hints at this underlying truth.

Does anyone here with a Buddhist background know more about this word? It's a nice one.

Question: *[new questioner]* Yes, it means 'suchness'. There is also a term, '*tathagata*', that the Buddha used to describe himself as 'the one who has gone beyond'.

Papaji: Yes, I have heard both words before. I don't know Pali, so

I can't really comment on these words with any great authority. 'Thus come' is another translation I have heard of this term. It is a reference to this instant, this present moment.

The Buddhists say, 'Gone, gone, gone beyond…'. You go to the other shore; then you go beyond the other shore; and then you go beyond the beyond. As you move towards the other shore, you are still in duality, still in the mind. You can contemplate your direction and your destination, but to finish the mind, you have to go 'beyond the beyond', past that place you can fix in your mind.

There is another word that is used to denote this moment, this situation when mind has gone. It is the exclamation '*Swaha!*' that follows the disappearance of the mind in the formless beyond. I have asked many people about this word without getting any satisfactory replies. This is the last utterance of the mind as it disappears, or the utterance that comes when mind has actually gone. It has no particular meaning. Mind cannot grasp or describe this state, so the word that comes from that place cannot be given a meaning that can be understood by the mind.

After the awakening, the utterance is there. What can we cling to in that place? Who or what can cling to the wisdom, the enlightenment, the emancipation, the freedom that is there? Even this word is useless there. Everything is finished here. *Samsara* and nirvana have gone, because they exist in relation to each other. The mind ends; manifestation ends; the creator ends; creation ends. The 'indweller' has gone entirely. This is the total release from the mind, from the never-ending cycle of birth, death and manifestation. It happens in an instant.

39

There have been instances in which a single vision changed and transformed a person's life

Question: I was sitting in my room last night and there was a very beautiful energy there. Suddenly, I had a very strong feeling, a very strong sense that Ramana was in the room. I didn't see him; it just felt like a very strong presence. It felt so real while it was happening, but afterwards I started to wonder if this was some sort of hallucination.

Papaji: You had a vision of someone who is free, liberated. Even if you didn't actually see a physical form, it is still a kind of vision. A liberated being came to you in the form of a presence that appeared to be pure and subtle thought. But when you returned to your old foolish mind, you interpreted the meaning in the context of your past training and called it a vision. And then you doubted it and called it 'a hallucination'.

Question: The reason I am asking this question is that whenever I meditate in a place that is associated with a particular spiritual figure, I tend to see images of that person. When I was in Dharamsala, I saw the Buddha, and when I was in some Christian places, I saw Jesus. That's what I am wondering: if these events are hallucinations, or something else.

Papaji: The outer dress, the form of the vision, may be different, but the power behind them is the same. You can dismiss such things as 'hallucinations', but there have been instances in which a single vision changed and transformed a person's life.

There was a diamond merchant whose wife used to give away all his wealth as alms to whichever beggars came to her door. This so annoyed the merchant, he took to locking up all his valuables whenever he went out. Whenever he left home, he would lock up the whole house except for the kitchen in an attempt to prevent his wife from giving away all his wealth.

One day, while he was out of the house, working in his shop, a brahmin priest came to the door and asked for alms. His wife had nothing to give him apart from the jewellery she was wearing.

She took off one of her earrings and said to him, 'Take this and sell it. You can use the money to look after yourself for a while.'

The priest gratefully accepted it, but when he went to sell it, he ended up in the shop of the diamond merchant whose wife had given him the earring. The earring had a diamond in it, so the priest had just taken it to the nearest diamond merchant. Since the merchant knew that his wife wore identical earrings, his first thought was that this priest must have stolen the earring from her. However, he didn't want to make any accusations before he had any proof. He took the priest back to his house and asked his wife if she could produce the earrings that she normally wore.

His wife, who did not want her husband to know that she had been giving away valuable jewellery to a complete stranger, told him that she still had them both and that they were in their *puja* room. Since the husband never went there, she thought she could safely say that they were there.

However, on this occasion the husband insisted on checking. They went to the *puja* room and found both earrings in a small pot that contained an offering to the deity. The family deity was Vittal, Lord Krishna. The merchant went back to his shop, satisfied that the priest was not a thief.

The meeting with the priest somehow transformed the diamond merchant. The events of the day changed him from being a miserly businessman who begrudged his wife's charitable activities to a man who no longer had any interest in money or material possessions. He sat in his shop for some time before coming to a momentous conclusion.

'These diamonds are not bringing me any happiness. They just make me a miserable and worried man. I will renounce the world of possessions and profits and become a *sannyasin*.'

He closed his shop, went home and announced to his wife that he had decided to renounce the world and live as a wandering monk.

This is not some fictional children's tale that I am telling you. This is the true story of a saint, Purandara Dasa, who even today is widely revered in Karnataka. Books have been written about this story; even films have been made about the events which happened that day. Purandara Dasa left home and became one of the most famous saints of Karnataka. He also became well known as a Carnatic musician, and the songs he composed are still widely sung today.

You could say that the merchant 'hallucinated' an earring in his wife's *puja* room that wasn't really there, but I prefer to regard this as a life-transforming vision. When something like this happens, the power of the Self is interceding in your life to push you in a new direction. A true vision is one that changes your life. Some versions of the story say that it was Krishna himself who took the form of the priest to bring about the transformation of the miserly merchant.

You could take some drug and have hallucinations that tigers are attacking you. When you get back to normal, you haven't been changed or transformed, you are just happy that you are no longer under the influence of a hallucinatory drug. A true vision compels you to move away from an old life to a new life. Its effect is purifying and long-lasting.

You can see demons and monsters that fill you with fear, but how many people can say that they have seen the divine in a vision, and that this vision has transformed them? Very few. To have a true vision of the divine you need to have a very sattvic mind. A divine, transforming vision can only manifest to an utterly pure mind. To such a mind an image of God can appear, an image that is so strong, the mind itself will disappear. The vision appears to that pure mind, and in response that pure mind dissolves and disappears. The mind will disappear, and the vision that prompted its disappearance will disappear along with it.

Question: I feel that a message came to me while I was having this vision. An instruction to do something. Should I trust it? Should I do what it says?

Papaji: Did you write it down at the time it happened?

Question: No.

Papaji: You should have. These visions take place in a state that is neither waking, nor dreaming nor sleeping. These kinds of communications are worth noting down. Because the mind is not working normally in that state, it may not later remember accurately what was going on.

40

This fire of knowledge will bring about understanding and knowledge

Question: I feel I have an incredible grace in my life. I have everything I could ask for, but even so old habits still persist, and I don't know how to facilitate the process of just letting them go. They tend to be very subtle things, old frames of mind, or certain emotional patterns. That kind of thing.

Papaji: What you need to eliminate is not the habits themselves but the sense of doership that attaches itself to them. Habits, by themselves, are not harmful. What is harmful is the idea, 'I have these habits' or, 'I am performing these activities'. Habits will continue after enlightenment. They will not obstruct the enlightenment because they are just patterns of behaviour that the body has been programmed to do. You have a store, a warehouse full of activities that you have to undertake. That is the destiny of the body, and while it continues to live, it will fulfil that destiny. When doership goes, you will no longer be interested in what the body does or doesn't do. In that moment of enlightenment there will be a conflagration that will burn up your sense of doership. Along with it the store of karma for future lives will also be burned, bringing your incarnations to an end. This fire of knowledge will bring about understanding and knowledge. It will burn so thoroughly, tendencies will no longer land in the memory and be the cause of future karma and future lives. The mind will be burned, and when that happens there will be no place to store the tendencies, desires and habits.

If you have attained this state, the various habits will continue, but they will not plant seeds that have to be harvested as future lives and future karma. Your life and its destined script will be like a bullet that has been fired from a gun. The initial velocity of the bullet causes it to travel a certain distance and then drop to the ground. Afterwards, it will not jump up and rush off again. The destiny of a life in which the mind has died is like the momentum of this bullet. It will carry the person to the end of his physical life, but after that the body will die, and there will be no more rebirth.

Question: The habits already seem to be less strong than before. They don't seem to have the force they used to.

Papaji: When freedom comes, all these things will seem like a dream, something distant that doesn't really touch you. Some reactions may be there, problems will come and be dealt with, but they will not make deep roots that will cause you suffering or bring about future reactions.

Question: I can sometimes feel that this is happening.

Papaji: When doership is absent, suffering will also be absent. Doership will die at the moment that freedom arises.

Question: You said earlier that I was 'committed' to these habits. That's how it feels sometimes.

Papaji: 'Commitments' are to something that belongs to the past. These impressions which are responsible for your current birth all come from your past. They have brought you suffering and a continuous sense of doership, but it is not all negative. There is a credit side as well as a debit side. You must have been working towards freedom in your past or you would not be here today. You may not think that you have been very successful, but unless you have millions of merits accumulated from past lives, the thought

'I want to be free' could not arise in you, and you would not be here today asking these questions. It has been said that you need a mountain of merits the size of Mount Meru before this desire can arise in you. From where has this desire 'I want to be free' arisen? This desire is a beautiful desire, and it is one that is rarely expressed.

When you were growing up, how many people talked about this desire to you? When you went to restaurants with your friends and relatives, what did you talk about? Mostly each others' problems: divorces, families, relationships, jobs, personal dramas. Did you ever sit down with a member of your family and hear him or her say, 'I am looking for freedom and I am desperate to get it. How much longer do I have to wait? It did not happen today. When will it happen?' Did you ever participate in conversations of this kind?

Question: Not very often.

Papaji: *[laughing]* I think you are exaggerating. This is such a rarely expressed sentiment, I doubt you heard it even once while you were growing up. I am not talking about some intellectual discussion in which two people exchange ideas on what freedom might be and how it might be attained; I am speaking of two lovesick people who are hurting inside because they cannot find a way to become one with freedom, their beloved. Many people speak about this, but how many of them are actually suffering inside because they cannot reach this elusive goal? That's very, very rare and very, very precious. This desire comes from a place that is not controlled by the mind. Mind cannot absorb or digest a desire like this, but at the same time it cannot stop it from arising and demanding your attention. When this desire for freedom makes you sick with longing for it, it has the power to bring about that freedom that it desires so badly. Just want it badly enough.

41

You have to be serious, and you have to want freedom to the exclusion of everything else

Question: Can you explain the distinction between *videhamukti* and *jivanmukti*?

Papaji: *Jivanmukti* is freedom that comes before the death of the body. While you are still alive you know and experience that you are free. Your work is over, and you will live in freedom for the rest of your life. *Videhamukti* means that freedom only comes at the moment of the death of the physical body. I just had a conversation with Kavita about tendencies and one's commitment to them. You may know that you are free, and you may even experience it directly from time to time, but if these tendencies still bother you and catch you from time to time, then you are not truly free. You will hitchhike from attachment to attachment until the moment of your death. However, if these residual attachments are not strong, and if you have directly experienced the Self consciously during your life, it is possible to come to the full state of freedom at the moment of your death. This is what is known as *videhamukti*.

There are very few *jivanmuktas*, very few.

Question: Ramana Maharshi?

Papaji: Yes, there are so few, if you survey the whole history of spirituality, you will still only come up with a small number of names. We still revere historical figures such as Sukadeva and King Janaka as great *jivanmuktas* because this state is so rare. In *jivanmuktas*, *prarabdha* karma has been ended and freedom has been definitively attained.

Question: These people who have become *jivanmuktas* must have come to their last lives with very little karma. *Jivanmuktas* such as Ramana Maharshi must have used up their karma quickly and then become enlightened.

Papaji: No, this is not the way it works. It is the other way round. Karma does not end with freedom; it is freedom that ends karma. Karma is not spent little by little until there is none left. There is no end to karma. When liberation comes, there is a great bonfire that burns all past karma and all its future consequences. When freedom, *jivanmukti*, has been attained, impressions are no longer stored, and when impressions are no longer stored, new karma is not created and births are no longer possible. A *jivanmukta* knows that he is free. He knows that irrespective of what he does in his life, he will always be free. There is no possibility of losing this state.

Others may have the experience of the Self, but it is not permanent. There is forgetfulness, which takes one back to the mind for a while, followed by recollection of one's true nature, which takes one back to the Self. This is not *jivanmukti* because in this state the mind and its tendencies have not been permanently eradicated. A person who oscillates between the mind and the Self while he is alive can become *videhamukti* when he dies, but he is not a *jivanmukta* while he is alive.

Question: So the *videhamukta* has to try to maintain his Self-awareness by effort, whereas the *jivanmukta* does not?

Papaji: Whether one has attained the state of *jivanmukta* through effort or no effort, one knows that one is free of karmic bondage.

There is no more bondage and no more ignorance. Karma will continue to make the body perform its activities, but it will not cause bondage since there is nothing and no one left who can be affected by this karma.

For those who are not fully established in the Self, pending karma can be moved forward to a future life, but the *jivanmukta* does not have this possibility. This means that the destiny he has to live out in his final incarnation often includes painful episodes, things that have to be gone through because they cannot be put off to a subsequent life.

Question: But in the case of the person who has the experience of the Self and then loses it, is there nothing he can do to become a *jivanmukta*? Or does he just have to wait until the end of his life and hope that he will become *videhamukti*?

Papaji: Sometimes it is your karma to have commitments and obligations and to be caught up in them. When this happens there is nothing you can do about them.

After final liberation one can sometimes see how all of one's karma was connected to past activities and events, but prior to that it just catches you, and you have to endure it.

There is a story about the Buddha. While he was walking in the forest he developed a headache. When he told Ananda about it, Ananda offered to go to a nearby village to look for some medicine.

The Buddha replied, 'No, wait. I don't need any medicine. I know why I have this headache. Two hundred and thirty-five lives ago I lived in a village in which the monsoons had failed. The village pond slowly dried up, and when there was just a small pool of water, the remaining fish started to flap around in the mud. All the boys in the village began to stone the fish, just for fun. I was one of those boys. I hit a fish and caused a major injury. That is why I am having this headache now. Let me suffer. This is something that has to happen to me.'

When freedom comes you sometimes know why certain problems have come to you, but you can't stop them from happening. All these things have to be worked out. When freedom comes, there is no real suffering because there is no longer an 'I' who identifies with the body that is suffering, but the body still has to go through these events.

Question: *[new questioner]* Is this Buddha story a myth, or did it really happen?

Papaji: You call your present state 'real' and these old stories you dismiss as a 'myth'. So long as there is a dream, there is a myth. In a dream a snake appears to be a real threat to you, and its bite causes you suffering. You run to a dream doctor to get an injection because you think this will end your suffering. But when you wake up, you know that your dream story has no more validity than a myth. When you know that your present state, this world you call reality, is just a myth, a fiction, it will be over for you, and it will be as if it never ever existed. This is the ultimate truth: nothing ever existed. You cannot understand what I am talking about when I speak to you like this because nothing I say is part of your experience. So, instead, I will talk to you in this place where you find yourself, inhabiting this mythical realm that you take to be so real. If we start from where you think you are right now, you may be able to see where you need to end up.

Suffering is a good place to start, because everyone believes that he suffers in one way or another. The Buddha taught that all are in suffering, because that is where everyone thinks he is. His own quest began by seeing suffering in his own city. He saw a sick man, an old man, a dead body and became aware of the suffering that his family was trying so hard to protect him from. He formulated a teaching that started from the statement that all are in suffering, and then he taught a way by which that suffering could be ended. When you believe in a myth, you have to start with that myth and then move away from it. This dream world you live in is a myth, a fantasy. Since you take it to be true, I will accept your complaint that you are suffering in it, and I will give you advice on how to end your suffering and become free. But while I am telling you all this, never for a moment do I actually accept that you are really suffering, nor will I ever accept that the world you claim you are living in is in any way real. For you this myth is true. *Samsara*, creation, all the gods: they are all real for you because you have not seen through the myth you have imposed on yourself.

Question: *[new questioner]* Ramana Maharshi spent several years sitting in obscure corners of Tiruvannamalai after he first arrived there. He seemed to be in a state of *samadhi* for most of the time. He wasn't teaching during this period, mostly because he was unable to communicate with anyone. During these years of intense meditation or *tapas*, did nothing change inside him? Was his experience of the Self deepening or stabilising during this period, or did it stay the same?

Papaji: His enlightenment was complete and irrevocable before he ever came to Tiruvannamalai. It happened in his house in Madurai when he was sixteen years old.

Question: So he was a *jivanmukta* before he came to Tiruvannamalai?

Papaji: Yes, it doesn't take time to be free, and it doesn't take years to stabilise in it. It happened in his family house, and there the boy Venkataraman 'disappeared', leaving only the Self. Due to some past tendencies he had a great attraction to Arunachala, so after a few weeks he made his way there and never returned to his family. He sat down there as a fully realised *jivanmukta*, closed his eyes and became immersed in some meditative state.

After you have realised the Self, true meditation can start. In that state there is nothing to understand or gain, so that which cannot be understood, the Self, pulls you into itself and makes you focus on it unswervingly. When all your attention is pulled into the Self and focused there, this is true meditation. Other people meditate to achieve something. There is the meditator, the object that is meditated on, and the act of meditating. A transaction is continuously going on between these three entities. This is not true meditation. It is a transaction, organised and sustained by an entity that is trying to attain something.

I believe that real and constant meditation can only take place after freedom has been discovered. This is what Ramana Maharshi was engaged in after he came to Tiruvannamalai. He was sitting quietly, in solitude, simply enjoying and celebrating the Self. He was not eating, and hardly anyone knew who he was. For years he sat like this. He was not trying to achieve something, or trying to deepen his experience or understanding. He was simply celebrating his freedom by becoming fully absorbed in it.

Question: So if no one had taken the trouble to take him out of that underground cellar he was in, he might have spent the rest of his life there?

Papaji: He was discovered and carried out. He had a destiny to teach, so someone had to find him and bring him out for the world. He was so reluctant to play that role, he tried to run away a few times, but eventually he realised that it was his fate, settled down, and an ashram grew up around him.

Question: *[new questioner]* Can one lose the benefits one gets from meditation, the progress one makes, or do the benefits slowly accumulate, even when it appears as if meditation is not going well?

Papaji: If you are following some form of meditation, you have a goal. If that goal is not attained, you have not lost something, you have simply not attained your goal. If you die without accomplishing your goal, you will carry on in a subsequent birth, and you will keep going until your work is complete. If you have this strong desire for the Self, and if you have meditated hard to achieve it, then your next birth will be in very favourable circumstances. You will choose a womb and circumstances that are favourable for your progress. Freedom is not the work of one life. This is why I say sometimes that the desire for freedom does not arise except in very rare circumstances. That desire is the result of millions of lives. It is not a random and uncaused whim that has just appeared in your mind. Millions of lives have brought you to the point where you have a desire for freedom, and not just sensual enjoyments.

All beings are addicted to sense enjoyments. Some of them call themselves 'religious' people because they are devoting themselves to God, but if you examine their beliefs and practices, you will find that they are doing their rituals and meditations so that they can enjoy themselves in heaven. They are so addicted to sense enjoyments, they are working hard to attain an eternal guaranteed supply of them.

Other 'religious' people end up studying the scriptures and mastering their contents. Their pleasure is the enjoyment of knowledge. I have seen and met many people who are like this. They can give you a good explanation of any line of scripture that you can quote, but the desire for freedom is not in their minds. I have some friends in the south who are like this. Some devotion may be there, but the desire for freedom is absent. It arises in very, very few people.

Question: So these people are not candidates even for *videhamukti*?

Papaji: No, because that desire for freedom is not there. Without that desire, it cannot happen. A few people have that desire, but it is mostly a weak desire. They are not serious enough, sincere enough or honest enough to focus exclusively on that desire. They make a little progress, then succumb to some desire, get distracted, and revert to their old state. This happens again and again. A few steps forward are followed by a few steps back, steps that put you back into the traps of the mind. Many lives can come and go like this without any real progress being made.

Even those who have been very decisive, who have moved towards their goal without getting distracted, can falter when they near the end of their journey. Mind will still be there, and there will be a strong desire to continue to use the mind. These people will come face to face with the Self, but the mind will still be there, evaluating and planning. They will think, unconsciously, 'I have come this far by my effort, and now I have to use this same mind that brought me here to understand what is happening, and to decide what I have to do next'. This will cause them to falter and keep them away from their goal, and as they fail to reach that goal, that same mind will become busier, trying to work out why it is not getting what it wants. It will be a very rare person who can drop the evaluating mind and merge into that nothingness, without thinking about it in any way.

You have to be serious, and you have to want freedom to the exclusion of everything else. It is just a joke if you think 'I want freedom', and then go back to all your old habits, or think that you can attain it by meditating for half an hour a day. Many people come here and say 'I want freedom', but they cannot keep their attention on this goal for any length of time. You walk down a road, determined to go somewhere, but on the way you see a dance performance by the side of the road and stop to watch it. Within a few minutes you have forgotten the purpose of your journey. This is how it is with most people who say 'I want freedom'. The determination to focus on the goal and not be distracted is not there. Mind is very tricky. It can fool you at any step of the journey. It can distract you when you have decided to work for freedom, and when you come close to that meeting with your own Self, it can trick you into believing that you are hallucinating and make you believe that what you are seeing or experiencing is not worthwhile.

When you come to that meeting with your own Self, the mind will not only succeed in persuading you that what you are doing is wrong, it will try to make you head off in a different direction, one that will just get you lost in some mental labyrinth. It might create a vision of your favourite deity for you, one that you will fall in love with, and by doing so it will keep your attention away from the formless Self. The mind knows what will seduce you, and if you get close to freedom, it will use its tremendous power of manifestation to create something that will cheat you and keep you away from the Self.

This is the mind. Everything that you see is this mind. All manifestation, all the past, the present and the future, all the gods, the heavens and the hells – all these things are mind. What a power this mind has! It will pretend to help you by giving you visions or pleasurable inner states, but it will do everything in its power to keep you away from that thought-free encounter with your own Self. When there are no thoughts, mind has no power to divert you. When thoughts are there, you will inevitably get tricked by them. You think that you are running and controlling your mind, that you are directing it for your own benefit, but the truth is, the mind is running you. Mind is a dangerous tiger, full of lethal power. You have to learn to ride this tiger, this immense power, without getting destroyed by it.

You need a strong determination to succeed, and when that determination is there, blessings will come that will keep you on the right path, focused on your goal. If you are serious, help will come.

A few years ago I met a man in Rudraprayag whose seriousness of purpose brought him the help he needed. For me, this story started at Lucknow railway station where I had gone to get on a train to South India. In those days there was only one particular carriage, attached to another train, that would take you to Madras direct. I had bought my ticket, but the Madras carriage had not been attached to the train, and no one at the station knew where it was. I abandoned my trip to the south and bought a ticket for Rishikesh instead. When I reached Rishikesh, I bought a bus ticket for Rudraprayag, which was a twelve-hour bus ride away. Pilgrims take this road to get to some of the high Himalayan pilgrimage destinations, but this was the middle of winter. Rock avalanches and snow blocked all the roads to the high-altitude destinations, and Rudraprayag was about as far as the bus could go. Why did I go there? I have no idea. I had no business there, and I was completely ill-equipped to deal with the cold winter weather. Rudraprayag is over 6,000 feet above sea level and it is not a pleasant place to be in mid-winter if one is not properly equipped. I had packed my bag with clothes that would be suitable for the warmth of South India, but something made me get on that bus even though I knew I would be in for a long, cold ride.

As soon as I got off the bus I went into a nearby restaurant to get something to eat. One man, who appeared to be very well dressed, followed me in and asked if he could speak to me. Because of the speed with which he had latched onto me, I assumed he must have been an agent for some local hotel, or some other local place that wanted my business. In winter not many people go to these hill towns, and there is strong competition for the custom of anyone who shows up.

I said, 'Let me eat. I am very hungry. I have just spent twelve hours on a bus with no food. Please wait.'

He went outside and waited for me there until I had finished eating.

As I walked out of the door he said, 'I apologise for bothering you before you had even had a chance to eat, but I felt a strong urge to come up to you and speak to you. Let's go down to the bank of the river and talk there. It's a very nice place to sit and talk.'

Rudraprayag is where two rivers, the Mandakini and the Alaknanda meet, and the river bank really is a very nice place to sit, even in winter. I followed him down to the river, wondering what his business might be.

'I am an engineer from Pune,' he began, 'from the Military Engineering Service. I had a Guru who passed away last year and before he died he told me that I would be enlightened in this very life. I am not enlightened, but I know that my Guruji loved me and that he would not lie to me. This promise has been bothering me for some time, but what could I do about it?

'Twenty days ago he appeared to me in a vision and said, "Go to Badrinath". What was I to make of an instruction like this? The road to Badrinath is closed and it will not be open for at least a month. The temple there is not open. Even if I managed to get there on foot, what would I do when I got there? There is nothing happening there at this time of year. At first I thought that this might be some sort of self-induced vision, a product of my desire to see my Guru's form again. Also, the instruction my Guru gave me was very odd because he himself never went on a pilgrimage in his whole life, nor did he recommend that anyone else go on one. At first I thought, "This is such a ridiculous thing for my Guru to tell me to do, it must be some sort of mental trick".

'But then I thought, "This man is my Guru and he may be trying to help me". I took twenty days' leave and arrived here this morning. Because of my engineering background, I spoke to the government engineers, the ones who maintain all the mountain roads here, and I was allowed to stay in the government rest house. They told me that a bulldozer is working on the road to Badrinath and that it will not be possible to go anywhere for at least two days. When I saw you arrive, something inside me said, "This is the reason why you have come here. This man is the person you have to see."'

You see how these things happen? I was diverted from a trip to South India by a missing carriage and ended up in a restaurant talking to a man who had been sent there by his Guru.

I was curious to know why, out of all the people who were available to him in the town, he had picked me.

'There are many *sadhus* here,' I said, 'people who look as if they might be able to help you in your quest for Self-realisation. Why did you immediately walk up to me, a visitor in ordinary clothes, and tell me this story?'

'Yes, there are many spiritual-looking people here. This place is famous. Adi-Shankaracharya wrote *Vivekachudamani* near here, and there are still many scholars and *sadhus* in the neighbourhood. I have seen many of these people in the last few hours, just walking around, but no one attracted me the way that you did.'

I persisted: 'But what did you see that made you take that decision?'

'I don't know,' he replied, 'but I think it is the grace of my Guru and the grace of all the *mahatmas* of the past and present that brought me to this place and made me approach you. Other than that, I don't know. I can't give you a sensible, rational reason. I have told you what my Guru promised me while he was alive, and I have told you that he sent me on this strange pilgrimage. I believe that he sent me here to fulfil his promise. I also believe that my Guru is still guiding me, even though he is no longer in the body, and I further believe that he has sent me here to meet you today.'

This man was still quite young, maybe about thirty-five, but he had a strong drive for freedom, and that drive had made him undertake this strange journey. We sat together by the side of the river, mostly in silence, for about an hour, and in that meeting he saw for the first time the Self that his Guru had promised him he would see.

He invited me to stay with him since his accommodation was warmer and better equipped than mine, but I turned down his invitation.

'Thank you, but "No",' I said. 'I will go back to Rishikesh. I now know why I came here. My business is finished. I can go home.'

How does something like this happen? It was not a random meeting. Some power scheduled that meeting and brought us together in that strange place because that man had a strong drive to attain the goal that his Guru had told him he would attain. Help is available everywhere. If you are honest in your search, how can the Self not give you the proper guidance that you need? But if you are not honest, you will be led astray. You will be fooled and cheated. But don't be too upset if you get fooled and cheated because that is also just what you need.

Question: *[new questioner]* This story prompts a question: 'Is it necessary to be continuously with a physical Guru?'

Papaji: If you don't understand the language of silence that the Guru in your Heart is speaking to you, then go to a Guru who speaks your own language. He will tell you, 'I am within you as your own Self'. If you can't understand this message and experience it for yourself in the Heart, then you have to find an external Guru who can give you this important message and then reveal to you the truth of what he is saying. The true Guru is always within you, but most people need to have an external Guru who can reveal this to them. In truth, there is no 'within' and 'without'. That is just your imagination. The true Guru is within, abiding in silence and speaking the language of no-words. Try to understand this language, but if you can't, find someone who translates that silence into words, words which will point you back to the silence where no words are spoken. This is all there is to the Guru-disciple relationship. If you can't discern the inner Guru, it will appear to you in a form you can see, and it will speak to you in a language that you can understand, saying, 'I am within you as your own Self'.

The true Guru never leaves you. Wherever you are, he is within you as your own Self. When I left Ramana Maharshi in 1947, I was not 'leaving my Master' because I knew that he would be with me wherever I went.

There had been a lot of trouble in the Punjab, and most of my family were still living there. Since I had not been reading any newspapers, I didn't even know what was going on there.

One of the devotees told the Maharshi that my family was stuck on the wrong side of the new international boundary between Pakistan and India, and when he heard this the Maharshi advised me to go home and look after them.

I didn't want to go because I had completely fallen in love with the Maharshi. I felt that I couldn't live without seeing his form.

We were walking on the hill together while this conversation was taking place.

'Sir,' I said, 'before I came to meet you I had a wife, children, brothers, sisters and parents. Now that I have met you, all these people have become a dream. I am not attached to anyone any more, except you.'

The Maharshi replied by saying, 'If you want to call it a dream, why are you afraid of it? If you can see that it is a dream, then you can transact your dream business with these dream people.'

I could see the logic of what he was saying but I didn't want to leave because I had become infatuated by his form and presence.

'I am completely attached to your form,' I said. 'That's the only relationship I have left. I am so physically attached to you, I cannot leave, even for a few hours. When the doors of your hall are open, I am inside, staring at you. When they are closed, I am camped outside your window, hoping to catch a glimpse of you. During the night I sleep on your front veranda because I can't bear to be any further away from you. I am absent for about one hour a day, eating or in the bathroom. The rest of the time I am here with you. How can I leave?'

He looked at me and said, 'I am with you wherever you are'. These are the words I remember him saying. I immediately understood what he was saying. The 'I am' that the Maharshi spoke of, referring to himself, was my own Self as well, so how could I ever be away from it?

I could not argue any more. I prostrated before him, walked around him three times, prostrated again, collected some of the dust from under his feet and put it in my pocket. I went back to my home town, picked up my family and took them all to the safety of India on the last train that left Pakistan. After that I never had a chance to go back to Ramanasramam because my family were destitute refugees. I had to support them all by working here in Lucknow. I didn't need to go back because I understood that 'I am with you wherever you are' means that my Master is always inside me, as my own Self.

Question: I have just one simple question. Why did you pick up the dust from under the Maharshi's feet?

Papaji: Gratitude. It was an expression of my absolute, unconditional gratitude.

Glossary

ananda	bliss; the bliss that is a consequence of experiencing the Self.
baba	a *sadhu*, particularly those in North India.
bhakta	a devotee.
bhakti	devotion to God.
Brahman	the impersonal absolute reality of Hinduism.
Brahma	the Hindu god of creation.
darshan	to see or be seen by a Guru or God.
dharma	there are several shades of meaning that depend on the context. It may mean right action, moral duty, divine law, or religious tradition.
ghats	bathing places adjoining sacred rivers or tanks. They usually take the form of paved stone steps that lead down to the water.
gunas	see sattvic.
Guru Purnima	an annual festival, usually in July, that celebrates or commemorates the Guru.
japa	the repetition of God's name or of any other combination of sacred words or syllables.
jiva	the soul; the individual self.
jivanmukta	a liberated being; sometimes this term implies someone has realised the Self while still alive, rather than someone who attains liberation at the moment of death.
jivanmukti	the state of the *jivanmukta*.
jnana	true knowledge; direct knowledge of the reality that is the Self.
jnani	one who has a direct awareness of himself as *jnana*; an enlightened being.
Kohinoor	a large diamond that spent several centuries of its celebrated life in India. It is now part of the crown jewels in London.
kundalini	psychic or spiritual energy that moves in a subtle channel that begins at the base of the spine and rises to the *sahasrara*, a centre in the subtle body that is located just above the top of the head.

kosas	usually translated as 'sheaths', these are the five entities or bodies that the ego functions through according to some schools of Indian philosophy.
mahatmas	great souls, great beings.
math	a Hindu institution, usually dedicated to the memory of a famous saint. It is sometimes spelt 'mutt'.
maya	illusion; the power that makes the unreal world appear to be real.
moksha	liberation; more specifically, liberation from the cycle of birth and death.
pranayama	breath control; yogic breathing exercises.
prarabdha	one of the three subdivisions of karma; the destined acts that one has to perform in one's life as a result of actions and reactions pending from previous lives.
puja	ritual worship of a Hindu deity.
punyas	spiritual merits earned from previous actions, usually performed in previous lives. A good store of *punyas* produces favourable circumstances for one's life, whereas the opposite, a large amount of *papams*, leads to an unpleasant existence.
rishi	a seer or sage.
sadhana	spiritual practice; the means by which a spiritual goal is attained.
sadhu	a Hindu who has renounced the world in order to seek enlightenment, or some other spiritual goal.
sahaja	natural; the *sahaja* state is the state of enlightenment in which one can engage in the world in a normal and natural way.
sahasrara	see *kundalini*.
samadhi	a state of trance-like absorption in which one is aware of the Self, but unaware of the world or one's body; the grave of a saint.
samsara	the continuous round of birth and death to which the *jiva* is subjected until it attains liberation; also, more generally, worldly life.
samskaras	tendencies or habits of the mind, particularly those that one has inherited from a previous life.
sanga	association; *satsang* is association with the Self.
sannyasin	a member of the fourth Hindu *asrama* or stage of

	life; a Hindu who has renounced the world to live as a celibate monk in order to attain liberation.
satsang	'association with *sat*'; *sat* is usually defined as 'truth' or 'reality'. It is the permanent unchanging being that is the substratum of all beings and all manifestation. *Satsang* is either association with someone who has become one with *sat*, or association with one's own inner *sat*.
sattvic	the adjective from *sattva*, which means purity, or harmony. The three *gunas*, *sattva* (purity) *rajas* (activity) and *tamas* (sloth) are, according to many Indian schools of thought, the fundamental and ever-changing qualities of both the mind and manifestation.
siddhis	supernatural powers, particularly those that have come as a result of yogic exercises.
tapas	arduous spiritual practice, often involving bodily mortification. Its aim is to burn off spiritual impurities.
turiya	the fourth state; the underling substratum in which the three states of waking, dreaming and sleep alternate.
turiyatita	beyond the fourth; see *turiya*.
vasanas	mental tendencies or habits; the latent urges and desires of the mind that compel one to behave in a particular way.
Vedas	the primary and oldest scriptures of Hinduism.
videhamukta	one who is liberated at the moment of death.
videhamukti	the state of being liberated at the moment of physical death.
yagna	a vedic rite; a sacrificial offering.
Yama	the Hindu god of death.